THE QUIET ASSASSIN

THE QUIET ASSASSIN

THE DAVIE HAY STORY

DAVIE HAY

WITH ALEX GORDON

BLACK & WHITE PUBLISHING

First published 2009
by Black & White Publishing Ltd
29 Ocean Drive, Edinburgh EH6 6JL

1 3 5 7 9 10 8 6 4 2   09 10 11 12

ISBN: 978 1 84502 266 2

Typeset by Ellipsis Books Limited, Glasgow
Printed and bound by MPG Books Ltd, Bodmin, Cornwall

CONTENTS

ACKNOWLEDGEMENTS

I would like to thank the majority of players, managers, chairmen and directors I have met in my career. For so many of you, far too many to name individually, I am glad our paths have crossed in life. It's been a long, varied journey and I have so many fond memories.

Peter Rafferty is a great Celtic fan who has been a friend through thick and thin for many years and I would like to acknowledge his support and presence in my professional and personal life.

I would also like to thank my co-author Alex Gordon for his expertise in putting this book together. I'm delighted to say our friendship, which was always strong, has developed even more so. Tuesdays won't be the same again without me and Alex getting everything down in print. It's been hard work, but, along with his wife Gerda, we have had a lot of fun, too.

I could never forget all the wonderful supporters I have encountered, home and abroad. I may not know all your names, but, rest assured, you will always be special to me. I'm grateful for everyone who has played their part. Thank you.

DEDICATION

This is for Catherine, my wife, who has been the one constant in my life since we first met. She has been by my side through the ups and downs, the good and the bad, the laughter and the tears. She has been my biggest ally when she understands I have been hurt. Sadly, that's happened a few times. I can take the pain and Catherine has probably hurt more on these occasions, but she has always offered me unstinting support. Hopefully, she knows exactly how much she means to me and always will.

Also, our departed parents; my mum Catherine and dad David and Catherine's mum Margaret and dad Patrick Docherty.

Our wonderful daughters Allison and Caroline and their husbands Tommaso and Damien. And our grandchildren Scarlett, Vincent, Grace and Louis who have been the best-ever additions to our lives.

My brother Brian who has been a rock and Catherine's sisters and her brother Patrick.

FOREWORD
BY BILLY McNEILL

Davie Hay was second best to no one. Undoubtedly, he was one of the best players I have ever had the privilege to call a team-mate.

He was a winner from day one. You could see his determination and character even as a youngster beginning to make regular appearances in the Celtic first team in 1969.

Davie was a joy to play alongside, a genuine 100 per cent competitor. His undoubted class shone through right from the start and I, for one, thought it was a sad day for the club when he went to Chelsea in 1974. I can tell you that if the players had had their way he would never have been allowed to go anywhere for any amount of money. He was a massive loss to the team.

I believe Davie also contributed magnificently to the continued success of Celtic from the late sixties into the seventies. It was imperative that the team kept its momentum after the European Cup success in 1967.

Father Time takes no prisoners and teams have to evolve and change. Players have to move on and, again, it is vitally important that you have youngsters coming through who can prove they are up to the challenges ahead. Davie was one of the ones who surpassed himself when it came to getting out there and doing the business. There were never any doubts that he would go all the way – none whatsoever.

Of course, he was known as The Quiet Assassin and, he might not thank me for this, but it was a fairly apt title. Off the field, he dodged the spotlight, but, on the park, his hunger for success was unquenchable and undeniable. He was a very determined young man and I can never remember him pulling out of a 50/50 tackle. Not once. He shirked nothing and bowed to no one. Right from the start, reputations meant nothing to Davie.

He was as hard as they come, but was never dirty. If you look closely at his disciplinary record you will see he was rarely in trouble with referees and that tells you all you need to know. However, there were a few opponents out there who knew they had been challenged when Davie went for the ball. Don't think, though, for one minute that Davie Hay was just all about muscle power. That would be doing him an awful disservice. He was an excellent player with bundles of energy and drive who could get up and down the pitch all day while he was also a fine user of the ball.

If you were in trouble, you could always be sure Davie would be around to give you some assistance. He was as honest as the day was long. He was a fabulous colleague on the pitch, but he was just as dependable away from the action. He has always been as truthful, fair and honourable a man you are ever likely to meet. Davie, as a matter of fact, is a rarity in football inasmuch as no one has a bad word to say about him. His honesty goes before him and, again, that is huge testimony to the man. He has proved he has principles over and over again. The accolades he receives are richly deserved.

Of course, I took over as Celtic manager from Davie in 1987 and, as you might expect, it was very much a time of mixed emotions for all concerned. I made it abundantly clear that Davie had to be told before I would meet the board. I knew Davie thought along the same lines as myself that Celtic was our club.

It didn't make it any the easier that he was a decent guy and a bloke for whom I had a genuine fondness. There was a lot of unnecessary suffering all round at the time.

I had telephoned him four years earlier to wish him all the best in the job when I moved to Manchester City. I had nothing whatsoever to do with Davie leaving Celtic and I know he realises that to this day. I would never have done that to him as he would never have done that to me. It's not in our natures. However, if any two people knew how much it meant to be manager of Celtic it was Davie and me.

In fact, I was grateful to Davie for signing centre half Mick McCarthy from my old club Manchester City just before he left. Mick was a player I rated extremely highly during our time together at Maine Road and my predecessor had chosen well. Thanks, Davie! Naturally enough, I have watched my old team-mate's career unfold over the years and I am positive he has given the same commitment to each of the clubs he has been associated with that he always demonstrated at Celtic. I would say Davie was a talented and tenacious teammate and, as I pointed out earlier, it was a joy to play alongside him. As a human being, he is first class, no doubt about it. It is my privilege to consider him a friend.

If you ever needed someone to fight your corner I would have no hesitation putting forward one name – Davie Hay.

INTRODUCTION

I couldn't possibly have realised it at the time, but I had just received an injury that would lead to my playing career effectively ending before I celebrated my thirtieth birthday. Well, I was only eight years old when the accident happened.

I was playing cowboys and Indians with a pal of mine, Tom Downes, in his family's home at 15 Moncrieff Street in Paisley – right next door to our tenement. Unluckily, for me, I was chosen to be the guy who wore the white hat for the day. I was John Wayne. My mate became Geronimo. How different might my career have been transformed if I'd had the toystore bow and arrow that day? Back in 1953 all the kids followed the Western television programmes. You had to watch the likes of *The Lone Ranger*, *Wyatt Earp*, *Gunsmoke*, *Laramie*, *Wagon Train* and so on. Those gun-tottin'cowboys were our heroes long before football stars took centre stage. In those days, you played football and, when you had time, also acted out the part of your small-screen Western idols.

That particular afternoon was to prove to be a fateful one for yours truly, although I have to say I absolve my boyhood friend Tom of all blame. It was a complete accident. We were just kids having fun and, unfortunately for me, I was in the direct line of one of his arrows. I recall it vividly. His mum was still at work and we had the place to ourselves. I had a plastic gun my parents had bought me for a Christmas gift and I was pointing it at Tom and he was threatening to fire arrows at me. All good knock-about fun. Until . . .

I was behind the couch when I suddenly emerged and pointed my toy pistol at my friend. He was taken totally by surprise and, panicking, let loose an arrow. He didn't mean it, of course, but he hit me smack on the eye. I fell backwards as pain instantly stabbed at me. I lay there, feeling more than just a little bit uncomfortable. But you know what kids are like; you believe you can bounce back from anything and take on the world. However, I didn't feel too good. My sight was blurred as I tried to focus on Tom. Of course, I didn't think it was serious. 'Everything will be OK in a moment,' I thought as my pal fussed over me.

How wrong could I be? Ten minutes passed. No improvement. Another ten. I still wasn't getting a proper image of Tom. Half an hour afterwards and things weren't getting better. Panic? No, I was too young to get over-anxious. You skinned your knees when you fell playing football in the school playground. Blood would pour everywhere, but you would dry it with a handkerchief and just get back into the game. I wasn't alone. Where I grew up in Paisley it was the same for everyone. You would play games that lasted until the twelfth goal, switching ends at six goals. It was rough and tough and you would have thought we were all playing for an enormous win bonus. You would throw yourself into tackles, getting battered and bruised by guys a lot older and bigger than you, but, hey, this was entertainment. It's what you did for enjoyment when you weren't watching the Westerns on the telly.

So, even at a very early age, I proved I could take a knock or two. This was different, though. I couldn't simply take a cloth and dab at the wound. I admit I was beginning to get more than a trifle concerned. Eventually, the horrible thoughts kicked in. 'What if I am going to be blind in this eye?' The more I struggled to focus, the worse it seemed to get. Now I was worried. 'Tom,' I said, 'I think I've got a wee bit of a problem.' I didn't realise I was such a master of the understatement.

My mate did his best to calm me down. His mother came home from work, took one look at my damaged right eye and almost shrieked the house down. I recall her saying, 'My God, what's happened here? David, are you all right?' Clearly, I wasn't. She went off to the kitchen and came back with this huge roll of bandage and began encircling my head with it. I don't know how many yards she used, but by the time she was finished you could probably stretch it the distance of a football pitch. And back. I was beginning to look like the top half of The Mummy. My head clunked to one side under the weight. 'You'll be fine, David,' she urged. 'You'll be fine.' Apart from having an extremely sore eye, I thought I was about to be suffocated under the welter of all that cloth. I felt anything but fine, believe me.

'You will be OK, David,' I was reassured time and again. 'Things will be fine.' Now Mrs Downes was a lovely, kindly lady with so many wonderful qualities. Unfortunately for me, soothsaying was not among them. I had to attend the Paisley Eye Infirmary for a fortnight afterwards. I was far from fine. I am blind in that right eye today.

1

IN THE BEGINNING

So, there I am perched precariously on a window ledge about forty feet from the ground and a raging neighbour is coming up the tenement stairs threatening to do all sorts of damage to my person. I am about ten years old and I can tell you I am more than just a shade nervous about the outcome if my irate pursuer gets his hands on me. I am looking down at the ground and wondering if I should take a chance and make a jump for safety. It seems an awful long way down.

OK, how did I find myself in this fairly risky and, to me, possibly life-threatening, position in the first place? Football. The sport has given me a fabulous life, full of wonderful, treasured memories, triumphs and traumas, too, along the way. It's all part of life's rich tapestry, I have told myself more than once. I have played in World Cup Finals, a European Cup Final, I've won silverware as a player and a manager and I am glad to say I have thoroughly enjoyed most of my career. I had no thoughts of the future that evening, though, as I clung onto the tenement wall for all I was worth. In fact, I wondered if I had a future. My irate neighbour was determined that I was going to pay for someone kicking the ball against his window while I was playing in the streets with my mates. Actually, I was not the guilty party, but try telling that to Mr Angry. I'll never know why he picked on me as his prey because, even if I do say so myself, I was the fastest kid on the block. I could outrun anyone, but that didn't deter this bloke. I was firmly on his radar and I was the one he had selected for punishment and retribution.

I raced off as I saw my pals scatter in all directions. I couldn't believe it when I looked over my shoulder and there was this middle-aged bloke in an open-necked white shirt, braces, dark trousers and, for some obscure reason I have never forgotten, tartan slippers, pounding after me. 'He'll give in soon enough,' I assured myself. I was wrong. Maybe I had upset his dinner and he didn't look the forgiving sort. There was little point in stopping to try to explain my innocence. I got the drift he wasn't in the mood to listen to reason. My heart was about to explode through my chest when I decided to try to sneak up the entrance of a nearby close. 'He won't find me here,' I thought. Wrong again. Did you ever see that movie *Butch Cassidy and the Sundance Kid* with Paul Newman and Robert Redford? The charismatic bank robbers kept squinting over their shoulders as they rode their horses through prairies and when they glanced backwards there was a grim-looking character with a white hat leading a posse; dogged and relentless. 'Who are these guys?' asks Sundance as they take off again.

Well, that was how I felt that particular evening in the dark streets of Paisley. I just could not shake this stubborn bloke. As I fled up the stone stairs I stopped to hear if he had detected the path of my survival plan. I was standing on the second floor landing, doing my best to control my breathing. There was silence. I was hoping to hear him chasing past. All was quiet; too quiet. Then came a voice, 'I know yer up there, ya little bastard. Ah'm coming to get ye.' It didn't look as though he had left even the merest margin for debate. What to do? There was no option – I was going out the window. My original intention was to try to hang onto the ledge by my fingertips, manoeuvre myself into a good position, if there was such a thing in this situation, and gently drop to the ground, hopefully landing on my feet. Then I looked down, peering through the darkness. 'No thanks.' I reckoned the guy might have a ten-stone advantage, at least, so squaring up to him didn't seem the brightest way to survive this delicate situation.

Out the window it was, then. I could hear him huffing and puffing, grunting and groaning as he made his way slowly up the stairs. The race was over and he was going in for the kill. I stepped gingerly onto the ledge that ran about six yards along under the windowsill. It stuck out about a foot or so. As quietly as I could, I pushed the window back into place to give the impression it was closed. I eased myself along this precipice until I was out of sight. I could still hear him shuffle ever upwards, muttering his threats. 'Ah'm going to get ye, ya little bastard. Yer gonnae get a right good skelp.' I moved as close to the edge as I possibly could and suddenly I found religion. 'God, I'll never be bad again – HELP!' Silence. And then footsteps coming down the stairs. 'Bastard,' was the word that seemed to be repeated all the way to the front of the close. I didn't believe this was the time to argue the fact that I was not, in fact, born out of wedlock. I didn't move; I was petrified. Then some more silence, but this time welcome. I remained on that ledge for about another fifteen minutes or so before edging back to the window. I popped my head up, half-expecting to come face to face with my would-be assailant. There was no sign of him. As quietly as I could, I clambered up, opened the window, slid through the gap and dropped to the floor. There was something more than just a little welcoming and reassuring in having a solid floor beneath my feet.

I moved to the stairwell and took a furtive look round the corner. I stood there for a while, my heart still doing the rumba in my ribcage. When I was convinced my pursuer had given up the ghost I ventured down the stairs, through the opening to the close and out to freedom, taking a huge gulp of air while doing so. I embarked on the longest route home I could think of, just in case my running mate was hanging around. Thankfully, this persistent character had gone back to his cold fish and chips, or whatever treat lay in store, and I was in the safety zone. Ah, growing up on a housing estate in Paisley in the fifties was, indeed, memorable. If possibly a little dangerous. But I loved it.

I made my debut on Planet Earth on 29 January 1948, the first of two sons to David and Catherine Hay. I am brother Brian's senior by two years. Home was the bottom floor flat in a four-storey tenement at 13 Moncrieff Street, not far from St Mirren's old ground at Love Street. You may find this hard to believe, but I did not play an organised game of football until I went to my secondary school, St Mirin's Academy.

I was five years old when I went to my first school, St James's Primary. Imagine my disappointment, though, when I was informed there was no such thing as a school team. Even back then, I was mad about football and just couldn't get enough of knocking that little sphere around. We had a kickabout before, during and after school and it was always my greatest ambition to be a professional footballer. I really mean that. I would sit in the classroom and scribble into my jotter, 'I want to be the best player in school.' I would repeat this over and over again. I was utterly convinced I could make the grade.

For a start, I was super-fit. I had a milk run in the morning before school and used to trek around the streets delivering to people's front doors. I had to carry two heavy containers about with me as the milk van slowly followed me. My heart sank when I had a delivery to the top of a tenement building where I realised the order for two or three residents would be three pints each. However, I set about my task with a fair degree of gusto and tried to carry out my duties as swiftly as possible so I could get to the school playground for a quick game of football before the bell rang at 9am to signal the beginning of that day's work. Then it was lunchtime – or as we said in Paisley, dinner time – and once more someone produced a ball and we were out kicking it around. Four o'clock and the end of my intake of knowledge for the day and it was football again. I also had a job selling newspapers – the *Evening Times* and the now-defunct *Evening Citizen* – at a corner of Paisley High Street to bring in a few bob to the Hay household.

Dad was an engineer with Rolls-Royce and he would often take me to see St Mirren in their home games. Mum was employed by a company that made cushions and suchlike. It may be polit-ically incorrect in this day and age, but I recall there were a lot of Asian people working in the factory. Now that didn't bother anyone where I came from, but there was a funny incident when my mum, known as Catty, was informed that Nehru had died. 'Oh, which department did he work in?' She didn't know that her colleagues were discussing the death in 1964 of Jawaharlal Nehru, who just happened to be the President of India! I remember, too, that my mum worked in a pub on occasion. That almost became my profession at one stage when things went just slightly awry on the football front, but I'll deal with that in another chapter. Back at school, I became an instant hero with all my classmates. How did I earn their undying gratitude? Simple – I clobbered the school bully!

Football, as you might expect, had something to do with it. I would play anywhere to get a place in our teams for bounce games. One day I was put in goal. I didn't grumble; I was involved and that was all that mattered. Anyway, the bloke who used to terrorise the rest of us was actually a bit on the small side. Strangely, though, he seemed to have this power over so many people, me included. He fancied himself as a wee hard man and most of us kept out of his way. Remember, too, these were the days of the old black-and-white gangster movies and the main mobsters were played by diminutive actors such as James Cagney,

Edward G Robinson and George Raft and they were all menacing blokes who hardly towered over the good guys. Humphrey Bogart, too, played a baddie on occasion and he never exactly scaled the six feet mark either. It just appeared to be a trend – the smaller you were, the more dangerous you appeared to be.

As luck would have it, the day I was put in goal the other team got a penalty kick. Guess who was the player given the task of trying to get the ball past yours truly? Aye, the poisoned dwarf. I set myself, he hit it hard and low, but I got down to get my hand to the ball and I grabbed the rebound. I heard this high-pitched yell, looked up and there was this crazy guy running towards me. I didn't get the impression he was about to congratulate me on my goalkeeping skills.

Honestly, I didn't have a clue what to expect and I don't know who I surprised most, him or me, by my next reaction. As he came flying in my direction, I acted instinctively and punched him straight in the face. Crunch! He collapsed in a heap. I stood there, still holding onto the ball. Then suddenly there was cheering from everyone present, including the school bully's own team-mates! I soaked up my new-found adulation as my conquest got slowly to his feet and ran away. The following day, though, I was hauled before a disapproving headmistress. I knocked on her door, was invited in and was surprised to see this wee guy who had previously intimidated everyone at the school sitting there with his father. He had gone home and told his dad I had set about him. The cheek of it when you consider what that little nyaff used to do to us. There was a happy outcome, though. The headmistress took no action against me and the would-be tough guy behaved himself from there on in. Oh, by the way, I was never asked to play in goal again. As the hero of the school I could pick my own position in the team!

I don't know how my dad swung it, but I was often allowed to get away early to watch St Mirren play midweek fixtures in those days, normally Scottish Cup replays. These were the days before floodlights, so, more often that not, the games would kick off early. My father must have known the headmistress or someone in power because he would turn up at school and whisk me off to Love Street. I remember a day when we missed each other. The Saints had a big game on and I simply presumed I would be let away early. I must have gone out one door as my dad came in another and, with kick-off time fast approaching, I made my own way to the ground. There was a little space where you could crawl through and get in for free. I took up my usual position and my dad arrived shortly afterwards. 'What happened to you?' he enquired. 'I got fed up waiting,' was my rather cheeky reply. It was the first time I had gone to a match on my own and I felt like a grown-up.

I lived for football and another amusing incident I recall while growing up in Paisley was the fact that the entire English FA Cup Final was replayed in Scotland on a Sunday – twenty-four hours after the Wembley occasion had been seen across the border. That was a must-see. We didn't have a television at the time, so I would watch it in my friend's house. He was called Michael Pierotti and his family owned the local fish and chip shop. They must have been doing well if they could afford a television set, I reckoned. There was one slight problem, though. We used to imagine we were catching the action live, so you had to do your best to avoid discovering the actual score beforehand. We really didn't want to know that Newcastle United had beaten Manchester City 3-1 in 1955 or Manchester City had won 3-1 against Birmingham City a year later. So, when we went out to play the inevitable game of football on the Saturday evening you had to tell all your mates not to discuss the Wembley game. They were sworn to secrecy so Michael and I could enjoy the action 'live' the following day.

Sadly, there were a lot of young nutters around the Paisley

schemes as I grew up. There was one gang – I can't remember their name – who used to come in from their territory and roam around our patch. There must be something about me, but I was the guy they most wanted to beat the living daylights out of. Again, thanks to all that running up and down the stairs delivering milk, I was exceptionally fit. I would see these halfwits coming for miles and give them a body swerve. Sometimes they got close, but I was too fast for them and would always escape. They did all sorts of things to the unfortunates they caught. They would tie them to a fence, with their arms spread out, and then they would 'torture' them. They didn't actually do any mortal harm, I'm glad to say, but they would punch their captives in the gut, sometimes throwing in a slap in the face if they were in a particularly grim mood. I wasn't having any of that.

However, one day one of their so-called gang members came to our door at Moncrieff Street, a building, sadly, that has since fallen to the wrecking ball as the council modernised that part of the world. Anyway, tentatively, I opened the door and saw this idiot standing in the hallway. He growled, 'We've got Brian.' Displaying marvellous family concern for my younger sibling, I answered, 'So?' I was then informed, 'We'll let him go if you take his place.' I pondered this for all of a nanosecond and then said, 'No thanks!' With that I slammed the door shut. Sorry, Brian! They never did catch me.

Holidays back in those heady days were mainly spent at Whitletts in Ayr. My mum and dad would rent part of this house where the residents, a family called the Wilsons, had a family of eight. I recall we were joined by my Uncle Jim and Aunt Nan and another family from Edinburgh for the same fortnight. It must have been a helluva size of a house to take us all. Inevitably, the ball would come with us and we would spend the bulk of the two weeks kicking it around any patch of land we could find. Brian wasn't a bad footballer and had a good pedigree at Junior level where he played fullback for Beith, Kilsyth Rangers and Ardrossan. He quit at the age of twenty-six to concentrate on his studies and is now a chartered accountant. Ironically, I thought my career might also be in bean-counting and I worked for a firm in Glasgow after leaving school. Actually, and I'm blowing my own trumpet here, I was quite good at school. I was better than average at most things, but I couldn't draw to save myself. Pablo Picasso wasn't the only one to give people three eyes, two noses and a couple of mouths. I could do that, too, without any trouble. Football was always my main aim, though. I don't regret giving accountancy a try because it was there that I met my wife, coincidentally called Catherine, the same name as my mum. We must have gazed across a spreadsheet and fallen in love at first sight!

Like every kid growing up in a grey, old housing scheme, I really looked forward to our summer break away in such an exotic place as Ayr. As I got older, the family then switched the annual holiday to Blackpool and I'd never seen such a spectacular place. All those bright lights, the Tower, the arcades, the beach, the donkey rides, the candy floss, the Kiss-Me-Quick hats. Who needed Vegas when you had this wonderful place virtually on your doorstep?

Another source of enjoyment was our days on the old Renfrew Ferry. My pals and I would get on the vessel and it would take us across the Clyde to Yoker where people paid their fare as they disembarked. Naturally enough, we would stay on the ferry and it would carry us back across the water, toing and froing from one side to another, until we had had enough of our grand cruise and went home for our tea without paying a penny. Ironically, I still go on the Ferry these days as it is now an excellent restaurant berthed at Anderston Quay in Glasgow. I pay my way now, though!

Back then, there were so many never-to-be-forgotten fun days with my family and friends, but things were beginning to get serious on the football front. Celtic were about to come calling and life would never be the same again.

2

HOOP HOOP HOORAY

I believe I might have been Jock Stein's first signing for Celtic. He arrived as manager from Hibs in March 1965 and I put pen to paper to become a part-time player at the club a month later at the tender age of seventeen. However, instead of the east end of Glasgow I could have been plying my trade in the west end of London if Tommy Docherty had had his way.

Let me explain. I was doing quite well with St Mirin's Boys' Guild and one of my young colleagues was a bloke called Chris Connor. As it happens, Chris's dad, Joe, did a bit of scouting for Celtic. He would come along to see his boy playing, giving him encouragement and so on, but, thankfully for me, I managed to attract his attention. I was delighted when Chris told me his dad liked what he saw of me. I always gave 100 per cent out on the football field and it never mattered in which position. However, when I saw Joe on the touchline on match day I think the sleeves got rolled up another inch or so. One day he sauntered over to me and asked, 'Would you like to train with Celtic?' He framed it in such a nonchalant way he could have been asking me the time. 'Yes,' I snapped without hesitation – I wasn't going to let an opportunity like this pass me by. 'When?' I queried. 'As soon as possible,' came the reply I so wanted to hear.

As you'll have gathered already, I was a bit of a St Mirren fan and had never given an awful lot of thought to playing for anyone but them. For whatever reason, they never came knocking on the door. I didn't exist as far as they were concerned. Fair enough. But the thought of going to Celtic, the famous Glasgow Celtic, almost made me weak at the knees. Joe arranged for me to train on Tuesday and Thursday evenings and things were run at the time by three great ex-Celts, Johnny Higgins, Alec Boden and Frank Meechan. They looked after the youngsters and I have to say they were absolutely superb to me. I couldn't get enough of training at Celtic Park those two nights a week. There were about thirty or forty kids and they all wanted to impress. They were all ready to live the dream. Alas, for some, it never materialised. The first time I turned up for a training session was not the first time I had ever been at the ground, though, and I have to admit I never saw a football game there. However, I have to say Celtic Park has always been special and unique to me. It's difficult to explain. There is a real football feel about the place. It is a proper stadium and I recognised that from a very early age.

The school once sent us through to Glasgow on a Wednesday evening to report to Celtic Park where we were given collection cans for nuns at Moredun Convent. These sort of things were the norm back then. We were taken into the gym where we could change our gear and then take our place at our designated spot outside and rattle these cans under the supporters' noses as they made their way to the game. So, I thought it was rather ironic that on my very first evening as a youngster about to step onto the football ladder, fingers crossed, I was ushered to that very same gym. I smiled to myself. I couldn't have thought in my wildest dreams that I would be returning to this place with the possibility of signing for the great Glasgow Celtic. But it almost didn't happen.

Tommy Docherty, who would later manage me with the Scottish international team, was in Edinburgh to take in an Under-23 game and I was asked to go through to meet him. He was boss of a very good Chelsea side and, to me, was a typical garrulous Glaswegian. He was a genuine bubbly character and he was working wonders with a young team at Stamford Bridge. He had introduced a lot of fresh-faced Scottish talent and somehow, through the excellent scouting system he had put in place, he had got to hear about me and was showing an interest. My dad, myself and a guy called Adam Busby, of St Mirin's Guild, were invited through to meet him in a hotel in the capital. It was all very exciting, but, deep down, I knew I wouldn't be signing for Chelsea. Or anyone else for that matter. Apart from Celtic, of course.

The Doc, as he was known to everyone, was fully aware I had been training with Celtic, where he started his own playing career before moving across the border to Preston North End. He must have known the appeal of being involved with Jock Stein at such a famous club. He didn't even attempt to twist my arm. He made an offer, an excellent one as I recall, but suddenly I blurted, 'I would rather sign for Celtic.' That was that. The Doc simply nodded, shook my hand and said, 'Have a good career.' I believe my dad and Adam Busby were still given their expenses for making the trip through. Ironically, I did join Chelsea nine years later, of course, but it would cost them an awful lot more than a signing-on fee.

Sean Fallon, who had been appointed as Jock's assistant at Celtic, got to hear about my meeting with Tommy Docherty. He might have been in Edinburgh that night, too, to watch the same game. Honestly, I don't know to this day how he got to know about my meeting with the Chelsea boss, but I suspect Joe Connor might have had something to do with it. If Joe thought it might get Celtic moving that little bit faster in signing me, he got it absolutely right. Suddenly, I had completed the forms and I was on my way on an epic sporting journey. One of the first things Big Jock did at the club was to start pruning the staff. He wanted the coaches to concentrate on a smaller group of players. He reckoned they should spend more time with certain individuals and, of course, it worked. I was lucky enough to get the nod. Many of our group were allowed to move on and, if fortune had smiled on them, they might just have gone on to do wonderful things in the game at Parkhead.

Jim Holton, for instance, trained with Celtic while I was there. He was a big, raw centre half, but wasn't taken on. Jim went to West Bromwich Albion, kick-started his career and was signed by Tommy Docherty – that man again! – for Manchester United. He was also my teammate in the Scottish team in the unforgettable World Cup Finals in 1974 when we returned home unbeaten, the first nation to be knocked out without losing a game. It wasn't a record we particularly wanted. Jim was a rock in that defence and the fans would sing, 'Six foot two, eyes of blue, Big Jim Holton's after you.' He was proof that a few will slip through the net. No one is going to realise the potential in every youngster, that's not possible. Some take longer to mature than others. Some can bloom overnight after struggling for so long. It just happens.

I came through the ranks and eventually made it into the reserve team that was labelled The Quality Street Gang. And little wonder when you look at the names that were around at the time. I'm talking about the likes of Kenny Dalglish, Danny McGrain, Lou Macari, George Connelly, John Gorman, Jimmy Quinn and Vic Davidson. Davie Cattenach, later to become a good pal, was there, too, but he was ancient – two years older than me! A place in the first team seemed miles away at the time as I just concentrated on trying to get a game in the second eleven. It was a fabulous time to be learning your trade. I remember a Reserve League Cup game against Partick Thistle around that time. We had to win by seven clear goals to emerge from our section which also included Rangers. Strangely, we went into that encounter believing we could get those goals. We didn't think anything was beyond us.

Big Jock boosted the side by bringing in Bertie Auld and Joe McBride. It was awesome playing alongside two guys who had been my heroes only a year or so beforehand. We were eight goals ahead at one stage and coasting. I learned a thing about being a genuine professional that evening. Wee Bertie, a European Cup winner in 1967, was urging us to keep going forward. He gave us pelters if he thought we weren't going to go flat out for the entire ninety minutes. 'Come on, we've got time for another couple,' he exclaimed. Actually, we got another four to triumph 12-0 and I think that game more than emphasised and underlined the young talent Celtic had coming through at the time. With a little help from Bertie and Joe, of course.

That reserve team started to attract reasonable crowds as the Celtic fans wanted to know about a bunch of lads labelled The Quality Street Gang. Jock nurtured us along at his own pace, but he liked to give us a flavour of the big time by taking us away to Seamill every now and again with the first team players. They got to stay in the hotel, but we were crammed three to a room in a small house next door. I have to put my hands up here and say there was a certain amount of devilment about my young colleagues, including me, of course. We weren't bad lads, of course, but we took a risk or two with Big Jock.

I recall we were down in Ayrshire and the club were taking us to see Morton play a Texaco Cup tie at Cappielow. It was a tournament, now defunct, that included Scottish and English teams who had missed out on Europe. During that stay, Jock would always keep a close watch on the first team players. He was strict and being a teetotaller could never quite understand the lure of alcohol. He positively frowned on players he reckoned overindulged. What would he have said one evening when I was sent out to a nearby off-licence to buy a half-bottle of white rum for me and my pals? We were sitting at a table away from the first teamers and were topping up this drink with Coca-Cola. Jock would look over and see this bunch of choirboys sipping at their cokes. He would nod his approval and continue to survey the older players. I recall Davie Cattenach, George Connelly, Jimmy Quinn and myself had a few drinks, but Kenny Dalglish and Lou Macari, teetotal like Jock, abstained. How would the Celtic manager have reacted if he had known what we were up to? Simple. He would have buried us! Honestly, it was just a wee bit of devilment and, may I say, that outlook served us all well as we were coming through the ranks and sorting out opponents along the way.

I was combining football with accountancy at a firm called Kelman Moore and Company who were situated in Glasgow's St.Vincent Street. Would you believe they also did the books for Celtic Football Club? So, I could see what was going on over at Parkhead as far as finances were concerned. However, as I started to make a bit of a name for myself in football, someone at the firm thought it might be a good idea if I didn't see too much about the financial state of affairs at my club. As I've said, that was where I met my wife Catherine and I have to say she has been an absolute rock in my life and my career. Things can change dramatically and drastically in football, but Catherine has been one constant in my life.

One thing worried me, though, and as I was emerging at Celtic, I had to keep a secret from Big Jock – I was short-sighted. It was a tough enough task trying to get into that top side, but can you imagine how much more difficult it would have been if the manager had discovered I had any sort of impairment? I admit I had a wee problem under floodlights. I used to wear these contact lenses that covered your pupil. They were virtually undetectable and Jock never found out, thank goodness. Actually, I wasn't the only one who wasn't coming clean with the boss. I discovered Lou Macari, too, had contact lenses and he revealed all to me one night on a trip up to a game at Dundee. Actually, that could have been the occasion of one of my most embarrassing moments in football.

After the game, Lou asked me to help him get one of his lenses out. We waited until the coast was clear and went into a little cubicle. We were standing there, in this extremely small and cramped space, and I was bending over Lou. God forbid if anyone had opened the door and spotted the two of us in there together. It might have taken some explaining!

There was an opticians near where I worked in St.Vincent Street and they were pioneering a new type of contact lens that actually filled your entire eye and not just a little cap over the pupil. I decided to give them a try. I think it took about a day to get the things in place and then I asked Catherine what she thought of her new-look husband. She cried, 'For goodness sake, you look like Marty Feldman!' The aforementioned Marty just happened to be a bug-eyed comedian at the time who was more than just a little peculiar looking. 'Get them out before you frighten someone,' added my wife. And they were gone.

I was enjoying life, I was making good friends on and off the pitch, the football was top-class, the camaraderie between the players was splendid and I had an inkling I was getting closer and closer to that precious first team place. No one in The Quality Street Gang would admit it, but I think there was a race going on to see who would be the first to get the big call-up. As it happens, Jock Stein, with his usual immaculate sense of timing, introduced myself, Lou Macari, George Connelly, John Gorman and Jimmy Quinn in his line-up for the League Cup tie against Hamilton Accies at Douglas Park on 25 September 1968. As I recall, goalkeeper Bobby Wraith also got a first team opportunity and I don't think he played again. Jock was known to be a bit of a gambler away from football – it was no secret that he liked a punt on the ponies – but he wasn't exactly sticking his neck out on this occasion.

It was a two-legged affair back then and we got the nod for the second game after Celtic had overwhelmed their unfortunate opponents 10-0 a fortnight beforehand. Remarkably, there were only two scorers on that torrid evening for Accies keeper Billy Lamont. Stevie Chalmers and Bobby Lennox both claimed five apiece in the destruction of their rivals. So, Jock thought we couldn't possibly lose such a massive lead and in we came for our first game in the spotlight. I'm delighted to say we won again, this time 4-2 with Joe McBride (2), John Clark and Pat McMahon on target. Whatever happened to McMahon? He was Jock's first signing for the club after we won the European Cup in 1967. He joined from Junior outfit Kilsyth Rangers and once again Chelsea boss Tommy Docherty was pipped by his old club. I remember McMahon being an extremely stylish midfield player, slow but precise, and you would have thought Celtic would have been a natural club to promote his talents. Pat was also a superb guitar player and was often found with his nose in a good book. After a year or so, he moved onto Aston Villa. He came off the radar when he joined American outfit Portland Timbers, but he had all the skill in the world and should have done so much more at Celtic.

It was the following season that I was to make my breakthrough on a consistent basis. I started sixteen league games and made one appearance as a substitute. We won fourteen, drew one and lost one. We scored a truly astonishing fifty-five goals in those confrontations – over three goals per game. We racked up scorelines such as 8-1 and 5-1 against Partick Thistle, 7-1 vs Raith Rovers and 6-1 vs Motherwell, but had to be content with taking four off Morton and Ayr United while netting three against an exceptional Aberdeen team. We drew one blank, a goalless draw with Hearts, and my solitary league defeat came against

Hibs when they triumphed 2-1 in Glasgow. Big Jock encouraged my versatility and played me mainly at right or left back in these games, but I got a midfield berth, too, in four other encounters.

You may find this hard to comprehend but Jock also turned me out as a striker in some reserve games. There was no way he believed that this would be my preferred position, but he reckoned I would learn a thing or two about how opponents would play against you. I had a few stints at centre half as well, and I have to say it was an education facing someone and seeing how they dealt with a player coming at them. It was all knowledge that I would put to good use as my career progressed.

In the midst of all those league appearances there was one that stood out – the Old Firm clash with old foes Rangers at Ibrox on 20 September. I was from Paisley, but, of course, I knew all about the intense rivalry between these two giants and the friction among the fans, too. I never got caught up in the Catholic and Protestant divide for one simple reason; my father was a Protestant and my mother a Catholic. Brian and I attended a school in my mother's faith, but, you never know, it could so easily have gone the other way. Davie Hay of Rangers? Somehow doesn't seem right, does it?

The game at Ibrox passed in a flash. I had looked forward to being involved in this fixture since walking through the front doors of Celtic Park and it really was a special moment. Jock put me into midfield that day and I suppose you could take an informed guess and say it wasn't for my pretty ball-playing skills. I was there to get in about it, win the ball and distribute it as swiftly as possible without any frills. There were the usual collisions along the way and the ball must have been black and blue by the end of a rather frantic ninety minutes. Making the memory even sweeter was the fact we won 1-0. I remember the goal well. Harry Hood, as gifted a frontman you could find, showed some lovely skills in the box as he shimmied one way, went the other, dummied a Rangers defender and stroked the ball with elegant ease between the goalkeeper and his near post. Nice one, Harry, and thanks for the win bonus.

It would be fair to say that money wasn't exactly cascading into my bank account, but I wasn't grumbling. I was doing something I thoroughly enjoyed and I believed the financial rewards would come later. Catherine and I bought our first flat which was situated at Uddingston Cross for a whopping £600. We sold it about a year later for £650 and already I knew how to play the property market! That apartment consisted of a living room, kitchen and a bedroom. Believe it or not, we had an outside toilet. I was dedicated and disciplined and I was always in bed by nine o'clock on a Friday night. My treat to myself on the day prior to a match was a can of Irn Bru, a Mars bar and a single nugget purchased from Pacitti's Cafe which was just down the road. Catherine loved looking out of the window and there was a pub right across the road called The Anvil. I would retreat to bed at the designated hour, but all I could hear from Catherine was, 'Come and see this, David,' or 'Look at the state of this bloke.' I would shout back, 'Leave me alone, I'm trying to sleep.' Married bliss!

I picked up my first senior piece of silverware a year later when we beat St Johnstone 1-0 to lift the League Cup. However, I wished I had been anywhere else rather than the Hampden dressing room before the kick-off that afternoon.

3

HAMPDEN SURPRISE

I had played in five League Cup-ties at the start of season 1969-70, but had missed out on Celtic's 2-1 semi-final replay over a dogged, determined Ayr United side who had, in remarkable fashion, carved out a 3-3 draw in the first game. Goals from Harry Hood and Stevie Chalmers edged Celtic into the final where they would meet a very good St Johnstone team which contained some excellent individuals at Hampden on 25 October. At best, I thought I might get a place on the substitutes' bench and, remember, you could name only one stand-by player in those days. I believed it was more likely that I would be taking my place in the stand, though, to watch the action among the supporters. It came as a bit of a shock, then, when the team was read out just before the game: Fallon, Craig and Hay . . .

My mind went numb. I didn't see it coming, that's for sure. We had prepared for the game at Troon and Jock Stein hadn't given me the merest hint I would be selected for the Cup Final. The team continued: Murdoch, McNeill and Brogan, Callaghan, Hood, Hughes, Chalmers and Auld. Substitute: Johnstone. I thought, 'Wait a minute, back up there. Who's playing at left back? Hay? Me? Are you sure?' I was dumbfounded, but deep embarrassment set in about an hour from the kick-off. Tommy Gemmell, still a true friend to this day, had been dropped. And if I didn't anticipate being selected, I can tell you our extrovert left back certainly didn't anticipate being given the axe. Big Tommy, one of the best in his position in the world in his prime, had played in all ten previous ties in the tournament and threw in three goals for good measure, one being the winner against Rangers at Parkhead in a crucial game in the qualifying section.

Tommy had been his usual breezy self while we were gearing up for the match down at the Ayrshire coast. He was undoubtedly a huge favourite with the fans and was the proud possessor of one of the most pulverising shots in the game which he put to good use on a regular basis. Who will ever forget that outstanding equaliser in the European Cup success against Inter Milan in 1967? Not me and I watched the game on a black-and-white television back in Bothwell with Catherine who was my girlfriend at the time. Now here I was at Hampden ready to replace Gemmell just over two years later. It was hard to fathom.

As we prepared to go out and face our Perth rivals, Tommy, one of the calmest guys you have ever seen in your life when it came to getting ready for a big game, was at the Hampden entrance, giving out tickets to family and friends and having a chat with the fans. He would normally appear about forty minutes or so before kick-off, get into his strip, do a couple of stretching exercises and then run out with the team, geared up and raring to go. Not a care in the world. I was putting on the No.3 shorts, normally reserved for Tommy, when he appeared at the dressing room door. I remember he was wearing a long white coat with a belt and he looked like he could have been a Hollywood star. He was the epitome of flamboyance on and off the park. On this occasion, though, I saw his face drop. Jim Kennedy, a former player at the club, used to distribute the complimentary tickets to the players who would not be getting a game. I was looking for a place to hide as I felt for my teammate. What had he done wrong? Why was he dropped?

To this day, Tommy believes it was a punishment from Celtic

for being sent off on international duty a week beforehand when Scotland lost 3-2 against West Germany in a vital World Cup-tie in Hamburg. I remember the incident vividly. The Germans scored their third goal late on, with about fifteen minutes or so to go, and Tommy was haring onto a ball in one of his favourite areas, about twenty yards from goal. Helmut Haller, their midfielder, took the legs from Tommy and he went down in a heap. A clear free kick? You would have thought so, but the referee, rather amazingly, waved play on. It was a truly awful decision and I know exactly how my Celtic teammate felt as he got back to his feet. Reason goes straight out of the window. He chased after Haller and put him up into the air. This time the match official actually got his decision right; Tommy had to go. It's often the way of things, isn't it? The guy who instigates the incident gets off completely free and the unfortunate who has blown a gasket and retaliates is the one to receive the red card. It's just possible Celtic's board may have been extremely unhappy at one of their players being ordered off and they might have perceived it as bringing shame upon the club. If that was the case, then I think it was a brutal way of dealing with the situation. No matter what Tommy did in West Germany, he deserved better treatment from the club. No argument. There are other ways of letting a player know he is dropped. To my mind, that's not one of them. Tommy was so upset that he slapped in a transfer request the following day and it did take a bit of gloss off our triumph.

St Johnstone weren't the most fashionable outfit, but they had a knowledgeable manager in Willie Ormond, who would be my boss when Scotland got to the World Cup Finals in West Germany in 1974 – and I'll tell you a lot more about that fabulous adventure in a later chapter. They had first-class players in the likes of John Connolly, Henry Hall, Kenny Aird and Fred Aitken. They also had resolute characters in Benny Rooney, who had started his career at Celtic, John Lambie and Alex Rennie. They also had a reasonable keeper in Jim Donaldson, although, like a lot of his breed, he could veer towards the eccentric.

So, I was pumped up and looking forward to claiming my first medal. It could have been in happier circumstances, of course, and Tommy and I still talk about that afternoon to this day. However, I was there to do a job for the club and I was up against Aird, who reminded so many of our very own Jimmy Johnstone. He was a tricky, little outside-right with red hair and it was easy to make the comparison. He was good, but not in Jinky's class and I hope he doesn't mind me saying that. I don't think ANYONE was on the wee man's level of quality.

The game was fairly uneventful, especially when we scored in only the second minute with a close-range effort from Bertie Auld. That settled the nerves and invited the Perth outfit to take the game to us. There was bad news, though, when striker Stevie Chalmers, as gutsy a front player you could ever meet, broke a leg and had to be stretchered off. He was thirty-two years old at the time and I believe that was one of his last first team appearances for the club. It always shakes up a team when they see someone in obvious distress. But we had to keep our concentration against a Saints team that was geared up for attacking football with so many flair players. However, we soaked it up and kept them busy at the back with our own forward play. John Fallon, who had taken over from the injured Ronnie Simpson in goal, made a couple of decent saves to repel our opponents. And that was that. I went up those famous Hampden steps to the presentation ceremony and was handed my medal and the trophy to wave to the Celtic crowd. It was a marvellous feeling, believe me. 'I want some more of this,' I thought.

I did play in two other finals before the end of that season in the European Cup and the Scottish Cup. Alas, both were to end in defeat and I soon realised what a cruel game football could be.

4

A POINT TO PROVE

Jock Stein winced when he heard the ballot for the 1970 European Cup semi-finals. Celtic were drawn to play Leeds United while Dutch side Feyenoord would take on Polish outfit Legia Warsaw. Now if anyone believed our manager was displaying any sort of trepidation or foreboding at facing the side the English press were already acclaiming as the best in the world, they could not have been more wrong. Jock, in fact, secretly hoped Celtic and Leeds United, managed by his good friend and intense rival Don Revie, would meet in the showdown for European football's most glittering prize in the San Siro Stadium in Milan on the evening of 6 May.

Our astute boss knew we could beat the English champions. He was utterly convinced that the final in Italy would be the ideal setting, with the world looking on, to show once and for all that Celtic were a force to be reckoned with. It used to irk Jock that Celtic never got the credit, particularly from across the border, that he firmly believed we deserved. Not surprisingly, everyone at the club agreed with him. It annoyed the players, too, because we knew we were superior and we just wanted the opportunity to display our skills against Revie's outfit. Fate, though, dealt us a duff card and I am convinced to this day that cost Celtic their second European Cup in the space of three years.

We simply had to be content in putting Leeds United in their place in the two-legged semi-final. And, of course, that's exactly what we did. We were supposed to be intimidated by the Elland Road side. We had been written off by the English scribes as 'no-hopers' and we didn't really need an extra incentive to go out there and wipe the floor with this much-vaunted collection of highly-rated individuals. Jack Charlton, their World Cup-winning centre half, should have known better, but he, too, went on a television sports programme to more or less dismiss us. Oops. Those words would come back and bite him big-style.

So, you can take it from me that it was a fairly determined Celtic squad who embarked on the train at Glasgow's Central Station as we headed for Yorkshire and our first-leg meeting at Elland Road on 1 April. Or April Fool's Day, if you prefer. Someone was going to be on the receiving end of soccer's equivalent of a custard pie. To a man, we couldn't wait for the action to start. We were a team on a mission with a massive point to prove. Revie, like Stein, was a fox. He was always looking at ways of getting a psychological advantage over opponents, even down to berating the state of his own side's pitch and saying it wasn't conducive to good football at that late stage of the season. He knew we liked to play the ball on the carpet, but he was wasting his time if he thought we were going to take in any of this clap-trap. We weren't about to change the style that had become synonymous with our team.

Leeds also had this hard man image. Norman 'Bites Yer Legs' Hunter, for a start. What sort of nickname is that? And, sadder still, he seemed to revel in this juvenile, daft moniker. Do you think for a split second his reputation meant a thing to the likes of Bobby Murdoch or Bertie Auld? Or me, for that matter? Don't get me wrong; Leeds United were a very good team. Excellent, even. But they weren't at the same level as us and we knew it. They, too, would soon come round to our way of thinking. The off-the-field shenanigans went on right up until the kick-off. We were informed they had complained about our white socks to the referee. They were the same colour as Leeds', of course, but no one made any mention of it until just before the start. As our kit men hadn't packed alternatives we had to borrow orange socks from our opponents. If that, too, was designed to faze us in any way, shape or form, it was another error on their part. We could have played in our civvies that night and still won.

'Right, bring it on,' was our message to the Leeds players as the whistle blew to start the contest. Within a minute we were a goal ahead. My pal Big Geordie, George Connelly, struck a fine effort from just inside the box, it clipped their defender Paul Madeley and swirled away from the stranded Gary Sprake, Leeds' Welsh international goalkeeper. I'm convinced Geordie's effort would have hit the target, anyway, without the slight deflection. I saw their players looking at each other. 'What's going on?' they seemed to be saying. They were top dogs in England and I believe their sheer presence and all the ballyhoo surrounding the team frightened the life out of some opponents. They were probably terrified to cross the halfway line and here we were a goal ahead in the away leg of the European Cup semi-final. They looked just a little gobsmacked.

Geordie netted another, but, although he was clearly onside, the referee ruled it out for someone, I think it was Jimmy Johnstone, straying into an offside position. I've seen them given, as they say, nowadays. No matter. The game finished 1-0 and I don't think our goalkeeper Evan Williams had a save of any note to make throughout the ninety minutes that we controlled for lengthy periods. Wee Jinky was majestic. He scampered up and down the wing, wriggling away merrily with those mesmerising snake hips and the left-hand side of the Leeds defence was getting a torrid time. It didn't get any better, either, for our opponents a fortnight later when a crowd of 136,505 crammed into Hampden Park for the second instalment. Honestly, even now, almost four decades later, I can still feel a surge going through my body when I think back to that utterly unbelievable evening in that grey, old fortress. The hairs on the back of my neck still stand to attention at the recollection. The only game at our national stadium that comes anywhere close to that occasion as far as I'm concerned was the night Scotland beat Czechoslovakia 2-1 to cement our place in the 1974 World Cup Finals in West Germany. Our country had been out in the international wilderness for sixteen long, miserable years until that victory catapulted us back into the big time.

I'm getting ahead of myself, though. At Hampden on 15 April we had a job to complete. We were only halfway through and, of course, Leeds were a dangerous team who had made all sorts of noises about turning the tie around. There was still cash going on them getting to the San Siro. Some people have more money than sense. Mind you, we did get a jolt in the fourteenth minute when their inspirational skipper and my Scotland colleague Billy Bremner levelled the aggregate scores with an absolute screamer. Hampden had been awash in green-and-white beforehand and our supporters were in party mode. The place had been rocking for hours before the kick-off and the celebration parties up and down the country had already been planned. Pubs had been booked for 'lock-ins'. Hotels were standing by for a rush at full time. And then wee Billy tried to go and spoil things for the very team he grew up supporting as a schoolboy in Stirling.

It was a mighty effort from Billy, and Williams had absolutely no chance as it soared high into the top right-hand corner of his goal. Now here's a strange thing. Even at that particular moment, I did not believe for one second that we would lose the game. Billy had probably done us a favour by scoring so early as it gave us seventy-six minutes to fight back and this Celtic team could inflict an awful lot of damage on our opponents over that period of time. I'm fairly certain our keeper didn't have another save to make that evening. We rolled forward in numbers and the Leeds players were chasing their tails for a great deal of the match. Jinky once again took centre stage. He frustrated the life out of their defenders as he edged forward in that very individualistic manner of his, hips veering this way and that, and then suddenly the shoulder would go down and he was darting off as a hapless defender was left tackling fresh air. He did it time and time again.

Leeds could be a physical team and, yes, some of their more frustrated and exasperated players tried to kick our wee touchline terror, but it was all to no avail. Simply put, he was unstoppable. I actually began to feel sorry for Terry Cooper, their English international left back who would play in the World Cup Finals later that year. He would face the likes of Brazil's Jairzinho and not be given such a runaround. It was an electrifying, pulsating performance from Jinky and one I will always remember with the utmost fondness. I really liked that wee man.

Thankfully, I had a role to play in our equaliser two minutes after the turnaround. I was pushing forward down the right as often as I could with Jinky tying up their left side in knots. That freed space for me and I bombed up and down the wing as often as I could. It was only recently that my son-in-law Tommaso Angelini, who had a spell with Lazio in Italy, saw that match. 'My God, you were quick,' he exclaimed. And, after watching the footage, too, I had to admit even I was impressed by my pace. I ventured forward for the umpteenth time, gained a corner kick on the right and worked a short one-two with Bertie, who delicately swung in the sort of tantalising cross that every defender absolutely abhors. It was between the goalkeeper and his central defence. Does the keeper leave it to the man in front of him? Does the defender depend on his keeper coming for it? All you need is that moment's hesitation and you are in trouble.

Sprake elected to stay on his goal line while Charlton stood transfixed on the six-yard line. Big Yogi, John Hughes, was alert to the opportunity. He dived forward, got the merest of touches to Bertie's astute cross and suddenly his header was nestling in the net. Charlton shouted at Sprake. Sprake shouted at Charlton. Presumably, they would sort it out later in the dressing room. Not that we cared. Hampden was engulfed in bedlam as the crowd, still a record for a European tie, went into orbit. It was awesome. I glanced up at one of the stands and it looked as though it was bouncing. What a feeling. I've been a coach, an assistant boss, a manager, a chief scout, an agent and a director of football, but, believe me, there is nothing to touch playing. Especially on nights like that.

OK, so we are 2-1 ahead on aggregate and the final is looming in front of us. What do we do now? Shut up shop and defend what we have? Or do we go and get another? Remember, this was Jock Stein's Celtic we're talking about. There was no debate among the players. 'Let's get a second,' was the battle cry. 'Let's finish it.' And we did. Jinky, our tormentor-in-chief all night, set up a chance for Bobby Murdoch on the edge of the penalty area. David Harvey, another who would later become a Scottish team-mate, had taken over in goal after Sprake had twisted an ankle. David's timing could have been better. Murdy, with that powerful frame of his solidly behind any strike, walloped the ball first time and it was merely a blur as it zipped low past the stranded stand-in. Game, set and match, I think. Maybe, just maybe, we would now get the credit and acclaim our football deserved. Even the English media had to admit their 'world champions' had been played off the park twice.

We had reached the semi-final after beating Swiss champions Basle 2-0 on aggregate, somewhat fortunately dismissing former European kings Benfica on the toss of a coin after a 3-3 draw over the two legs and overcoming Italian aces Fiorentina 3-1 in the last eight. Leeds had been banished to oblivion and we would discover Feyenoord had edged past Legia Warsaw.

No one could have anticipated what that Dutch triumph over the Poles would actually mean to us. Until it was too late.

5

SHADOWS IN THE SAN SIRO

If only Jock Stein had got his wish and we had been drawn against Feyenoord in the European Cup semi-final of 1970. I am not being churlish, but I know we would have beaten our Dutch rivals over two legs. They might have caught us cold in the first game, but we would have seen them off in the second, trust me. It's been a long time coming, but I can only apologise to all Celtic supporters everywhere for our feeble, appalling, miserable performance in the 2-1 European Cup Final extra time defeat in the San Siro on 6 May 1970. I still feel a mixture of embarrassment and anger when I think back to that night in Milan. We let down everyone connected with the club.

Celtic were mere shadows of themselves in the San Siro. We were over-confident, there was maybe an unusual hint of arrogance. Unforgiveably, we might even have underestimated our opponents. Big mistake. We believed we had done the hard work in dismissing Leeds United in the semi-final and it was only a matter of turning up, going through the motions and then collecting the coveted silverware. Or so we thought. Everything went wrong before and during that confrontation. You would have been forgiven for believing we were gearing up for some sort of bounce game at the end of a gruelling season such was the uncharacteristic ineptitude in our preparation. We are all in the dock and guilty as charged. And I include Jock Stein, our manager who was normally so meticulous and thorough in going through the minute details of opponents before a big game.

For some obscure reason, Big Jock did not prepare as he normally would against the Rotterdam outfit. Maybe he was as culpable as his players in already believing we were the best team in Europe and no upstarts from Holland would stand in our way of conquering soccer's elite for the second time in three years. I don't think anyone should be sacrosanct or spared from criticism after by far the worst memory of my playing days. The better team won on the night and no one can debate that. The trophy went to the side that deserved it. How much different it would have been, though, if we had scraped a draw in the San Siro. And, remember, we were just three minutes from the end of extra time when they got the winning goal. The alarm bells were ringing loud and clear throughout the two hours of action against the Dutch. We were well and truly knocked out of our stride by a very competitive bunch of players – future Celtic manager Wim Jansen among them – whose concentration was absolute and their determination abundant.

I'll never know why Jock changed the side from the one that beat Leeds United in the second leg at Hampden. Actually, it's unfathomable and I am not having a go at the man to whom I owe so much just for the sake of it. Bobby Murdoch, George Connelly and Bertie Auld made up the core of that team as a midfield three. They sparked off each other and had the styles of play that dovetailed and complimented perfectly. Murdy was simply marvellous; a complete team man. His range of vision and the ability to thump devastatingly accurate passes all over the place was breathtaking. Big Geordie had frightening skill. He lacked pace, but he made the ball do all the work. Bertie was immense and would always accept responsibility. He and Murdy went into the tie against Leeds United up against the likes of

Billy Bremner and Johnny Giles, two extremely gifted individuals. Apart from Bremner's goal at Hampden – and Bertie has already held his hands up to accept responsibility for not shutting him down quickly enough – he was mainly deployed in a defensive midfield role over the two legs. Giles, too, was spending too much time chasing back for his own liking against Celtic. In truth, they were largely anonymous and that was down to the fact that Murdoch, Connelly and Auld were ruling the roost.

Then, inexplicably, Big Jock dropped Geordie for the final and put him on the substitutes' bench. He went with the two in midfield – Murdy and Bertie – that had worked so wonderfully well in Lisbon in 1967. This was a different game, though. Feyenoord were exceptionally strong across the middle of the park where their main man was Wim van Hanagem, who was dismissed by Jock as being a 'poor man's Jim Baxter'. It was unlike our boss to misread a situation, but on this occasion he got it wrong; very wrong. Our line-up played right into their hands. We had Jinky, Willie Wallace, John Hughes and Bobby Lennox as a four-man frontline, but with the Dutch's stranglehold in the middle of the park, they were starved of any reasonable service. Normally, I could get forward when Jinky was buzzing, but the wee man was being suffocated by their defence. They double-banked and even treble-banked on him. They tried to force him inside into an already cluttered midfield where they had players waiting to pick him off.

Feyenoord played a pressing game all over the park and we were struggling to get into any sort of rhythm. They worked our defence well and didn't give us a moment's respite. Ove Kindvall, their Swedish striker, was keeping Billy McNeill occupied while Jim Brogan had picked up an early foot injury that curtailed his movement a bit. Tommy Gemmell was getting forward, as usual, but our cavalier fullback also had his work cut out deep in his own territory.

Even our wonderful support seemed to be strangely subdued in the 53,000 crowd. The klaxon horns of the Dutch fans drowned them out and the entire atmosphere appeared to be geared towards Feyenoord. Rather remarkably, we scored a perfectly good goal that would have certainly stood today with all the technology we can call upon. Bobby Lennox got free on the left-hand side of their penalty box and hammered an unstoppable effort wide of their keeper, Pieters Graafland. Before we even got a chance to let loose a sigh of relief and celebrate we noticed that experienced Italian referee Concetto Lo Bello was blowing for offside. If you ever get the chance to watch TV replays of that goal again you will no doubt be astonished to find our speedy little frontman was played onside by THREE Dutch defenders. He was too fast for his own good sometimes.

And yet we still took the lead on the night through another whizz-bang effort from Big Tommy on the half-hour mark. Murdy neatly back-heeled a free kick to our rampaging defender and from about twenty yards he smashed it first time with his mighty right foot. The keeper actually looked a bit distracted by the match official who had taken up a strange position behind the Feyenoord defensive wall. He probably wouldn't have saved it anyway, as it thundered its way low into the net. That was probably the worst thing that happened to us that evening! If we were more than just a shade arrogant at the start, we were even more so now. We knew we hadn't been playing well, very little was coming off for us in our forward plays, and yet we were a goal in front. We could do no wrong.

That unlikely notion didn't last long – all of three minutes to be precise. Our defence made a mess of trying to clear a free-kick from the right and it bounced around until their skipper Rinus Israel got in a header. The ball looped high over Evan Williams and nestled in the far corner. I know better than most that football is all about ifs and buts. However, if we had held that lead until half-time there is no saying what the outcome of the game would have been. We could have gone in at the interval, had a good talk about what was happening out on the park and where we could hopefully put things right. It was still dead-locked at the turnaround and the dressing room was strangely quiet. There were a few in that Celtic team who liked themselves to be heard, but not on this occasion. I still think we believed deep down within ourselves we would beat them. 'The first-half was a bit of a fluke,' seemed to be the thinking. 'They can't be so good in the second-half.' Or 'We can't be that bad again.'

The Dutch klaxons were blaring once more as we trooped out for the second period and do you know something? Yes, they could be so good in the second-half. And, yes, we could be so bad. It was like stepping back into your worst nightmare after a brief fifteen-minute interlude. Hanagem, who went on to win over one hundred caps for Holland, was hitting passes with that gifted left foot; Jansen was playing like a man possessed; running, fetching, passing, shooting. Kindvall was still a handful for our central defence and we were gasping for air. Now I knew what it must have been like to be a Leeds United player facing us in the semi-finals. Bluntly put, we were getting a going over; a real doing. It was a painful experience, believe me.

Mainly thanks to our overworked goalkeeper Evan Williams we held out to take the game into extra time. If it had been about 4-1 or 5-1 for Feyenoord at the time no one could have argued. We defended as best we could against what appeared to be a never-ending onslaught from an eager collection of ambitious, well-primed professionals who sensed blood and knew victory was within their grasp. I recall one outstanding save from Evan as Jansen drove forward before unleashing a rasping drive from about twenty-five yards that looked destined for the roof of the net. Evan took off, twisted in mid-air and, quite magnificently, held onto the effort. In another game on another night that sort of brilliance would have inspired his teammates. Not this game and not this night.

Three minutes remained when the ref awarded the Dutch a free kick halfway inside our own half on the right. What happened next would have any self-respecting, defensive-minded coach sucking out his fillings and clawing out his hair. Murdy picked up the ball as soon as Lo Bello whistled for the foul and handed it to an opponent. Within seconds the Dutchman had placed it on the ground, took a quick glance up and propelled the ball towards the ever-lurking Kindvall. We didn't even get the opportunity to erect a defensive wall or pick up a player. Big Billy was left all on his lonesome as the ball homed in on its target. Our skipper couldn't set himself for one of his trademark clearing headers and as he back-pedalled he threw up his hands in desperation. His actions broke the flight of the kick and the ball dropped perfectly for the inrushing Kindvall. He raced in, Evan left his line, the Swede got a touch and his effort sailed serenely and precisely into the inviting net. And that was the end of our European dream. Those bloody, infuriating klaxons started up again and kept going all the way through the presentation. We were devastated.

There is absolutely no way that I would blame our world-class midfield man, but if only Bobby Murdoch hadn't been such a good sport. He could have let the ball run on and the Feyenoord player would have been forced to go and fetch it himself, giving our defence the time to get in place. Honours are won and lost in such a manner. As I have said, Feyenoord deserved their victory and there are no arguments from this quarter. However, I can assure everyone our Dutch opponents would have seen another Celtic, the real Celtic, in the replay. We would have made them pay for what they put us through at the San Siro. Also, we would have been only too aware of their true abilities and that was something we were not afforded in the countdown to that dreadful night.

Mistakes were made and, my God, were we made to pay for them. The Celtic fans deserved so much better. We failed them miserably that evening. It's a horrible recollection I would dearly love to obliterate from my memory banks. But, deep down, I know I never will.

6

OLD FIRM DUELS AND JEWELS

Whisper it, but I saw an awful lot of Rangers in action when I was growing up as a schoolboy in Paisley. Now I am fully aware that this startling admission – revealed for the first time – will send eyebrows rocketing skywards among the thousands of Celtic fans who have been nothing short of magnificent to me throughout my career. So, before I am accused of being a closet Ibrox fan, I better jump to my defence and come clean. My parents reckoned it was safe for my pals and me to make the short ten-minute train journey from Paisley to Govan. Celtic Park in the east end of Glasgow was a different proposition altogether. They weren't about to allow their son to trek halfway across Glasgow to take in a football game, but Rangers and Ibrox were OK.

I even witnessed Jim Baxter's debut for Rangers at Ibrox on 13 August 1960 when I was twelve years old. Slim Jim, as he became known, had figured prominently in the sports pages that summer after signing from Raith Rovers for £17,500. It was a Scottish record transfer fee and, to me, it was astronomical. How good was this guy who had cost a king's ransom? My pals and I had to see for ourselves. We jumped on the train at Paisley Gilmour Street with loads of Rangers supporters and made our way to Govan. I recall Rangers were playing Partick Thistle in a League Cup section game and there were 51,000 packed into the ground to get a glimpse of Baxter. He wore the No.10 shirt that afternoon and sauntered through the game, looking as though he had been a fixture in the Rangers line-up for years. Two goals from Jimmy Millar and a single from Alex Scott gave the home side a 3-0 win. I was well impressed by what I had seen. As I grew older I saw the light!

I was eleven years old the first time I saw Celtic in live action. My dad and I were at Hampden on 4 April 1959 for a Scottish Cup semi-final and St Mirren won 4-0. I also witnessed another Cup meeting between the two sides in March three years later. It was a second interesting sighting of the team that would become such a huge part of my life. The Saints triumphed 3-1 and the tie was disrupted as fans spilled onto the track. I should have known then, at the age of fourteen, that it was never going to be dull when Celtic were around!

Old Firm meetings were normally bone-shuddering, nerve-racking, tension-laden affairs. If you were fortunate, they were also morale-boosting. No quarter was asked or given. For so many of our fans, this was THE game. I knew a few who didn't care if we won the League title, the Scottish Cup or the League Cup – just so long as we took care of Rangers when we locked horns. Sad, really, but I had a fair idea of where they were coming from. It meant so much to these guys to get one over our rivals from across the Clyde. They call it bragging rights these days. It meant you could go to your work on Monday while the other half went into hiding. Greatest derby match in the world? You better believe it. Nothing comes remotely close. It may not always be pretty or easy on the eye, but these encounters, often played at a ferocious, frantic pace, were the ones that appealed so much to the man who means the most in football, the paying customer. They lapped them up then and they still do today. And they will tomorrow, irrespective of the actual quality that's on display. It's the Old Firm and there's not a game like it on this planet.

I didn't get off to the best of starts against Rangers as I recall we lost a Glasgow Cup-tie 4-3, but I am proud to tell you that I never again lost a game at Parkhead either as a player or a manager to them. That particular run kicked off on a freezing cold 3 January afternoon in 1969 in the east end of Glasgow; a typically tense encounter that ended goalless. I played right back that day, but earlier in the season I was in midfield when we played at Ibrox and triumphed 1-0 with a neat goal from Harry Hood. So, if you wipe out the Glasgow Cup loss, I started with a win and I finished with a triumph, too, as a manager when we beat Graeme Souness's side 3-1 on 4 April 1987 at Celtic Park with Brian McClair (2) and Owen Archdeacon on target.

Old Firm encounters were the acid test, as far as I was concerned. There was no hiding place in these often torrid affairs. You could thunder through the emotions against our lifelong rivals. Of course, there is always the fear of failure, but you cannot allow that to turn your legs to jelly. I have witnessed guys in that dressing room before kick-off who have done fair impersonations of nervous wrecks. They have looked as though they would much prefer to be elsewhere. Then the whistle goes to start the game and these same blokes instantly become masters of all they survey. It's a startling, mind-boggling transformation and you have to experience it to even attempt to understand it.

I have to admit I looked forward to these no-holds-barred confrontations. We were known as a team who liked to get the ball down and knock it around, but we could be physical, too, when it was warranted. John Greig was the epitome of a Rangers player back then. He was all hustle and bustle, putting himself about all over the pitch and giving everything for the cause. He could put in the welly, too, as Jimmy Johnstone could have told you! I'm not saying he was dirty, but he was hard and there is a world of a difference between the two. In one of my first games against the men from Ibrox I upended their skipper around the halfway line. The look on Greigy's face was priceless. He might have been querying, 'Who the hell is this young upstart?' You could say I was just putting down a marker. He chased after me later in that game following another clattering challenge from yours truly, but he calmed down and what could have been an unsavoury incident passed, thank goodness.

Players flying into tackles really got the fans going. You could make yourself a hero with a goal or two, but I realised the supporters also relished a player who would not hang back when there was a ball to be won. You would get almost as big a cheer for dumping an opponent on his backside as a player scoring a goal. Naturally enough, I can look back at these derbies and smile at some memories and scowl at others. I recall playing three games in three weeks at Ibrox at the start of season 1971/72 and Celtic won the lot – and I admit I was extremely fortunate to remain on the pitch in the last encounter. We were drawn against Rangers in the League Cup qualifying section and were also due to play them in the league. Major renovation works were going on at Parkhead at the time, so we had to play them three times on their ground. We won the first 2-0 on 14 August when Wee Jinky and Kenny Dalglish scored. We all knew Kenny had been a bit of a Rangers fan as he grew up in the shadow of Ibrox Stadium, but he didn't hesitate when it came to taking a penalty kick against them. He was utterly cool and composed as he strode forward purposely and slotted the ball into one corner as Peter McCloy took off for the other.

A fortnight later and we were back in Govan and this time we triumphed 3-0 with goals from Bobby Lennox, Tommy Callaghan and Kenny again. Then it was league business on 11 September and another victory, this time 3-2 with efforts from Johnstone, Lou Macari and, yes, you've guessed it, Dalglish. He was beginning to enjoy scoring against his boyhood idols. Three excellent victories and I managed to get booked in all three. I completely lost it when I was cautioned in the league game by Falkirk referee Alastair MacKenzie. I don't think my reputation was doing me any good at the time and I got the impression the match official couldn't wait to get my name in his little black book. He pulled me up for a relatively innocuous challenge and went to his pocket for his book. I just about went ballistic. I had a full head of steam as he motioned for me to come over. It would be fair to say I was raging. Luckily enough, I can't remember what my frank exchange of words were exactly, but there was no doubt that the name Alastair MacKenzie would not be figuring on the Hay Christmas card list any time in the future. Even Greigy tried to intervene as I came close to exploding. I was The Incredible Hulk for about five minutes! However, that was all part and parcel of Old Firm clashes. Sometimes they were a bit towsy, but they were always memorable for one thing or another.

After my first two appearances against Rangers, I played in a League Cup-tie at Ibrox on 13 August in 1969 when we lost 2-1, despite another fine effort from Harry Hood. We got our revenge a week later when Tommy Gemmell got the only goal at our place. That was the year when I would go on to pick up my first winners' medal – at Big Tommy's expense! We met up with our old chums again in the Scottish Cup quarter-final at Parkhead and I was fortunate enough to get on the scoresheet as we romped to a 3-1 win. Now I was never going to be noted for my goalscoring, so I have perfect recall of the ones that did hit the back of the opposition's net. The pitch that day was just a sea of mud, but that didn't prevent two sets of players piling into one another and giving it everything for ninety minutes. My magical moment arrived in the second-half as I carried the ball forward from the old inside-left position. I made up my mind early that I was going to have a go. I leathered the ball goalwards with all the power I could muster from about twenty-five yards.

Their keeper Gerry Neef made an acrobatic attempt to push my attempt over the bar, but there was only one destination for that ball as soon as it left my boot and that was the roof of the net. It wasn't a bad goal, even if I do say so myself! Johnstone and Lennox were our other scorers in a day when you had to be brave and courageous in monsoon conditions.

How did we celebrate that extraordinary victory? Most of the younger players were invited to an evening wedding reception at St. Margaret Mary's in Glasgow's sprawling Castlemilk housing scheme! Our young teammate Tony McBride was getting hitched later that day and had extended invitations to a lot of the lads he played alongside as we battled to come through the ranks. Tony was an exceptional talent, but, rather sadly, he lost his way and was allowed to leave Celtic early. I have no doubt whatsoever that he could have been part of The Quality Street Gang. Tony had been the most sought-after youngster in Britain after scoring two goals for Scotland Schoolboys against their English counterparts at Wembley. Manchester United were ready to offer him the moon to go to Old Trafford. Their manager at the time was Sir Matt Busby, a good friend and confidante of our own Jock Stein, and he even travelled to Castlemilk in an effort to persuade Tony to try his luck with United. Sir Matt was wasting his time. Celtic were Tony's team and I don't think the Parkhead management had to try too hard to tempt him to sign for them. But, for whatever reason, he was given a free transfer in 1971. Possibly, football came too easily to Tony. However, there are a lot more requirements if you are to make it in the game than just mere skill. You have to apply yourself and be dedicated. You have to be prepared to make sacrifices and you must have the correct mental attitude. Maybe Tony didn't possess that outlook. He might have taken things for granted and expected everything to fall into place. That doesn't happen in football, believe me, and Tony, who was obviously something of a free spirit, was allowed to leave.

That was the week before we were due to play Aberdeen in a league game in Glasgow on 6 November. I am reliably informed that Tony, bedecked in a huge woolly green-and-white scarf, was in the Celtic end that day cheering us on. I played that afternoon as we drew 1-1 and, but for the grace of God, it could have been Tony McBride performing in the hoops. I suppose football is littered with stories like Tony's, more's the pity.

We got to the Scottish Cup Final that year, but lost 3-1 to Aberdeen at Hampden after one of the most diabolical refereeing performances in the history of the game from Airdrie's Bobby Davidson. The players realised there was always a bit of friction between Big Jock and the match official. However, the ref's display that afternoon is one that is burned into my memory banks for all the wrong reasons. I doubt if he would have got away with it today because of the television exposure. Certainly, there were some very puzzling decisions, to say the least. I'll elaborate on that particular confrontation in another chapter.

We continued the good work against our ancient adversaries Rangers when the next season kicked off. Bobby Murdoch and John Hughes scored in a reasonably comfortable 2-0 win at our place on 12 September, but we were given a real jolt in the next match, the 1970 League Cup Final when we lost 1-0 at Hampden. No one, including the bookies, saw that one coming. We were clear favourites and I have to say our already-confident outlook was boosted further when we were told Rangers would be without skipper John Grieg. He was by far their most inspirational player and we believed he would be sorely missed. We would never underestimate the Ibrox side, but we thought our name was on the trophy that year. We had beaten Hearts and Clyde twice and drawn on two occasions with Dundee United in the qualifying section. We then drew 2-2 with Dundee at Dens Park before walloping them 5-1 in Glasgow. We made really heavy weather of overcoming Dumbarton in the semi-final. We couldn't buy a goal in the first game. However, we netted four in the replay with the only snag being that they scored three themselves. That should have been a wake-up call to us.

It was another rain-lashed occasion at the national stadium and we had little to celebrate as a sixteen-year-old Derek Johnstone outjumped Billy McNeill and Jim Craig about eight yards out to get his head to a right-wing cross from Willie Johnston. To be fair to Derek, it was a perfect header that arrowed in low down to Evan Williams' right-hand post. An Old Firm dust-up would never be allowed to pass without some sort of talking point and referee Tiny Wharton provided it when he rejected our claims for a stonewall penalty kick in the second-half. Lou Macari was clean through on the exposed Peter McCloy and the giant Rangers keeper brought him down. There was a marvellous photograph of the incident in a newspaper the following day that caught the image perfectly. Lou was up in the air and McCloy was clearly culpable. Much to our annoyance and Rangers' relief, Tiny waved play on.

The next head-to-head at Ibrox on 2 January 1971 is one that nobody will ever be able to forget for all the wrong reasons. It seemed almost incidental that the game finished tied at 1-1 with Jinky getting our goal and Colin Stein equalising in the last minute. There are defining moments in your life that make you understand your priorities and this was one of them. Sixty-six fans lost their lives that afternoon when a passageway collapsed at the Rangers end. It's difficult to comprehend such a scale of disaster when you are so close to it. We were devastated when the news filtered through. The number of casualties was rising by the minute. It was a black day for sport.

We met Rangers again later that season in the Scottish Cup Final and Derek Johnstone scored once more. However, his late equalising goal merely forced a replay and we won the second game 2-1. We were leading 1-0 in the first match through a typical strike from Lennox. That looked good enough to bring the silverware home to the east end of Glasgow, but there was a distinct communication breakdown between George Connelly and Williams as an Ibrox player hoofed a clearance down the park. Our guys hesitated and Johnstone looked as though he was chasing a lost cause. However, as luck would have it, the ball took an awkward bounce and seemed to hold up in the wind. Williams rushed from his goal and was caught in no-man's-land as Johnstone got his head to the ball to nod it over our keeper's upstretched arms. It took an eternity to roll over the line and it was back to Hampden for the replay the following Wednesday.

You might already have got the impression that the players thoroughly enjoyed beating Rangers and we would dine out on triumphs for some considerable time. But the guy at Parkhead who loved more than most to turn over the Ibrox side was none other than Jock Stein. He would tell the public that beating Rangers was just the same as beating anyone – you still got two points, as it was back then. However, this was not what was said in private. Jock didn't like them at all and he would be all smiles after a win over Rangers. It meant so much to him to put them in their place. It was almost an obsession with our gaffer. So, you can take it from me that he was far from happy with our slack play that had gifted Rangers their equaliser in the fading moments of that game when it looked well and truly over.

We made no mistake in the replay although, as ever, we threw them a lifeline near the end that made it a tense and nervy finish for us. We were given the Rangers team sheet in our dressing room and we all looked a little puzzled when we saw who was listed at right back. It was a youngster called Jim Denny and their manager Willie Waddell had decided to give him his debut in place of the injured Alex Miller. I think Denny had just signed that season from Junior club Yoker Athletic. He was immediately pinpointed as a weak link. We were two goals ahead by the interval and Wee Jinky was in one of his most exhilarating moods. There was nothing defenders could do when the wee man was in that sort of form. The ball seemed to be superglued to his toes as he teased and tormented Rangers down both flanks. Lou Macari swept in a close-range effort from a left-wing corner-kick to give us an early advantage and Harry Hood netted the second via the penalty spot after Jinky had been sent sprawling by a panicking Ronnie McKinnon. We were well in control, but once again Derek Johnstone upset our defence at a high ball and Jim Craig turned it into his own net. We were furious. 'Not again,' we all thought. We held out, though, and the trophy was bedecked in green-and-white ribbons again.

As I have said, these encounters could be fought in ferocious fashion and I recall incurring the wrath of the Rangers support in one game at Ibrox. In fact, it ended with them chanting my name, but, unfortunately, with the addition of 'is a bastard' at the end of their little ditty that rocked around the stadium! What had I done to provoke such a response? Well, I clattered into Sandy Jardine and somehow he ended up going clean over my shoulder. He landed awkwardly and was down for some time as he received treatment. That's when the Ibrox choir decided to exercise their vocal chords. Funnily enough, Sandy – who could also dish it out, by the way – became a very good friend during our international days together and, of course, we were both in the 1974 World Cup Final squad in West Germany.

There was another time when I went in hard on a Rangers player and, again, he went down looking as though he had had ten tons of bricks dropped on him. Big Jock Wallace was the Ibrox manager at the time and he came bounding out of the dugout, racing to where I was on the touchline. Now Jock was a massive guy who had been a trained soldier but I wasn't for backing down. I gave him a look that said, 'What are you going to do about it?' Thankfully, he didn't come onto the pitch because that would have made for a very interesting confrontation. Like Sandy, though, he became a friend when we were both managers of the Old Firm.

Don't get the impression it was all fury and no football in these games. There would be the usual threats and counter-threats from both sets of players. 'I'm going to do you.' 'Not if I do you first.' That sort of thing. But there were some extremely entertaining meetings.

I've already talked about the start of the 1971/72 campaign when we won three out of three at Ibrox. In fact, we had a clean sweep that term as we also overcame them 2-1 in the league match at Parkhead on 3 January. Jinky scored for us, but it was deadlocked at 1-1 when our left back Jim Brogan, of all people, raced unchallenged into their box as he followed a long cross in from the right. Jim got his head solidly on the ball and his effort flew into the net for a last-minute winner. Good timing, Jim!

I wasn't smiling a year later when we went down 2-1 in the league at Ibrox despite a Dixie Deans goal. It didn't get much better, either, when we lost 3-2 in the Scottish Cup Final in the most bizarre of circumstances on 5 May at Hampden. As usual, it poured down from the heavens, but we still took the lead through a deft flick from Dixie to Kenny who fairly hammered it past McCloy into the net. We were sloppy, though, shortly afterwards and allowed Alex MacDonald time and space on the left to sling in an inviting cross and Derek Parlane sent a header wide of Ally Hunter. Alfie Conn, later to become a Celtic player, got their second when he, too, was given far too much leeway as he ran through the centre of our defence before tucking his effort low past Hunter.

We got a penalty kick when John Greig punched a shot from

Dixie off the goal line. The Ibrox skipper must have been relieved that he didn't receive an automatic red card as would happen these days, of course. George Connelly stepped up, casually sauntered forward and fired the spot kick wide of McCloy. I was watching a rerun of the game the following day and I had to smile when I heard the TV commentator's take on the penalty. I recall he said, 'Up comes Connelly and he rarely misses.' He had never missed a penalty kick, in fact. That was the first he ever took!

At 2-2, the game could have gone either way as the clock ticked down in the second-half. We conceded a free kick midway inside our own half on the left. Tommy McLean was a bit of an artist with deadball efforts and, of course, we had all been well warned about Derek Johnstone's prowess in the air as he had demonstrated far too often against us for our liking. McLean flicked it into the packed penalty area and, unbelievably, Johnstone was given a free header. He glanced the ball down to Hunter's right. It eluded his grasp, struck the inside of the upright and ran tantalisingly along the goal line. Our collective sighs of relief were a bit premature. No one had picked up their defender Tom Forsyth at the other post. Tom used to score as frequently as the eclipse of the moon, but he couldn't miss this one. Or could he? He was about a yard out when he stabbed his right foot at the ball. He didn't make a clean contact, it got stuck under his studs and then agonisingly rolled over the line. What a sickener.

I was destined to play only three more games against Rangers and, happily, we won the lot. I was in the side for the opening league game of the 1973/74 season on 15 September at Ibrox. Wee Jinky scored the only goal of the encounter and we enjoyed an identical scoreline in the 5 January match in the east end of Glasgow. Bobby Lennox, so often the slayer of our deadly rivals, was on target once more that afternoon. Earlier we had beaten them 3-1 in the League Cup semi-final with Harry Hood grabbing a classy hat-trick. However, as I came off the pitch after the January fixture, I couldn't have believed that I would not face those guys again for another nine years. This time, of course, I would be in the Celtic dugout as their new manager.

I was in charge of my first Old Firm fixture on 3 September 1983 while my old adversary John Greig was in the opposition's dugout. He would later be replaced by Jock Wallace, of course. I liked Big Jock. He was a gruff individual to some, but I mixed in his company on several occasions because managers of the Old Firm are often invited to the same ceremonies and functions. He was an honest guy, but, like Jock Stein and Billy McNeill before me, I was only too aware of what beating Rangers meant to our support. I couldn't have wished for a worse start to these games as a boss – Rangers were a goal ahead in the first minute. Ally McCoist sent in a whiplash effort from the edge of the box and I don't know if our keeper Pat Bonner was unsighted or not, but the ball sped straight through his legs into the net. Oh well, we had plenty of time to fight back. And that's exactly what we did, to claim the first Old Firm scalp of my managerial career with goals from Roy Aitken and Frank McGarvey. I believe I had a glass or two to celebrate afterwards!

It was on to Ibrox for our second meeting on 5 November and once again we triumphed, 2-1 again with fine efforts from McGarvey and Tommy Burns. We had to wait five months for our next league meeting, but in between there was the little matter of the League Cup Final scheduled for Hampden on 25 March. I am not one for making excuses, but it just wasn't our day as we went down 3-2. Rangers were awarded two penalty kicks and McCoist netted one and saw the other saved by Bonner before he followed up to tuck away the rebound for the winner in extra time. Ally claimed a hat-trick that afternoon and our goals came from Brian McClair and a spot kick from Mark Reid. We got our revenge in fine style as we trounced them 3-0 in a midweek game on 2 April. We played exceptionally well and deserved to win, no doubt about it. Goals from the McStay brothers, Paul and Willie, and another from Davie Provan gave us the points. We went down 1-0 at their place nineteen days later.

We didn't lose any of the four league meetings the following season, but three ended in draws. The first was at Ibrox on 25 August and ended scoreless. It was 1-1 at Parkhead on 22 October with McClair on target for us. The New Year's Day fixture brought us a 2-1 success with McClair and Mo Johnston getting the goals that mattered. Alan McInally, my £100,000 buy from Ayr United, netted in the 1-1 draw at Parkhead on 1 May. We still couldn't separate ourselves when the 1985/86 term kicked off. Peter Grant claimed our goal in the opening fixture at our place on 31 August, but we were hit by an onslaught at Ibrox three months later as we collapsed 3-0. It was a dreadful performance from us and I had no quibbles about the result. We got what we deserved that afternoon – zilch. We were far better prepared by the time the 1 January encounter came around at our place. I had let my players know in no uncertain manner that I would not tolerate a repeat of their awful display at Ibrox. Thankfully, they were listening. Centre half Paul McGugan headed in the opener and McClair – again! – got the second. That was a lot more like it.

The next derby duel was a jewel of a game – a truly remarkable 4-4 draw at Ibrox. The previous seven encounters had brought in fourteen goals at an average of two per game. And here we were watching an eight-goal spectacle. We had Willie McStay sent off in the first-half after a challenge on their awkward left-winger Ted McMinn. Actually, Willie might even admit this today, but he was getting a fairly tough time of it from McMinn and I had it in my mind to take him off at the interval. I didn't get the opportunity – the ref did my job for me! Brian McClair, Mo Johnston and Tommy Burns scored for us during a tumultuous tussle, but, with the game coming to a close, we were trailing 4-3 as they had scored through Cammy Fraser (2), Ally McCoist and Robert Fleck. It was inconceivable we could lose after leading twice in the game. Again, the ground conditions were very heavy and I'll never know where Murdo MacLeod summoned up the raw power to hammer in an unstoppable equaliser from about thirty yards past their keeper, Nicky Walker. Actually, it had been a thoroughly enjoyable ninety minutes' worth of entertainment and Jock Wallace and I agreed on that at the end. It was to be my old Rangers rival's last game in charge of the team in an Old Firm fixture. What a way to bow out.

People were writing us off in the race for the title that season and Hearts seemed to be on course for success. But I knew I had a good dressing room; a determined one, as well. No one at Celtic had given up the chase and I will talk at length about that truly astounding eight-game run-in that brought the championship home to Parkhead in another chapter. Season 1986/87 saw massive changes at Ibrox. Jock Wallace, of course, was out, Graeme Souness was in and he had been spending big money during the summer. We had finished with the title while our old foes had completed the season in fifth place behind us, Hearts, Dundee United and Aberdeen. Souness had been allowed to spend £750,000 in bringing in England captain Terry Butcher from Ipswich Town and another £600,000 on his international teammate Chris Woods, the Norwich City goalkeeper. He had also paid out a 'modest' £200,000 for Watford striker Colin West. It was quite a shake-up and remember, too, that Souness was player/manager, so he wasn't a bad acquisition, either, to the squad. It was going to be a monumental task to hold onto our trophy because I could only dream about the sort of money my opposite number was splashing around in the transfer market. My big summer signing was left back Anton Rogan from Irish club Distillery for about ten grand. It was good to see the Celtic board were taking note of what was happening across the road!

It was difficult enough accepting that Rangers had so much cash to splash in the pre-season, but their chairman, David Murray, also came up with the idea that he should give his team's supporters what was known as a 'Christmas gift' every year. That always took the shape of a new and expensive player. Of course, it is always a good time to strengthen your squad and a new face can give the place a lift. I recall that one such signing was England international Graham Roberts who arrived for £400,000 from Spurs. At one stage it looked as though Rangers would have more Englishmen in their team than Scots!

We lost the opening Old Firm game of season 86/87 1-0 with Ian Durrant scoring on 31 August at Ibrox. A goal from McClair helped us to a 1-1 draw at Parkhead on 1 November and then we went down 2-0 in the New Year's Day fixture with Ally McCoist and Robert Fleck on target. We completed the campaign with a 3-1 triumph on 4 April when McClair (2) and Owen Archdeacon scored. But the derby that will be imprinted in my memory banks forever was the League Cup Final at Hampden on 26 October the previous year. At one stage of that extremely controversial collision I came close to going up like Vesuvius. I was raging at referee Davie Syme when he awarded Rangers a penalty kick nine minutes from time after he had also sent off Mo Johnston. He tried to order off our young winger Tony Shepherd, claiming he had punched him on the back of the head. Actually, he had been struck by a coin thrown by an obviously irate fan. What a lot of nonsense to believe a player would wallop him in front of an audience of thousands at the ground and millions worldwide tuning in on the television. It was only after the linesman intervened that Tony was allowed onto the pitch again. The match official completely lost the plot with some of his decision-making that afternoon. That was a shame because up until he decided to take centre stage it hadn't been a bad game at all. They scored first through Ian Durrant, but we levelled with an absolute belter from Brian McClair. Brian's tally against the old enemy was nine in my four years as a manager. It was an impressive haul.

We were looking forward to the second-half, but Syme was making decisions that were baffling, to say the least. I could feel my blood beginning to boil. Mo got involved with their left back Stuart Munro and it was a mere case of handbags. The Rangers player went down and Syme was quick to flash the red card under Mo's nose. What on earth was going on? I was standing on the touchline at the time with the ball in my hands. For a split-second I thought about volleying it as powerfully as possible in the direction of the ref, but, thankfully, I had a swift change of mind. I guessed it would be an action that would send an already powder-keg confrontation into utter chaos. In all, the referee booked ten players that day and that would lead you to believe it was simply a kicking match. It wasn't – he just went card daft at one stage. The game was heading for extra time when Syme handed them a spot kick in the most remarkable of circumstances. A corner-kick came in from the right and Roy Aitken and Terry Butcher went for it at the back post. These are two big guys we are talking about and both were extremely passionate captains of their respective clubs. They were jostling with each other and it looked to everyone that it was a case of six of one and half a dozen of another. Well, everyone apart from Syme, who was, by the way, positioned at the near post and would have required x-ray vision to see through a crowd of players to witness what was going on between Roy and Terry.

I couldn't believe it when he pointed to the penalty spot. To be fair, even the Rangers contingent looked more than a little surprised by this absurd decision. Davie Cooper took the kick and sent the ball low into the corner of the net. And that was that. I was furious, absolutely livid. It was an outrageous bit of refereeing and it cost us the game and the trophy. When decisions are made like that it leaves a sour taste in your mouth. We had prepared well for that final. The boys had worked hard in training and I had poured over our tactics time and time again. I had plotted an offensive line-up that had McClair and Johnston up front supported by Mark McGhee and Alan McInally. Paul McStay, Murdo MacLeod and Shepherd were in midfield and fullbacks Peter Grant and Derek Whyte were given licence to get forward down the flanks when the opportunities arose. Murdo was also deployed to help out Roy in central defence. It looked to be working a treat until Syme made the decisions that backfired big-style on us. Afterwards I couldn't prevent myself from showing my anger. I just could not calm down. 'I think we should take Celtic to England,' I said, a bit ahead of my time. 'At least, we'll get a fair crack of the whip down there.' I meant it, too.

Sadly, I wouldn't get another opportunity to win silverware as manager of Celtic. I was sacked seven months later.

7

STRIKING OUT AT CELTIC

I made history when I became the first player to go on strike at Celtic late in 1973. I withdrew my labour for a fortnight in a dispute over wages and I firmly believed I was in the right. My pal George Connelly came out in sympathy with me for a week and suddenly Jock Stein had a mutiny on his hands! No problems with players for eighty-five years since the club had been formed in 1888 and suddenly two players are walking out within a fortnight. You couldn't make it up.

Back in those unenlightened times before Bosman, players were handcuffed to their teams. The clubs were firmly in command of your destiny and players were bought and sold like cattle. I know of some players who left Celtic who would have been quite happy to have spent their entire career in the east end of Glasgow. I should know what I am talking about because I was one of them.

Frankly, I didn't believe I was getting what I was worth at Celtic. I was on a basic £65 per week for playing for one of the game's biggest clubs with a fan base that covered the planet. Yet, when it came to pay talks there was no negotiation. You were told that was what was on offer and that was the end of it. The Celtic secretary at the time was Desmond White and I actually got on really well with him. He was a chartered accountant who had offices in Bath Street at the corner of West Nile Street in

Glasgow. As you might expect, every penny was a prisoner and I spent a lot of time in his company around that time trying my best to shake loose a few extra quid. It would have been easier picking up an elephant by its tail and hurling it the length of Sauchiehall Street. It was all a colossal waste of time. No matter what argument I put forward, Desmond was not responding. Listen, anyone who knows me will tell you I am not a greedy individual. Money is not a god.

The problem was simple. I had broken into the first team in 1969, played in a European Cup Final a year later and had gone on to become a regular selection for club and country. My head wasn't turned by what I heard Scottish players in England were earning. 'Good luck to them,' was my response. Leaving the club I genuinely loved wasn't a priority. I wanted to stay and get the rate of pay I thought I deserved. I told the club I thought I was worth £100 per week. As you might expect, they disagreed. I had missed some of the previous season through injury and suddenly I realised it was difficult to make ends meet on a basic £65 when you stripped your normal wage of bonuses and first team appearance money. I felt the pinch and so, too, did my family. I had to take action.

I had a lengthy conversation with Desmond White and basically it came down to him saying to me, 'Davie, if I give you £100 then I'll have to give the rest of the first team that, too.' I replied, 'Go ahead then. Give them what they are due.' The club had built their wage structure in such a way that it kept you keen and competitive and I didn't see anything wrong with that. However, if a player did receive a bad injury while on duty and doing his best for the team then it seemed a bit savage that his reward was a massive cut in wages. It was time to do something about it. I may have appeared laid-back to the point of horizontal to a lot of onlookers, but, believe me, I can be as impetuous as the next guy and I can hit the roof with the best of them. I can act on the spur of the moment as you will undoubtedly learn as you read on.

As far as I was concerned, Celtic left me with no alternative – I would go on strike. I told some of my teammates about my intentions. 'You can't do that,' they chorused to a man. 'No one walks out on Celtic.' Oh, yeah? Watch this space. I duly informed Jock of my course of action and I'm not sure if he thought I was calling his bluff or not. He soon discovered that I wasn't. I played in the 3-1 victory over Hearts at Tynecastle on 27 October 1973 and then missed the following five league games against East Fife, Ayr United, Partick Thistle, Dumbarton and Arbroath stretching from 3 November to 1 December. If my mates were missing me it didn't show – Celtic won the lot, including an 8-0 triumph over poor old Thistle when Dixie Deans hammered six past Alan Rough.

By that stage of the season you are fairly fit. All the hard work is done pre-season when you come back from your summer break and try to shed some excess baggage. Luckily for me, I have never had a problem with my weight. While I was on strike I trained on my own. I would go for lengthy runs and work out in public parks or gyms. I knew I had to be match-fit just in case I got the call from Big Jock. And that call did come – a couple of days before an Old Firm confrontation no less! Jock knew I would not back down from my stance and, by the same token, I realised full well the Celtic manager would not perform a U-turn, either. We had reached an impasse. We had to find some middle ground in which to negotiate and Jock used a journalist friend of his, the late Jim Rodger who was with the *Daily Express* at the time. Jim was a bit of a Mr Fixit in the days before agents. He was involved in a lot of transfer deals and I think he was behind Denis Law's move to Manchester United from Italian side Torino and the likes of Alan Gilzean to Spurs from Dundee and Ian Ure to Arsenal from the Dens Park outfit. He was fairly well connected. I respected him and he turned up at my door one day to say, 'It's time you were back playing. This is doing no one any good.' He was right, of course. He conveyed the message that I was prepared to return to the fold.

I was told to get down to Parkhead and prepare for the League Cup semi-final against Rangers at Hampden on Wednesday, 5 December. I thought I was ready to play, but feeling fit and being match-fit are two different things, take my word for it. 'You're in,' I was told and I duly turned out against our oldest rivals at our national stadium in a must-win game. I knew only too well that all eyes were on me. Some Celtic fans were in my corner, but I also realised there were a few who, as ever, sided with the club. I put all that behind me, determined to prove to Celtic that I was worth a wage hike. I'm glad to say we won 3-1 with a marvellous hat-trick from Harry Hood. It was a great feeling to be back, but I can now confess I was absolutely shattered after that encounter. I was just about out on my feet in the last ten minutes or so, but I managed to get through it. Jock knew what he was doing. He had pitched me in at the deep end and I had to respond in kind. I think I managed that. At the end of the game Jock patted me on the back and growled, 'Well done.' Praise indeed.

I still thought I had to move on to realise my value and just before I took strike action Celtic were willing to sell me to Spurs. I believe the White Hart Lane side offered something in the region of £200,000, a lot of money in those days, and I agreed to talk to them. I met their manager, Bill Nicholson, and I have to say I was impressed. There was no haggling over wages, either. I was told they would put me on a basic £165 per week and that would rise with bonuses. I would also receive a £10,000 lump sum from Celtic for accepting the transfer. I thought about it long and hard and I have to admit I was hugely tempted. At the same time I learned Manchester United were interested. Tommy

Docherty was never one to accept no for an answer. I waited for them to make their move and, with absolutely no disrespect to Spurs, I would have preferred a move to Old Trafford. My wee pal Lou Macari had told me all about the club and I knew he was enjoying his football alongside so many other Scots such as George Graham, Jim Holton, Martin Buchan, Ted McDougall and Alex Forsyth. The team had even been dubbed 'Mac-chester United' because there were so many of my fellow countrymen at the club. I have to say I could see me fitting in at United. Big Jock had other ideas, though.

He told me he would not sell me to Manchester United. I don't know if he was still upset by Lou's move to join Tommy Doc's clan the previous year, but he would not budge on his stance. 'You'll go where we tell you to go,' I was informed. Jock wanted me to move to Spurs and accept the £10,000 pay-off from the club. There would be no lump sum if I persevered in trying to get to Old Trafford. United, I was reliably informed, were willing to match any transfer fee that Spurs put in. Still, Jock was having none of it and, naturally enough, that angered me. I thought it was only right and proper that I could go where I liked and Celtic would get £200,000 for a player who hadn't cost them a penny. That was another factor in me walking out. I was in a quandary, though. The World Cup Finals in West Germany were looming in the summer and I realised I would not be part of Willie Ormond's squad if I wasn't playing regular first team football at club level. In short, Jock held all the aces. And he knew it.

I didn't have too many alternatives. I had to bite the bullet, get back into the Celtic side and forget all about a big-money transfer or a wage rise. I was a professional and I had to act in such a manner. Jock realised how much it meant to me – and every other player, for that matter – to turn out in those green-and-white hoops. No one wanted to leave, but at the same time everyone wanted what they thought they were due. That's why Lou left in the first place. He was aware of his market value and, like me, the club simply refused to make him an offer he couldn't refuse. I don't think Kenny Dalglish wanted to leave, either. Again, money was the sticking point and, after a summer of discontent, he eventually moved to Liverpool. Celtic banked £440,000 and never really replaced him.

So, I decided to forget all about London or Manchester and get on with taking care of business in Glasgow. I spoke to Catherine about the possibility of buying a pub after coming back from the World Cup. A friend of mine, Gerry Gallon, owned The Carousel Bar in Motherwell and he was willing to show me the ropes. I reckoned such an acquisition would help bolster my weekly wage because it was only too evident that Celtic were never going to give me an increase.

Little did I realise when I waved the newly-won Scottish Cup to the fans – we had just beaten Dundee United 3-0 on 4 May – that I would never play at Hampden again for Celtic. Things would take a rather dramatic turn, but before that there was the matter of the World Cup Finals in West Germany to be addressed.

8

THE INTERNATIONAL
BREAKTHROUGH

Scotland came home to a heroes' welcome after the 1974 World Cup Finals. Every Scottish player, manager Willie Ormond, his backroom staff and the SFA contingent could hardly believe it when we touched down at Glasgow Airport; out of the tournament without losing a game. The fans turned out in their thousands – some estimates were around the 10,000 mark – and I have to say there was a lump in my throat when I witnessed this awesome welcome. 'Christ, what would have happened if we had won the bloody thing?' came an enquiring voice from beside me.

I played in the games against Zaire, Brazil and Yugoslavia and it is a masterly understatement to admit I thoroughly enjoyed the tournament. Beckenbauer, Cruyff, Rivelino, Muller, Jairzinho, Kempes, Facchetti, Denya, Mazzola, Neeskens, Zoff, Lato, Cubilla, Netzer – they were all there. I was in good company. It was an unforgettable experience to mix with the crème de la crème of world football.

Let's start at the beginning, though, and my first call to represent my country. It was four years before the extravaganza in West Germany, 18 April 1970, to be precise, and I was given the nod to play at right back against Northern Ireland in Belfast. Naturally enough, being a proud Scot, I was thrilled at getting international recognition so early in my career. I was at Celtic

Park for training on the day Scotland manager Bobby Brown announced his line-up. I was getting a few slaps on the back from my teammates and then someone reminded me, 'You'll be up against George Best, of course.' I hadn't quite thought of that.

I could be in for a baptism of fire because the Manchester United genius was in the form of his life. He was dismantling defences on the home and European fronts and only three years earlier had shredded the Scottish rearguard with a spectacular solo display as the Irish triumphed 1-0. My old pal Tommy Gemmell recalled being terrorised for the first forty-five minutes and then being more than relieved when Best decided to switch wings for the second-half and then make life more than just a shade difficult for Eddie McCreadie, later to become my boss at Chelsea. George Best, on form, was an electrifying sight. I reckoned I was in for a busy afternoon.

I pulled on the dark blue of Scotland for the first time and lined up with this team: Bobby Clark (Aberdeen); Hay and Billy Dickson (Kilmarnock); Frank McLintock (Arsenal), Ronnie McKinnon (Rangers) and Bobby Moncur (Newcastle); Tommy McLean (Rangers), Willie Carr (Coventry City), John O'Hare (Derby County), Alan Gilzean (Spurs) and Willie Johnston (Rangers). Colin Stein, of Rangers, would later replace Gilzean. It was a simple 2-3-5 formation with fullbacks, wing-halves, wingers and target men. I recall the Irish didn't have a bad-looking team. As well as George, they had Pat Jennings, of Spurs, in goal and he was one of the best in the world. Terry Neill, who would later manage both Arsenal and Spurs, was at centre half while they had an imposing and wily old-fashioned centre forward in Derek Dougan, of Wolves. There was also a talented little midfielder called Eric McMurdie, who played for Middlesbrough.

I took my place in the No.2 position, looked up and saw Bestie standing in the wide-left berth. The referee blew his whistle and I thought, 'Here we go. Bring it on.' I have to say I was pleasantly surprised throughout my debut – mainly because Bestie went wandering here, there and everywhere. He obviously had a free role in the team system that didn't tie him down to playing ninety minutes haring up and down the left wing. Windsor Park that day was a quagmire and you could see Bestie was beginning to get frustrated trying to break down the barrier that was put in front of him. He probed away, jinking this way and that, but was getting nowhere. Controversy, of course, followed him around and once again he hit the headlines for all the wrong reasons. Referee Eric Jennings pulled him up for some offence or another and the Irishman disagreed, took exception, picked up a handful of mud and slung it at the match official. That was the end of the game for George. Off he went and we eventually won 1-0 with a goal from John O'Hare.

The drama of the day didn't end at the full-time whistle for yours truly. I knew my dad had travelled to Belfast for the game and I went over to wave to him and his friends in the crowd. There was a policeman on the track making all sorts of gesticulations to the supporters to point out the exits and usher them out of the ground safely. I got too close to the cop as he threw up a hand and caught me smack in the eye. I blinked as a contact lens immediately took to the air and dropped unseen somewhere in the morass of mud at my feet. If I wanted to waste an hour or so I could have searched for the object on a pitch that had been transformed into a wet, slushy mudbath, churned up by two sets of players going at it hammer and tongs for an hour and a half. A sudden thought came into my head. We were due to play Wales at Hampden four days later in the second of our three British Championship matches. I was desperate to turn out for my country at the national stadium but knew it was unlikely that the manager would select someone with only one good eye. Did I have a replacement? Thankfully, I did and was fit and raring to go for the next encounter. Actually, I would have had some explaining to do to the manager because, like Big Jock before him, he had no idea I wore contact lenses in the first place!

Bobby Brown, who would never be in Jock Stein's class as an astute coach, shook things up for the visit of the Welsh and gave me a midfield berth with Dunfermline's Willie Callaghan coming in at right back. Rangers captain John Greig replaced Frank McLintock and Willie Carr moved over to the left with Willie Johnston dropping out. There was a change in goal, too, with Hearts' Jim Cruickshank taking over from Bobby Clark. It was a fairly uneventful evening, as I recall, and it ended goalless. Three days later was the game every Scot wanted to play in – the meeting with the Auld Enemy England in Glasgow. This was what it was all about. It's never been any kind of secret that the Scots loved getting one over on the English. People still talk today about Scotland's 3-2 victory over Sir Alf Ramsey's side at Wembley in 1967, their first defeat after winning the World Cup the previous summer. No one needed any sort of motivation when England were in town. Liverpool's legendary manager Bill Shankly admitted he used to look down at that little lion on his shirt as he came out of the tunnel at Hampden or Wembley to face the English while he was a player. Shanks swore that lion motif would look up at him and say, 'Let's get intae these bastards!'

I remained in midfield as Brown went with this line-up: Cruickshank; Tommy Gemmell (Celtic) and Dickson; Greig, McKinnon and Moncur; Jimmy Johnstone (Celtic), Hay, Stein, O'Hare and Carr. Gilzean replaced Moncur during the second-half. It was quite breathtaking coming down the tunnel and looking up at the Hampden slopes festooned in tartan and swirling Lion Rampant flags. The English players must have realised that not many of their countrymen helped make up the 100,000 crowd. This was one of Sir Alf's last games before he took his troops off to Mexico to defend the World Cup that summer. Gordon Banks, the best goalkeeper I have ever seen, was calmness personified before the confrontation and, alas, he didn't put a glove wrong as we battled out a goalless draw. They also had the likes of West Ham trio Bobby Moore, Geoff Hurst and Martin Peters, Everton's Alan Ball and Manchester United's Nobby Stiles and, of course, they had all been World Cup winners four years earlier.

As usual, it was a fairly tense occasion and no player wanted to dwell on the ball or make a mistake. When I first came into the Celtic team that was also my outlook. I wouldn't say I was nervous, but I wanted to do the simple things well without being over-elaborate. My game would progress with the confidence that is gained by being a regular selection. Then you could try something out of the ordinary; then you could maybe indulge yourself a little. The one thing I do recall about the English game was the fact that we were denied a stonewall penalty kick. Brian Labone, their no-frills centre half, upended Colin Stein and the whole of Hampden – with the exception of eleven Englishmen, the substitutes, Sir Alf, his backroom staff and, alas, the match official – thought it was a certain spot kick. West German referee Ernst Horstmann, unfortunately, wasn't swayed by thousands of baying Scots and waved play on. It must have been one of the only times a Rangers player had been brought down in the box at Hampden and didn't get a penalty kick! So, it ended scoreless – the first 0-0 between the nations since the fixture was introduced in 1872.

I looked back on my three international games in the space of eight days and felt fairly pleased. We had won one and drawn two. I was also happy about the fact that we had kept a clean sheet in all three encounters. And that was something Scotland had not managed against the three home nations since 1926, so that was another reason for being reasonably cheerful. My mood changed rather dramatically only a year later.

I played in all five games leading up to facing England at

Wembley. That was another dream of mine. OK, the results before that encounter weren't too clever, but I don't think I was solely to blame. We started the European Championship qualifying section by beating Denmark 1-0 with a John O'Hare goal at Hampden. However, we lost two back-to-back away games in the competition to Belgium, 3-0 in Liege, and Portugal, 2-0 in Lisbon. Next up was the Home Nations tournament and we drew 0-0 with Wales in Cardiff and went down 1-0 to the Irish in Glasgow. Undoubtedly, the pressure was mounting on the manager who had just signed a new four-year deal the previous year.

Back then, there was no such thing as the Tartan Army and I would say the backing was mainly from Rangers followers. However, I was aware of being barracked by my own fans for the first time in my career when I turned out for Scotland. The bulk of the support demanded that Ibrox players got the nod and when I played I would invariably be keeping their own Sandy Jardine out of the team. It was the same, too, for Jimmy Johnstone. The Ibrox contingent would have been happier seeing Willie Henderson in the No.7 shirt rather than a genuine world class performer like wee Jinky. Kenny Dalglish got booed, too, but that stopped when he joined Liverpool. I wonder why? I struggled in our 11 November 1970 European opener against Denmark. I'm not one to make excuses, but I had got out of my sickbed to play that evening. I should have stayed at home with my Lemsips. The Rangers fans were on my case right from the off and I will also admit I was not having the best of nights. Eventually, they got their wish and Brown took me off and put on Jardine.

I was still in place, though, as Wembley loomed. But the manager had a problem, with Rangers skipper John Greig available. Now I'm not being paranoid, but I was only too aware that Brown had been a Rangers goalkeeper during his playing days.

There was no way he could drop Leeds United's Billy Bremner from his right-half berth – a position Greigy could play at club level – or Newcastle's Bobby Moncur from the left-hand side of the defence. He had played the previous eight internationals and, despite some dodgy results, had been a rock. Brown must have been in a lather. How could he fit John Greig into his team? Simple, drop Davie Hay! And that's exactly what he did with the Ibrox man getting the right-back berth against the English.

Yes, I was upset, but I wasn't about to throw a tantrum; I was never that precious. Clearly, I wasn't happy. However, I accepted the manager's decision although I didn't agree with it. I couldn't see any good reason for getting the chop. Good luck to John Greig, a bloke I liked, but he had played in only one of the three previous internationals – the defeat from Northern Ireland when he was unlucky enough to put through his own net for the only goal of the game! I watched the action from the substitutes' bench and we were cuffed 3-1. The fans cried for Brown's head and, after two successive 1-0 defeats against Denmark and Russia the following month, they got their wish. I played no part in either game.

The door then was opened for my one-time suitor, Tommy Docherty, and he quit Hull City where he had been assistant boss to Terry Neill to become Brown's successor. In fact, the SFA, never one to rush a decision, gave The Doc the job on an interim basis and it became permanent after he had victories over Belgium and Portugal in October and November. I knew I would get an opportunity under The Doc who was very much his own man and would not be swayed one way or another by voices from the terracing.

One of the first things he did was bring in Arsenal goalkeeper Bob Wilson and Hibs midfielder Alex Cropley, who became the first English-born players to represent Scotland in over 98 years. Of course, there was the usual murmur of criticism from some hard-nosed Scots, but they were wasting their time – The Doc was not listening. The world governing football body, FIFA, had rubberstamped their decision to allow players to represent countries of their parents or grandparents' birth and our new gaffer simply utilised the rule.

Only one player – Hibs' Pat Stanton – survived from Brown's last selection against Russia in Moscow on 14 June. Just under four months later Tommy Docherty had revamped the entire set-up and things were looking up. He named this side to play Portugal at Hampden: Wilson; Jardine and Hay; Bremner, Eddie Colquhoun (Sheffield United), Stanton; Johnstone, George Graham (Arsenal), O'Hare, Cropley and Archie Gemmill (Derby County). As my old Celtic skipper Paul McStay often said, 'There was a buzz about the place.' Scotland won 2-1 with goals from O'Hare and Gemmill. And I found myself with a new nickname, The Quiet Assassin! The Scotland gaffer seemed to think that summed me up very nicely. Thanks, Doc. Pele was The Black Pearl. Alfredo di Stefano was The White Arrow. Eusebio was The Black Panther. Puskas was The Galloping Major. Me? The Quiet Assassin. Tells you all you need to know, doesn't it?

Next up was Belgium and once again Tommy Docherty showed how cute he was. The game was being played at Aberdeen's Pittodrie Stadium and three Dons players were included in the team – Bobby Clark, Martin Buchan, later to join The Doc at Manchester United, and midfielder Stevie Murray, who would become a teammate of mine at Celtic. It helped swell the gate, of course, and it seems a simple tactic to come up with, but I bet it wouldn't have occurred to a few international bosses who went before Tommy. Scotland won 1-0 with a header from O'Hare and the game was memorable for something else – the first international appearance of a certain Kenny Dalglish. He came on as a second-half substitute for Cropley and we were all witnessing history in the making. He would go on to win 102 caps and chalk up 30 goals – a record he shares with the incomparable Denis Law who achieved his total in only fifty-five games.

These were exciting times to be involved in the Scottish international set-up and that hadn't always been the case. The Doc was an infectious, enthusiastic individual who was blessed with a quick wit. He was brilliant with one-liners and the dressing room was a happy place to be. He revitalised and revamped the place. The SFA agreed to a friendly against Holland on 1 December that year and we travelled to Amsterdam in good spirits. Ajax had just won the first of three consecutive European Cups with a 2-0 triumph over Greek outfit Panathinaikos at Wembley. They would later defeat Inter Milan, who had beaten us on penalties in the semi, by the same score in Rotterdam and completed the hat-trick with a 1-0 success against Juventus in Belgrade. An encounter against Holland, Johan Cruyff et al, certainly appealed to me. It seemed I was being fast-tracked through my football education.

The Doc started with Bob Wilson back in goal while Sandy Jardine, Eddie Colquhoun, Pat Stanton and yours truly formed the back four. Billy Bremner, George Graham and Archie Gemmill were in midfield with Jimmy Johnstone and Eddie Gray offering width on the flanks. Kenny Dalglish started his first Scotland game in the striker's role. I recall it was a fascinating match; full of superb football, encouraging attacking play and some outstanding individual touches. They scored first through Cruyff – who else? – but we came back to level when Graham knocked in a free kick from Bremner. It was stalemate with only three minutes to go and I'm afraid our English keeper made a hash of coming for a corner-kick. He missed his punch and Barry Hulshoff, a towering and formidable centre back, powered in to send a header thumping into the back of the net. Bob Wilson never played again for Scotland. I heard that later on he took to the after-dinner-speaking circuit and used to open with, 'Kenny

Dalglish and I won 104 caps between us.' Well, at least he retained his sense of humour.

I had hamstring problems throughout 1972 and dropped into the international wilderness. By the time I returned a year later, Tommy Docherty had been replaced by Willie Ormond. The Doc had taken Scotland to Brazil to play in something called the Independence Cup during the summer. Two goals from Lou Macari gave them a 2-2 draw with Yugoslavia in Belo Horizonte, there was a goalless draw with Czechoslovakia in Porto Alegre and then a narrow 1-0 defeat from Brazil in Rio with Jairzinho netting the only goal ten minutes from time in front of a crowd of 113,000 at the Maracana. Rumours were rife that our ebullient manager was about to depart and so it proved after he had guided his country to two successive World Cup qualifying victories over Denmark, 4-1 in Copenhagen and 2-0 in Glasgow where Dalglish scored his first international goal. The Doc found the lure of Manchester United too much to ignore and he duly packed his bags again and headed back across the border to Old Trafford.

Willie Ormond, who had done such a splendid job at St Johnstone including a European run that saw off the likes of SV Hamburg and Ujpest Dozsa during one fantastic season, was appointed. He was a likeable wee guy who had, of course, been part of the Hibs Famous Five of the Fifties that was made up of Gordon Smith, Eddie Turnbull, Lawrie Reilly, Ormond and Bobby Johnston. Unlike The Doc, Willie didn't embrace the spotlight. Tommy used to court the media and he was, as reporters say, 'good copy'. That wasn't Willie's style. Of course, he went about his job in a thoroughly professional manner and handed me one of the greatest nights of my international career when we over-whelmed Czechoslovakia to reach the World Cup Finals.

However, Willie couldn't have thought such a breathtaking breakthrough was in the offing after his first match in charge of his nation on 14 February 1973. The SFA had arranged a special

Centenary Game against England in Glasgow and it turned out to be something of a St.Valentine's Day Massacre with our neighbours winning 5-0 after being three goals ahead in the first fifteen minutes. Goodness only knows what was going through our new manager's mind and I am delighted to say I wasn't involved. I was in three months later as the Home Championships kicked off and two goals from George Graham propelled us to a 2-0 triumph over Wales at Wrexham. A crowd of just under 40,000 turned out for Ormond's first competitive game in charge and once again I was in midfield to face Northern Ireland. Alas, it was another defeat for Scotland, 2-1 with Dalglish scoring our consolation effort in the last minute after the Irish had raced to a two-goal advantage in the opening twenty minutes. Rangers keeper Peter McCloy didn't look too clever at the goals and was dropped to make way for Celtic's Ally Hunter for the one everyone wanted to play in – England at Wembley on 19 May. Willie Ormond might not have been the most demonstrative human being you might meet, but he was activated for this one, believe me. The five-goal drubbing in his debut match hurt like hell. He wanted his revenge. And he came so close, too.

He put out this side: Hunter; Jardine, Holton, Derek Johnstone (Rangers) and Danny McGrain (Celtic); Willie Morgan (Manchester United), Bremner, Hay; Peter Lorimer (Leeds United), Dalglish and Macari, who was replaced by Jordan in the second-half while Colin Stein came on for Lorimer. It showed six changes from the team walloped at Hampden three months earlier. We gave our fiercest foes a real fright that afternoon as the rain drizzled down in the capital. Our defence switched off once and that was enough for them to snatch a 1-0 victory. Alan Ball flighted over a free kick and Martin Peters ghosted in at the far post to send a header spiralling away from the exposed Hunter. Five minutes from time Peter Shilton produced a gravity-defying save to get up and push a wicked effort from Dalglish over the crossbar. We were beaten, but, on this occasion, far from disgraced. Better times were around the corner.

However, before we could pack up and look out the suntan lotion for our family summer hols there was the little matter of two quick-fire friendlies against Switzerland in Berne and Brazil in Glasgow. The game against the Swiss on 22 June meant very little and, to be honest, the players were just about out on their feet. We lost 1-0 and the only thing of note was the disappearing act by my big mate George Connelly. He checked in at the airport and then decided he would head back home. If you knew Geordie well, as I did, that sort of behaviour wouldn't be too surprising. He could act on impulse and he thought it better not to go on the flight. He didn't miss much and he got a rap across the knuckles from the SFA afterwards. Eight days later Brazil were in town, but this was not the same collection of players who became known as 'The Beautiful Team' three years earlier who played the sort of football that entranced millions throughout the globe as they lifted the World Cup in Mexico. It seemed that brute force had replaced the beauty.

They were gearing up for a World Cup being played in Europe and no doubt they would remember England in 1966 when they were kicked off the park. They had gone to that tournament as holders of the trophy, beating Czechoslovakia 3-1 in Chile in 1962, but they were swamped by Portugal and Hungary after their initial 2-0 success against Bulgaria. They had undergone a drastic change of game plan as they prepared for West Germany, although they still had skilful players such as Rivelino and Jairzinho in the ranks. But they had toughened up big-style, that's for sure. What a shame. If the 70,000 Scottish support turned up at Hampden that afternoon to watch maestros in action they were short-changed. Brazil won 1-0 when Derek Johnstone headed a right-wing cross past Peter McCloy. Now the big Rangers player was well known for his heading ability and he demonstrated that well enough against Celtic in my playing days, notably in the 1970 League Cup Final when, as a sixteen year old, he glanced in the only goal to leave us devastated.

He was asked what he was thinking by powering one into his own net, as perfect a diving header as you are ever likely to witness. Before the kick-off the referee ordered McCloy to change his yellow jersey as it clashed with those worn by the Brazilians. Believe it or not, there wasn't a replacement jersey of a different colour, so the SFA had to borrow a green one from Queen's Park. Johnstone replied, 'I looked up and saw a green shirt and thought I was playing against Celtic. I didn't hesitate in putting the ball in the net.' Aye, very funny, Derek!

Things would be a lot more serious the next time we locked horns with the World Cup holders the following summer. However, there was the little matter of getting to West Germany in the first place.

9

LOOK OUT WORLD –
HERE COME THE SCOTS

Scotland manager Willie Ormond's pre-match talk to the assembled players in the Hampden dressing room was succinct and to the point. 'Go out there and become legends. You have Scotland's destiny in your hands. Don't let down your country. Don't let down yourselves. Go on, get the job done.' No one was left in any doubt what was expected on this evening of 26 September 1973.

The bedlam from the stands was already reverberating around the place. Thump, thump, thump. We could hear the supporters banging their feet above us almost in unison, a rhythmic and hypnotic call to arms. It was tribal-like and I could see it was getting through to my teammates, including my great hero Denis Law, who at thirty-two, must have seen and heard it all. We all made the usual noises. 'Let's get in about them.' 'This is our night.' 'We'll show them.' It was impossible not to be sucked in to this intoxicating mixture of anticipation and expectation. The atmosphere before the kick-off was quite awesome and the shrieks and chants from the frenzied crowd were reaching an ear-splitting crescendo. Players go through all sorts of routines in the dressing room. Some would be fidgeting with their tie-ups. Others would be footering with laces. Some checked their studs for the umpteenth time. Through it all, though, was a remarkable degree of concentration from each and every one of us. This was our night. Then the referee, Harald Oberg of Norway, told us it was time to go.

Chests out, teeth gritted, jaws jutting, muscles flexed. We walked out of the dressing room and into the tunnel that leads out to the Hampden pitch. Willie Ormond had selected: Hunter; Jardine, Holton, Connelly and McGrain; Morgan, Bremner, Hay and Tommy Hutchison (Coventry City); Law (Manchester City) and Dalglish. 'Scotland . . . Scotland' was the cry that filled the still night air in Glasgow. I defy anyone to say that sort of enthralling atmosphere doesn't get the adrenalin going. The task before us was straightforward; we had to win to reach the World Cup Finals in West Germany in 1974. It was something we had failed to do since playing in the game's most glittering competition in Sweden in 1958 while I was still at St James's Primary School in Paisley. We had been in exile for sixteen years. We were all getting fed up with the old jokes. 'What do you call a Scotsman at the World Cup Finals? The referee.' It was time to stop the rot.

The crowd was restricted to 100,000 on instructions from the police authorities. Every single last one of that tartan-clad gathering seemed determined to make their voice heard. It was amazingly uplifting; pure, gorgeous, orchestrated mayhem. If the Czechs looked unnerved in this cauldron I couldn't detect it and I wasn't surprised. This was a first-class collection of players who would win the European Championship in Yugoslavia in 1976, beating the formidable West Germany on penalty kicks after drawing 2-2. They had acclaimed world performers such as goalkeeper Viktor, defender Pivarnik, midfielders Adamec and Dobias while frontmen Nehoda and Penenka were as dangerous as any in the world. This was going to be some contest. The first goal would be vital – and the Czechs claimed it in the thirty-fourth minute to silence the crowd for a moment or two.

It was a real calamity for our keeper, Ally Hunter. Nehoda

cut inside from the right and lashed what looked like a happy-go-lucky effort at goal. It wasn't particularly fiercely struck and Ally moved to his right to deal with the danger. I don't know if the shot swerved or dipped, but our keeper, who had been having an excellent season at Celtic, seemed to lose the flight of the ball. He got a hand to it, but it still swept past him and crossed the line. Ally lay there, looking aghast. He didn't need to be told he should have done so much better. In circumstances like that you have to feel some sort of sympathy with the goal-keeper. They normally only have one opportunity to keep the ball out of the net whereas an outfield player can misplace a pass, misread a through ball, mishit a clearance and still have time to atone for a mistake. That's a luxury the man wearing the No.1 jersey doesn't have. Ally was playing in his fourth and final international that evening. The loss of that goal affected his club form, too, and he was eventually replaced by Denis Connaghan. He never really recovered and that was a shame. It was such a momentous night for us all and he bore the brunt of losing such a horrendous goal.

Thankfully, we didn't collapse in the face of adversity. How could we with that inspirational crowd roaring us on? It was time to get the sleeves rolled up. That's exactly what we did. Jim Holton, a beast of a central defender who was utterly fearless in the air and on the deck, joined a packed penalty area as we prepared to take a corner-kick from the left. In it soared, Holton threw himself forward, the keeper was left in no-man's land, and the Manchester United man, who was once deemed not good enough for Celtic, got his head to the ball and his effort bulleted into the back of the net. It was just before half-time and it was the perfect time to score an equaliser.

Willie Ormond kept it simple at half-time. 'Keep doing what you're doing and we'll win,' he said. I'm not sure if he was 100 per cent certain in what he was saying, but it was what we wanted to hear. He asked us to step up the pace and we got a lot of the ball out to Tommy Hutchison on the left wing after the turn-around. He was a big, leggy lad who looked a bit ungainly, but, my goodness, was he effective as he ran at fullbacks and delivered balls into the danger zone. Willie Morgan was on the right and he sometimes liked to bring the ball inside – he wasn't an out-and-out winger in the mould of, say, Jimmy Johnstone. Billy Bremner went through his usual bristling bantam routine. There wasn't much of the Leeds United and Scotland captain, but he had so much spirit and courage. Nothing frightened him.

It was still stalemated at 1-1 when Willie Ormond went for more height in attack and took off Kenny Dalglish and put on Leeds United's Joe Jordan just after the hour mark. He was another who was so proud to wear that Scotland jersey. The clock was ticking down at a rapid pace. Twenty minutes to go and the Czechs were hanging on, packing their defence while still looking very threatening on the break. Five minutes later the roof came close to parting company with the Hampden stand. We had scored again. We were going to West Germany!

We were piling into wave after wave of attack and I had to remain disciplined in the midfield. Wee Billy was surging forward at every opportunity and I knew we had to be careful. On this occasion, Billy got into a shooting position on the right-hand side of the penalty box. He hit it low and true from an angle and it sped under the right hand of Viktor. Hampden held its breath. Was it going in? It seemed to take an eternity until the ball clattered off the inside of the post, ran agonisingly along the goal line and was scooped clear by a frantic defender. Thankfully, it didn't go too far and fell at the feet of the lurking Morgan on the edge of the penalty box. He didn't waste any time in despatching it back into the mix. Jordan, on the pitch just over twenty minutes, launched himself full length and his header was in the net before Viktor could move a muscle. It was a rollercoaster of a confrontation and we just went crazy at the final whistle.

The unassuming Ormond was standing on the touchline applauding our efforts when Billy raced off the pitch, grabbed him and pulled him into the middle of the celebrating players. Our boss was a shy man by nature, but he lost his inhibitions at that moment as we put him on our shoulders and paraded him around the ground. What a night. It was what football was invented for. The passion, the aggression, the compassion. It was all in evidence. A truly wonderful memory. We were going to the finals as Britain's sole representative, the standard-bearers. I even had the grand honour of captaining my country when we played them again in Bratislava on 17 October. I wanted a victory, of course, but it wasn't to be as Alex Forsyth conceded an early penalty kick and Nehoda swept the award past Leeds United's David Harvey, who had replaced the luckless Hunter. What a contrast in atmospheres in the two games. Whereas Hampden had been rocking to its foundations, only 15,000 bothered to attend in Czechoslovakia. The job had been done in Glasgow and, in truth, this was a routine exercise for most of us.

We had six more games to play, three Home Nations ties and three friendlies, before we would kick off the soccer spectacle against Zaire in Dortmund on 14 June. Still plenty of time for us to make a mess of our preparations.

10

MAYHEM AND MAGIC

If there's a banana skin out there, I would say there is every like-lihood Scotland will find it, step on it and land flat on our faces. It just wouldn't be us if we didn't make life difficult for ourselves. It just seems to be our nature. It was in the midst of this all-too-familiar backdrop that our World Cup squad took off for the colourful cavalcade that would be the World Cup Finals in West Germany in the summer of 1974.

Before that epic journey, I got the nod from Willie Ormond to again lead out my nation for a friendly against West Germany in Frankfurt on 27 March 1974. It was the ideal setting for us considering we would play two of our World Cup Finals games in this city. However, I can assure you that the temperatures in Frankfurt in March and the temperatures in Frankfurt in June are more than just poles apart. It was marvellous to be in the company of Denis Law again – I was in awe of this man. He was a god to me as I was growing up. He may have been coming to the end of his career, but he still had so much charisma and energy. It looked as though his international days were numbered when Tommy Docherty left him out of his sides for the two opening World Cup qualifiers against Denmark. He was overlooked, too, by Willie Ormond for his first six selections before being brought back for the 2-1 win over Czechoslovakia that would send us to the finals. That guy always had a fabulous sense of timing.

It was a great night for me to be skipper of a team that included the outstanding Denis Law. I recall we had a few new caps in Frankfurt, including left back Erich Schaedler, who played for Hibs and Dundee. His father was a German who had turned out for Borussia Mönchengladbach before becoming a POW in Scotland. Like all the best romance stories, he met and fell in love with a Scots lass and here now was Erich lining up against the country of his father's birth. West Germany took the game very seriously and fielded eight of their 1972 European Championship-winning team. We were two goals down by the interval, but Kenny Dalglish put a better complexion on the scoreline when he knocked one in from close range. Not exactly the perfect warm-up or scoreline we were seeking, but we also knew we could up the tempo with our more settled formation.

Denis picked up his fifty-fourth cap in the next game against Northern Ireland and that overtook the previous best held by Rangers legend George Young. Sadly, neither Denis nor his teammates had too much to celebrate as a goal from Tommy Cassidy gave the Irish a 1-0 win in Glasgow. Ormond ordered the players to watch the x-certificate performance again on film and he was clearly concerned that his side had scored only five goals in their last nine internationals. It worked a treat as we next beat Wales 2-0. Kenny netted a typical effort and Sandy Jardine slotted in a penalty kick. A crowd of 41,969 turned out for the game at Hampden, but that rose to 94,487 when England came calling four days later.

However, some strange things happened in between those two games. Once more, we had found the banana skin. Actually, it was all a bit of nonsense as the boys relaxed after the victory over the Welsh at the Ayrshire resort of Largs. Jimmy Johnstone, often the life and soul of the party, had possibly overdone the victory celebrations. It's legend now that the wee man was stuck in a small boat that was drifting out to sea. At first, Jinky was laughing, joking and singing, but the merriment came to an abrupt halt when he realised there were no oars in the boat. It was floating out of sight in the Firth of Clyde and I was one of the lads who suddenly realised there was genuine danger threatening our wee pal. Most of the players were there and Erich Schaedler and I jumped into another boat to head off in pursuit of Jinky. We got a few feet before we discovered there was a leak! Jinky was disappearing into the distance.

The Coastguard was called in the early hours of the morning to stage a rescue act and goodness knows where our outside-right would have surfaced otherwise. He could navigate his way through packed defences with a ball at his feet, but I'm not too sure if he was in the Christopher Columbus class when it came to finding land. The press got a hold of the story and suddenly a daft prank was front-page news. It was silly and, yes, ultimately even dangerous, but the guys were in high spirits and we were looking forward to playing England on the Saturday before taking in two friendlies in Belgium and Denmark and then onto West Germany. Boys will be boys . . .

Of course, some of the SFA hierarchy would have taken a dim view of Jinky's nocturnal seaside adventures and the only way he could answer them and his critics was to put on a display against England. Willie Ormond would have realised that the wee man, with his dander up, was a frightening proposition for any unsuspecting defence. Jinky was in the starting line-up – and that was bad news for England left back Mike Pejic who was never selected again for his country after being given a very public runaround by a little demon with something to prove. We lined up like this: Harvey; Jardine, Holton, John Blackley (Hibs), McGrain; Lorimer, Bremner and Hay; Johnstone, Jordan and Dalglish. Jinky was slaloming all over the place, zipping here and there and proving, as we all knew, he was world class when he put his mind to it. England were dismantled and undone as early as the fourth minute when a Jordan shot took a nick off the unfortunate Pejic and Peter Shilton was left stranded. And the English keeper was fishing the ball out of the net once again before half-time when an effort from Dalglish was deflected in by Colin Todd. We settled for 2-0 and, as we came off the pitch, that possibly was what Jinky was indicating with his two fingers to the members of the press, peering down from their gantry high above the old stand.

Two back-to-back 2-0 victories, so everything is fine and dandy? Remember, this is Scotland we are talking about. It looked as though Jimmy had been forgiven and he was in the side that kicked off against Belgium in Bruges a couple of weeks after the triumph over England. Jimmy even scored against the Belgians, but we lost 2-1 with their winner coming from a dodgy late penalty kick. That was not the end of the drama for the evening, unfortunately. On the flight to Oslo for the match against Norway five days later the crew decided to give us all champagne to mark our achievement of reaching the World Cup Finals. The bubbly flowed and, as so often happens on these occasions, it all got a bit out of hand. Jimmy and Billy Bremner were the guys who took the front page headlines this time around. Poor Jimmy, he couldn't get away with anything – he was always getting caught. Anyway, our captain and our world-class winger broke a curfew in a bar in Oslo and Willie Ormond was far from impressed.

Billy used to go everywhere with this portable record player and he and Jimmy had been dueting in the bar long after most of us had gone to our beds. Willie Ormond discovered they had gone AWOL and he ordered them back to their rooms. Words were exchanged in the heat of the moment and once again we had found that inevitable banana skin. Looking back, I have to laugh. Billy and Jimmy were most upset to have been treated the way they were by the manager. They took offence at being reprimanded! Reason went out the window as they decided they were not, after all, going to the World Cup. Remember, vast quantities of champagne had been consumed. I got wind of it and tried to talk some sense into them. They had gone to their rooms, packed their bags and were making their way to the lifts with the full intention of going home. Dishevelled and obviously the worse for wear, they were teetering about with their luggage undone while their clothes, sleeves, trouser legs and ties were hanging out of the bags.

Goodness knows how they were going to get back to Scotland. They had no air tickets and there was the little matter of the North Sea separating the two countries. That didn't seem to bother them too much at the time. Jimmy, in that condition, might even have been contemplating hiring a boat! Eventually, they were talked out of going home and returned to their rooms. I understood the seriousness of the situation, but it was comical seeing them standing there with their half-packed bags ready to make their escape. Neither Willie Ormond nor the SFA saw the funny side of things as the players surfaced the following morning. It looked as though they might be going home, after all, but this time it wouldn't be their decision.

The other players sympathised with Billy and Jimmy. We had all had a few drinks and I admit we let our hair down. We still had a few days to prepare for the friendly in Oslo and you could be absolutely sure we would be in peak condition by the time the World Cup kicked off. I believe there were some at the SFA who wanted the pair sent back to Scotland on the first available flight. The team manager didn't want to take such stringent and drastic action, of course. For a start, he would be without the country's captain for our first appearance on the biggest stage of all in sixteen years. Billy was our on-field organiser and invaluable as to how the team was set up. There was a lot of improvisation in those days and the players weren't always looking over at the dugout for instructions. Billy was brilliant at reading play. Ormond chose the players and laid down a formation, but Billy had the go-ahead to change that on the field if he believed it wasn't working.

The boss's great strength was picking players. He introduced the likes of Joe Jordan and Tommy Hutchison to the international set-up and that underlined that particular ability. However, there was still the need for someone to knit it all together and Billy was that man. We would miss him in West Germany in more ways than one. We would all take responsibility on the park, but Billy was the prime motivator. Jinky was Jinky. Ormond would know, too, that he could turn the game upside down with one shimmy of those swivel hips. Any country in the world – and I include Brazil – would welcome such a talent.

Thankfully, sanity kicked in. The players weren't being sent home. Instead, they got a stiff reprimand. Peace broke out. They both played as we beat Norway 2-1 with goals from Jordan and Dalglish and now, at long last, it was on to West Germany to make up for some lost time. We were all in the right frame of mind by the time 14 June rolled in and we faced Zaire in Dortmund in our opening game. Ormond had watched the Africans from the Congo Basin in a tournament in Egypt and told us how they lined up and basically how they played. To be honest, though, we were going into the unknown against the team known as the Ebony Leopards. I can tell you they had Kazadi, Kilasu, Kibonge, Kembo, Kidumu, Kakoko and Kabasu in their squad. A commentator's nightmare, I would have thought. It might have been better if we had opened against Brazil or Yugoslavia. We would know what to expect from these two nations and we could have a look later at Zaire and how they had coped with their opening match. We lined up like this: Harvey; Jardine, Holton, Blackley and McGrain; Lorimer, Bremner and Hay; Dalglish, Jordan and Law. Billy was in; Jimmy was out.

We were cautious to start with and that was understandable in the circumstances. It was a swelteringly hot evening and even Denis Law, making his first and, unfortunately, only appearance in the world's greatest soccer showpiece, had abandoned his trademark long sleeves for short ones. Everything was going according to plan when I slung a long ball into their box from the left. Joe Jordan, so adept in the air, knocked the ball down into the path of his Leeds United teammate Peter Lorimer – christened The Lash by Tommy Docherty – and he lived up to his nickname by thundering an unsaveable first-time effort into the roof of the net. That was in the twenty-sixth minute and we were celebrating six minutes later when we doubled our advantage. Billy swung in an enticing free kick from the right and the Zaire defence simply froze. Big Joe got round the back of them, nodded the ball down and their keeper Kazadi looked a little startled as he allowed it to squirm under his arm and across the line.

Hindsight is a wonderful thing and if we had known then that goal difference would be so crucially important in our group we would have put our foot firmly on the pedal in the hope of racking up a cricket score. No one told us to sit on our lead, but, subconsciously, I think that's exactly what we did. We had gone into the confrontation with the main thought of picking up a victory and, at two goals ahead, we were heading in the right direction. At the end of the day, it all came down to our naivety at this level. Zaire were clearly more at home in the heat and we finished the game simply happy to get that initial win. On the same evening Brazil, then the World Cup holders, had drawn 0-0 with Yugoslavia. After one game we were top of our section!

Frankfurt was our next stop as we faced the South Americans, many experts' tip to retain their trophy, on 18 June. It was around this time that I firmly believe the Tartan Army was being assembled, unwittingly or otherwise. We had seen it in Dortmund as

30,000 turned out to cheer us on. There was a carnival atmosphere before, during and after the game against the Africans. It was obvious, too, there were supporters from all over Scotland getting behind their country like never before. You were as likely to hear an Aberdonian accent as a Glaswegian. The banners around the ground told us there were fans from Edinburgh, Fife, Ayrshire, Dundee and even the Shetland Isles. It was a real team effort on and off the field. Ormond brought in Martin Buchan for John Blackley and Willie Morgan for Denis Law as his only changes from the Zaire encounter.

A crowd of 62,000 watched our goalless draw with Brazil and we were within inches of claiming a famous victory. Their goalkeeper Leao, later to manage his country, couldn't hold a stinging downward header from Jordan at his right-hand post. It eluded his grasp and Bremner, only a yard out, must have thought he was about to snatch the winner. The ball, though, came up off the keeper at a difficult angle, struck our captain on the shin and rebounded past the upright. It could so easily have bounced into the net. I enjoyed that game and I, too, came close to scoring. I picked up the ball around the halfway line and sauntered forward. Their midfielders were backing off, picking up our runners, and I realised there might be an opportunity for a pop at goal. I carried on and couldn't believe my luck as their defence parted in front of me. I was about twenty yards out when I decided to have a dig. I hit it firmly with my right foot and the ball took off. It was moving at a fair pelt, but Leao was right in line to leap high and knock it over the bar.

Wee Billy proved his worth to the team as an onfield decision-maker in that match. Brazil came out the traps at a pulsating pace and we were being overrun. They were dictating the game and taking control. Something had to be done before it was too late. After only fifteen minutes Billy gave instructions for Kenny Dalglish to drop off the front and come into midfield, leaving

Big Joe on his own in attack. It worked a treat. Kenny was always a tireless worker and he slotted in well to his new role. We got a point in a goalless draw and we were all in a confident mood before we discovered what had happened in the Yugoslavia v Zaire meeting. The Slavs ran amok as they raced to a remarkable 9-0 win. We must have softened up the Africans! It was 6-0 at the interval and Yugoslavia came very close to going into double figures. They now had three points as well as us, but, of course, now had a vastly superior goal difference. Brazil were on two after successive goalless draws.

We went into our next game against Yugoslavia four days later, again in Frankfurt. It was a Saturday afternoon kick-off and once again the soaring temperatures did us no favours. Our destiny, as it had been that unforgettable night in Glasgow against Czechoslovakia the previous year, was in our own hands. A win against the Slavs and we were through. A draw would leave us sweating on what the Brazilians were doing against Zaire in Gelsenkirchen at the same time. We went with the same line-up that had drawn against the world champions. For the third time, Wee Jinky had been overlooked.

This time 55,000 turned out and the Tartan Army was just about established by now. It was an extremely emotional afternoon and there was so much at stake. No Scottish international team had ever got past the group stages of the tournament and we were now a mere hour and a half from making history. Mind you, we were up against fairly impressive opponents in Yugoslavia whose side was littered with such gifted individuals as goalkeeper Enver Maric, defenders Vladislav Bogicevic and Josip Katalinski, midfielders Jovan Acimovic, Branko Oblak and Stanislav Karasi and frontmen Vladimir Petrovic and Dragan Dzajic, possibly their best-known performer.

It developed into soccer's version of a game of chess as both countries played it cagey. Their ability on the ball was incredible and they were a solid unit. We put in an awful lot of effort while trying to wipe out what was happening with Brazil from our thoughts and concentrate fully on our own game. At half-time we were told the South Americans were leading 1-0 through a goal from Jairzinho in the thirteenth minute. We were still ahead of them on goal difference at that stage. Just forty-five minutes to go.

We were probing and looking for a breakthrough, but the Slavs, with Maric looking extremely safe, were holding out. Then nine minutes from time came disaster. They scored through Karasi and our defence, which hadn't conceded a goal in just under four and a half hours in the competition, was undone. Hutchison was thrown on for Dalglish as we rallied and we got a deserved equaliser through Jordan a minute from time. We came off the pitch, perplexed and puzzled. Had we done enough? What was happening in Gelsenkirchen? Brazil had netted a second through Rivelino in the sixty-seventh minute and we all faced an anxious wait to discover the full-time score. Dame Fortune scowled at us with only eleven minutes remaining. Their right-winger Valdomiro fired in a cross from the touchline and the hapless Kazadi managed to push the ball into his own net at the near post. We were out! One more goal against Zaire in our opening match would have made all the difference. If only . . . if only.

I have to say I thought it was an absolute travesty that Jimmy Johnstone played no part in those World Cup Finals. That would have been his stage. He had the God-given ability to illuminate this competition. An onlooking world would have undoubtedly appreciated his dazzling range of skills. The tournament was designed for the likes of Wee Jinky. He didn't get a sniff and I still believe that was a massive error on someone's part. It looked as though he was being punished by the powers that be for his antics leading up to West Germany. If that is the case, then it is undeniably churlish to deprive a player his opportunity to perform at that level. Could you have ever imagined Northern Ireland reaching the World Cup Finals and not playing George Best? No, me neither. It wouldn't have mattered what George got up to off the pitch, he would have been first pick in any manager's team. It should have been the same with Jinky. I felt sick for my wee mate.

For a start, he should surely have got a place against Yugoslavia, even as a substitute. I can tell you the Slavs were in awe of the wee man after he tore Red Star Belgrade apart in a European Cup-tie at Parkhead a few years beforehand. Jinky was unstoppable that evening as he scored two goals and set up two others as Celtic swept to a whirlwind 5-1 triumph. Dzajic, Acimovic and Bogicevic were just three of the Red Star players who witnessed that devastating display. They lined up against Scotland and must have been more than slightly relieved, a bit mystified, too, no doubt, that there was no sign of the player who had just about single-handedly ended their European Cup campaign that particular season.

However, there was no sign of any disruptiveness from Jinky. I roomed with him for five weeks and I knew how deeply hurt he was to be shunned by his country. He wanted to stand up and be counted and to play his part in the wonderful adventure. Instead, he didn't get a look-in. That was sad. He was never to get another opportunity at that level. Neither was I. The game against Yugoslavia would prove to be my last for my country.

11

FAREWELL TO PARADISE, HELLO TO PROBLEMS

I was on top of the world when I returned from West Germany and had made up my mind that I would be staying with Celtic. I had discussed it fully with Catherine and I was going to accept what was on offer at Parkhead, buy a pub as a safety net and concentrate completely on getting on with business at the club that was always closest to my heart. There would be no more demands for a wage rise. There would be no more walkouts. I was, as always, prepared to do my utmost for Celtic and the supporters. Jock Stein had other ideas.

I was summoned to Parkhead on a Sunday morning to see the boss. Jock was actually sitting in his Mercedes in the Parkhead car park when I arrived. I sat in beside him and he turned and in a very matter-of-fact way said, 'I think it's better that you move on.' I was taken aback and didn't know quite how to respond. I looked at Big Jock. Clearly, he had made up his mind that he didn't want me in his first team any more. In truth, I was hot property after the World Cup. I was voted into a couple of those dream teams that are compiled by the international media. I was also the only player outside England who got a place in the prestigious Rothman's Team of the Year. I was hurt and that may seem a bit strange when you consider I went on strike the previous year and had already talked to Spurs about the possibility of a move. I hadn't had the opportunity to tell the club what I had decided with my family after coming home. Jock looked as though he had had enough of confrontations with me and also my constant visits to Desmond White's office in town when I stated I thought I was worth £100 per week.

Possibly he believed, too, that one dissenting voice in the dressing room can lead to others being unhappy with their lot. I sat in that Celtic manager's office years later and realised where Jock was coming from. Also, my teammates might have thought I had got the pay hike I wanted if they saw me staying at the club. That, too, can lead to all sorts of trouble from within. Jock, plainly, wasn't going to tolerate it any longer. Plus there was the fact that Chelsea were sniffing around and were willing to pay a hefty transfer fee for me. As Celtic had shown a couple of years earlier, they were happy to take £200,000 from Manchester United for Lou Macari. And Chelsea were prepared to pay £250,000 for my services. That was £100,000 higher than their previous transfer record fee when they signed midfielder Steve Kember from Crystal Palace in 1971. I agreed to talk to manager Dave Sexton and chairman Brian Mears and I was immediately impressed by the men and the club. There was the red carpet treatment right from the start. There was a chauffeur-driven Rolls-Royce waiting for me at Heathrow Airport when I arrived and I was whisked to the swish Claridges Hotel in London for our meeting. After the anticlimactic way my nine-year service at Celtic ended, I felt wanted.

The last thing Catherine said to me before I got on the plane at Glasgow Airport on 3 July was, 'Remember, don't sign a thing.' I didn't have an agent and I agreed with my wife that the best thing was to mull things over and discuss everything with her. So, I signed on the dotted line almost immediately! My basic weekly wage jumped from £65 per week to £215 and Celtic had thrown in £15,000 too, as a parting gift. To put my £250,000 fee in perspective, it matched the figure between Leeds United and Nottingham Forest when Brian Clough, during his tempestuous forty-four days at Elland Road, bought England striker Duncan McKenzie, a record for both clubs. It was only £10,000 short of the highest fee Chelsea had received from Southampton for Peter Osgood in March that year. Presumably, some of that cash went towards buying me. Remarkably, the great George Best was also on the move in July – agreeing to play two games for Dunstable Town. This was the same Irish genius who had scored that excellent solo goal to help Manchester United become the first English club to win the European Cup as they overwhelmed Benfica 4-1 during extra time at Wembley only six years beforehand. He was also the guy I faced on my Scotland international debut a mere four years earlier. The mind boggles!

I realised, too, I was going to a club that had a strong Scottish identity following the Tommy Docherty era. Charlie Cooke, that marvellously entertaining winger who had played in Scotland with Dundee and Aberdeen, was there. Eddie McCreadie was a bit of a legend with the fans. And there were the likes of youngsters Ian Britton and Steve Finnieston. Future England captain Ray Wilkins was emerging as a youngster with enormous potential and there were stalwarts such as Micky Droy, Marvin Hinton, John Dempsey, John Hollins, Tommy Baldwin and Ian Hutchinson. The guy I really got on well with was Ron Harris. He made me feel welcome in my new surroundings and I greatly appreciated that. I was gearing up for a new era in my career.

However, I might have realised 1974 was not going to be my year when my summer holiday with Catherine and daughter Allison in Cyprus was interrupted when I awoke one morning with some sort of commotion going on in the grounds outside our hotel. I heard a sound like a 'whoosh' followed swiftly by a 'whump'. I hadn't a clue what was going on as I rubbed the sleep from my eyes and moved toward the window. I pulled the curtains and peered outside. Catherine had awakened, too, and said, 'What's going on?' I answered, 'I'm still trying to figure it out.' Then 'whoosh' and 'whump' again. There was a plume of smoke rising somewhere in the background. Then a jet zipped by overhead and the entire hotel shook.

The sounds I had heard were bombs being dropped and explosions all around us. The shells didn't make those ear-piercing eruptions you get at the movies, but the deadly cargo still carried the same threat. 'I think we're being bombed,' I added, slightly dumbfounded by the dramatic and terrifying events that were unfolding before my very eyes. This fireworks display was far too close for comfort. 'Waken Allison, get your bags, we're leaving.' War had flared between the Turks and Greek Cypriots that divided the island and our so-called relaxing break was cut short pronto. We were evacuated from our hotel and taken to an airbase where tents were erected to allow us to stay for a couple of days before we were finally flown home in a military aircraft. Hardly the ideal preparation for my great adventure in English football.

It wasn't to get any better when the league season kicked off with a match against newly-promoted Carlisle United at Stamford Bridge on a sunny afternoon on 17 August. My new club had selected the occasion to unveil their new £2 million stand and 31,268 turned out for the big kick-off. Chelsea had toiled the previous season and had just escaped relegation. They had finished with thirty-seven points alongside West Ham and Birmingham City. That was one point better off than Southampton who went down with Manchester United and Norwich City. I had been used to chasing championships with Celtic, but now I realised my mindset would have to change drastically to concentrate on keeping Chelsea in the top division across the border. Easier said than done.

I pulled on their blue shirt for the first time on 3 August, exactly a month after signing, in a friendly against Feyenoord in Rotterdam. We lost 3-1 and Dave Sexton said, 'It will take Davie Hay some time to get used to us and it will take us some time to get used to him.' To be fair to myself, my pre-season training had been delayed because of my involvement in the World Cup Finals and I wasn't quite up to speed. Two weeks later I made my competitive debut against new boys Carlisle and it was hardly the most memorable of starts. We lost 2-0 and I realised a long, arduous campaign lay ahead. We played again in midweek and we shared six goals with Burnley. I had to wait another few days before I picked up a win bonus as we overcame Coventry City 3-1 at Highfield Road. We beat Burnley 2-1 after that and we were on a roll. Or so we thought. We came back to earth with a shuddering 3-0 defeat at Liverpool.

Believe me, I was desperate to repay Dave Sexton and his board for the faith they had shown in my ability. I was anxious to prove I was worth every penny of that enormous transfer fee. However, it was obvious the club was going to struggle. They didn't have the swagger or the style they had displayed in abundance only a few years earlier when they beat Leeds United 2-1 in a replay to lift the FA Cup and then emerge victorious in the European Cup Winners' Cup the following year, beating Real Madrid 2-1 in Athens after a 1-1 draw. This was a different team and we were still getting to know each other as twenty-five players were utilised during the league campaign. We just couldn't score goals and notched three on only four occasions. We never hit four goals in one game. There were a few doubles and singles, but we also drew a blank on sixteen occasions. Even now, it makes depressing reading.

We had started the long haul with Peter Bonetti in goal and he was a keeper I had always admired. Gordon Banks was my No.1, but I also rated Pat Jennings and Bonetti right up there with the best of them. However, our veteran shotstopper was coming to the end of a colourful sixteen-year career with the

London club that saw him eventually turn out in 495 league games. He was dropped for Welsh international John Phillips after only three games, but made a brief comeback to play five times in November. Chelsea lost three, including a 5-0 hiding against Newcastle United at St James's Park, and drew two. We conceded twelve goals and, sadly, that was the end of Peter's career at The Bridge. I couldn't have known it at the time, but I wasn't going to be too far behind him.

I was having problems with my vision. I noticed it in the last World Cup Finals game against Yugoslavia in Frankfurt that summer. The sun shone brightly throughout that afternoon and I was picking up some light images in my right eye. There had been no sign of problems during the previous matches against Zaire or Brazil and I didn't think too much about it. I thought I had just taken a knock and my range of vision would only be impaired for a short term. No such luck. I was playing in midfield and you need to be aware of everything that is going on all around you in that position. I knew I wasn't doing myself justice with my new team. To make matters worse, I received a gash on my leg that turned septic and I was forced to sit out six league games with the club having only one success during that period, a 1-0 win over London rivals Spurs and it took a penalty kick from John Hollins to give us that victory.

My mood wasn't lifted with the news that Dave Sexton, the manager who had bought me, was leaving the club on 3 October to be replaced by his assistant Ron Stuart who would then make way for Eddie McCreadie. I had one manager, Jock Stein, at Celtic in nine years and now I had racked up three in one season in London. Things did not auger well. Around this time I saw a doctor about my troublesome right eye. It was diagnosed that I had cataract problems, but, to be honest, I wasn't overly worried. Maybe I was getting used to playing with blurred vision. I made thirty-four appearances from forty-two league games and agreed to have an operation on my eye at the end of the season. My career, soaring a year beforehand, was now crashing around my ears. Apart from my personal problems, Chelsea were relegated to the Second Division. We completed a miserable season second from the bottom on thirty-three points, the same as Luton Town who had a better goal difference. Carlisle United were anchored at the foot of the table. Unfortunately, we had the worst home record of the twenty-two clubs in the division, four wins in twenty-one games. As we went down we passed Tommy Docherty's Manchester United on the way back up after a one-year banishment from the top flight. I didn't have time to wonder about what might have happened if Celtic had allowed me to go to Old Trafford.

My life was drifting towards a deeply unhappy phase and I couldn't believe it when I received a phone call in October from my dad to tell me my mother had passed away suddenly. Sadly, Catherine's father, Patrick Docherty, had died only three months beforehand. It was an extremely testing time for us both. Actually, I had been included in the Scotland squad for a game against Denmark at Hampden on 29 October when I got the shattering news about my mother. I thought the call from my dad had something to do with the international match. It was as low as I could ever feel in life with the sad passing of my mum and football took a distinct back seat as everything was put in perspective. Immediately, I pulled out of the squad and I was never selected again by Scotland. I had played twenty-seven times for my country, won ten, drawn five and lost twelve. The team scored twenty-two goals and conceded twenty-three. None of that seemed too important back in October 1975.

However, I still had a job to do at Chelsea. The cataract operation was a success and I was left wearing a soft lens in my right eye and a hard lens on the other. The doctors assured me the mixture of lenses would help with the balance of my vision.

They worked a treat, too. I was back in the team and, although we had dropped down a division, I was confident we could do a Manchester United and come bouncing back up after a short exile. I believed I was playing well again and I thought I wasn't far off the form that I displayed in the World Cup Finals the previous year. Eddie McCreadie was in the dugout and we had a great relationship. Then, without a hint of a warning, Eddie, after two years in charge, quit the club in 1977 and their ex-player Ken Shellito became my fourth manager at The Bridge.

It was all a bit bewildering, but I knuckled down and tried to perform at my best for the team. A month before the end of the season I took a kick in the face and then an elbow straight in my right eye. Suddenly I had another problem – a detached retina. I went to hospital and one doctor, after examining me, stressed my career could be in jeopardy. My heart sank. What had I done to deserve all this? Why me? I was in and out of hospital as I strived to overcome these problems. I was sent to Charing Cross Hospital for a specialist to have a look at me. I lived in Epsom at the time and used to pick up Ron Harris, who didn't drive, at his place in a nearby village called Ewell to go to training. Ron was with me as we were making our way home from training when I told him I would have to pop into Charing Cross Hospital for a swift examination before carrying on our journey homeward. The doctor discovered a small dot in my eye. He frowned and said, 'We'll have to take you into hospital. You've got a serious problem.'

'OK, Doc,' I said, not quite immediately grasping the severity or enormity of the problem. 'I'm just running my pal Ron Harris home, so I'll come back in the morning.' He looked at me, frowned and shook his head. 'Forget it, you're going into hospital imme-diately.' As I stood there taking all this in, a horrible feeling churning in my gut, he added, 'Your eye is so badly damaged you may never play football again.' I had to find Ron and tell him he would have to make his own way home and the next thing I realised I was being whisked off to a bed and being prepared for emergency surgery. It was hard to take it all in. 'How could my career be over at twenty-eight?' I asked myself. The first operation was not a success. Someone recommended an eye specialist in Cambridge and once more I underwent an operation. This time there was limited success; enough to give me hope that I could continue my career. My sight was never going to be as good as it was before the detached retina, but at least my vision had been stabilised. I was also told by the specialist that he did not believe there would be any further deterioration to my eyesight.

I must stress here that Chelsea were nothing short of excellent with me. Everyone went out of their way to be helpful and I appreciated all their kindness. It's still a pity they did not see the real Davie Hay, though. That rankles to this day. A set of circumstances conspired against me and there was little I could do. They embraced me at Stamford Bridge and they were good people to work with. They were employers who actually cared about their players. They must have been disappointed to shell out £250,000 for me and not get an instant return, but they were so understanding of my particular situation. They never once forced me into an early comeback and were extremely patient throughout. I really wish it could have all turned out so much differently.

Don't think it was all doom and gloom at Chelsea. There were some amusing incidents to bring a shaft of light into proceedings. I recall the club took us to the States as a thank you for winning promotion back to the top division in 1978. We were due to play San Jose Earthquakes and Los Angeles Aztecs and, somewhat bizarrely, my old chum George Best was allowed to play for both of them. Anyway, the players were enjoying a drink – in fact, a few drinks – in Vancouver and when we turned up at the airport the following day I thought it would be a good idea to have a refreshing orange juice. You don't sip orange juice in this part of the world; you go for a swim in it! The girl at the bar passed over about two litres of the stuff and, without thinking of the immediate consequences, I started to guzzle it. Not a good idea. I felt my stomach churning and I raced to the nearest toilet.

I got to the pan before I was violently sick. Sorry to impart this gem of knowledge upon you, but I threw up in spectacular style. Unfortunately for me, I have a couple of false teeth and the plate decided to part company with my mouth. I just saw them and thought they could be rescued. Alas, this particular toilet was equipped with one of those flushers on the ground that you operate with your feet and, yes, I stepped on it by mistake. Goodbye wallies! There's not really an awful lot you can do in the circumstances, is there? We were preparing to fly to Orange County – of all places – and I took my seat on the aircraft beside my mate Ron Harris. I went to the loo to check out the state of play. I came back and informed Ron I had lost my teeth down the loo. He obviously thought I had just been ill in the plane's toilet. He casually replied, 'Don't worry, Davie, we'll look for them on the way back!'

There was another time Ron and I went to the Epsom Derby. My teammate's mother, a typical Londoner, had a shop and she very kindly agreed to cash a cheque for me. I needed a few quid in my wallet to have a flutter. I'm not a gambler, but you can't go to a place like Epsom and not have a bet. We were watching the horses go by as they were paraded before a race when I recalled words of advice from Ron's mum as she handed over my cash, 'Watch what you are doing with your money – this is a notorious place for pickpockets.' I went to my back pocket and, yes, there was no wallet. I'd been dipped!

As far as the actual football was going, Ken Shellito had brought me back into the first team, but immediately I realised I had a problem playing in midfield. As I said earlier, you have to be keenly aware of what is happening all around you in the middle of the park. Eyes in the back of the head would have been handy, too! It was hopeless trying to perform to the high standards I had always set for myself. I found it easier playing at the back and midfield soon became a no-go area for me. My vision was never going to recover completely and, simply put, I had to accept that. I would never allow myself the luxury of feeling sorry for myself, but I was beginning to feel more than just a little cursed. And so my bad luck continued. I went over awkwardly on my knee during pre-season training and had to undergo a cartilage operation. I went to a rehabilitation centre run by the RAF as I tried to rebuild the knee.

I trained hard while refusing to admit defeat. Sometimes you just don't get the final say, though. A doctor told me bluntly that my playing career was over. The combination of my problematic eye and now a knackered knee left me on the scrap heap at the age of twenty-eight years of age. As I was preparing to leave his offices, he said, 'Sorry, David, to have told you that news.' Then he casually threw in, 'Why don't you try coaching?'

Why not indeed?

12

DIDN'T I DO WELL!

Where would I be today if I hadn't had a bit of a bust-up with England's 1966 World Cup hat-trick hero Geoff Hurst? I was doing some coaching with the Chelsea Youth team and Danny Blanchflower, who had taken over from Ken Shellito as manager in 1978, offered me the job on a full-time basis. I had been helping out, anyway, as I was trying to come to terms that I could no longer cut it as a player on matchday. Coaching was the next best thing and I found it enjoyable as well as rewarding.

Was there to be a happy ending, after all, to my troubled times with the London club? Fate once again stepped in. Danny left the club about six weeks later and was replaced by Geoff Hurst. It seemed as though they had a revolving door at Stamford Bridge for the managers. Hurst was the sixth in my five seasons there and that was as many as Celtic had had in close to a century! He suggested that I continue to work in that capacity on a trial basis. I had done the job under Ken Shellito and Danny Blanchflower and, as far as I was aware, they were delighted with the progress I was making. Hurst knew only too well, too, what I had been contributing at that level.

I got the impression he was doing a bit of empire-building and was preparing to bring in his own men. I didn't think I had anything to prove to Hurst or anyone else. I could have bit my tongue and gone along with it. It might have worked out, but I doubt it. I acted impulsively and basically told him where to stick his job. After five traumatic years at Chelsea it was all over. Just like that. I left The Bridge, said my goodbyes to the likes of Ron Harris, severed all connections, sold up in Epsom and came home to Scotland. It was a decision that I would not regret as it ultimately opened the door to the Celtic manager's office for me.

However, before that, there was a little matter of trying to get another job in football. If that failed there was no doubt that I would have gone into the pub business. Celtic were always closest to my heart, so you will not be surprised to discover that I got in touch with Billy McNeill to see if there was anything on the go at Parkhead. I met him at the ground to find out if there was a coaching post, but, of course, Big Billy had his full quota and the board back then, as I already realised, were not ones for taking people onto the wage bill just for the sake of it. Then fate stepped in once again in late December 1979. I had a chance conversation with David McParland, the former Partick Thistle manager who had also been an assistant to Jock Stein at Celtic at one stage. He knew my brother Brian and I mentioned I was looking to get back into the game as a coach. David was chatting to Ally MacLeod shortly afterwards and told him of my ambitions. Ally had just taken over as boss of Motherwell and was looking for an assistant. Hey, presto! Suddenly it was MacLeod and Hay in the Fir Park dugout.

I got on exceptionally well with Ally. Who couldn't? He was a thoroughly decent and likeable character, but I often wondered if he fully recovered from the terrible mauling he took from all quarters when Scotland fell from grace during the World Cup Finals in Argentina in 1978. Ally, then the international boss, of course, was christened 'The Fastest Gums In The West' and 'Muhammad Ally' by the media as he fired out all sorts of promises and predictions. The Tartan Army were caught up in the fever and the hype, not all of Ally's doing, I hasten to add. I recall him saying something along the lines of, 'I think we can come back with some sort of medal.' Somehow that got bent out of shape and translated to, 'We'll win the World Cup!' To my knowledge, Ally never said those words. Try telling that to the lynch mob when they come calling. Losing the first game to Peru was bad enough, but then there was all the front page stuff concerning Willie Johnston failing a drugs test. After that came a draw with Iran and Ally, on the bench, clearly going through all sorts of anguish with the world looking on. In typical Scottish fashion, we thumped an excellent Holland team 3-2 when it was too late. We were home and Ally was scarred for life. He took charge of the team for one more game – a 3-2 defeat from Austria in Vienna on 20 September – and was then replaced by Jock Stein.

Possibly the public image of Ally MacLeod was that of a court jester. Yes, he liked a laugh and a joke, but he was a football man deep down. I know what I am talking about from first-hand experience and I will be forever in that man's debt for what he did for me when basically very little was going to plan in my career. I owed him plenty and I am aware that everything that transpired later in my managerial life was thanks to him. Ally showed me the ropes about management. I soon learned that a manager's job wasn't to turn up every day, take training, pick the team, buy and sell players and talk to the media. There was a lot, lot more to discover about the job and I was fortunate enough to have Ally as the man to give me my grounding.

He had been a success at club level with Ayr United and Aberdeen and he seemed the logical choice to take over from Willie Ormond when he resigned his international post in 1977. He was ebullient, brash and charismatic. He was in charge when Scotland took a large stride towards the 1978 World Cup Finals by beating Czechoslovakia 3-1 at Hampden on 21 September 1977 with goals from Joe Jordan, Asa Hartford and Kenny Dalglish. He chuckled at the memory of how he celebrated afterwards. 'I found a wee chip shop in King's Park, close to Hampden, and I queued up with some of the Tartan Army to buy a fish supper. I could see them looking at me and enquiring, "Is that Ally MacLeod? Looks like him. Naw couldnae be!"' I could see a story like that would appeal to Ally.

The man was the extreme super-optimist. You got the impression he would have been disappointed if he had fallen in the River Clyde and not come out with a Rolex in one pocket and a salmon in the other. He was just that type of guy. I recall a Scottish Cup-tie at Dundee United at Tannadice when we were together. Jim McLean's team were firing on all cylinders at the time and we were a division below them and toiling a wee bit. 'We've got a chance, Davie,' he said. Actually, we had two chances – slim and none! We were four goals down inside twenty minutes and ended up losing 6-0. 'I thought we had a chance, Davie,' repeated Ally on the bus home. Actually, Ally would have thought that Motherwell's youth team back then would have had a chance against Brazil's 1970 World Cup-winning side in the Maracana. The word 'irrepressible' was invented for this man. I couldn't believe my eyes when I was manager of St Mirren and took in a reserve game against Queen of the South at Love Street one evening just to run the rule over some of our emerging talents. Ally was the Dumfries side's boss at the time and I wondered if we might bump into each other. We might have if I had been on the pitch – Ally was playing! He must have been about sixty. Now that's enthusiasm.

I was a willing listener when Ally spoke. He went through all the nuances of being a manager. How to handle the board and things like that. He taught me all about contracts and how to work out all the details with a player. That would certainly come in handy in my managerial career. Of course, I had my own ideas about training routines and the like, but Ally added a little here and there. I was learning all the time and I was enjoying it, to boot. I welcomed my brief spell at Chelsea with their young-sters and now I was working with more mature players, some around the same age as me at the time. I was thirty-one years old and there might even have been a few players older than me. I picked up a lot from Ally; he gave me a great education. Eventually, I succeeded Ally as manager of Motherwell when he was sacked after failing to win promotion back to the Premier League. Ally knew me too well to know there was no back-stab-bing on my part. That wasn't my style and he had been in the game long enough to realise these things happen. The board craved a place back in the top division and results had been bad. As I am now only too aware, they never have to search too far for the sacrificial lamb and rarely look further than the manager's desk.

The directors came to me and asked if I wanted to take over as manager. I felt sorry for Ally, I truly did, but I also knew this was too good an opportunity to reject because of sentimentality. I'm sure Ally would have urged me to take the job, anyway, to carry on his hard work that, unfortunately, went largely unre-warded. I accepted the post and took Motherwell into season 1981/82 and, after an exciting, enthralling campaign, we were back in the Premier League. I got on really well with chairman Bill Samuel, but he had to quit the club to concentrate on busi-ness commitments about four months into the season. We had a special relationship and that sparked events around the club.

If things are right at board and managerial level, the feelings work their way through to the dressing room and everyone is pulling in the same direction. That's what happened at the start of our promotion campaign. I recall we had a fabulous attacking team with the likes of Alfie Conn, Brian McLaughlin and a young Brian McClair. We were solid at the back, too, with that great club servant Joe Wark doing so well in knitting the defence together with his vast experience.

Mission accomplished. Promotion secured. I savoured the feeling of my first trophy success for only a few weeks before I told my wonderful board of directors I was leaving the club. So, it was farewell Fir Park and hello Florida. Or so I thought.

13

THE GREAT AMERICAN NIGHTMARE

How I wished I could have seen into the future in 1982 when I decided to chase the Great American Dream. I quit Motherwell and, looking back, I now know that was a blunder on an Everest scale. I had a superb board who gave me unstinting support and ambitious young players eager to get into the Premier League and show what they were all about. Upon reflection, I should have been there, too. Instead, I ended up buying a pub in Paisley and wondering if I would ever get back into football again.

At the end of our promotion-winning season, done with a bit of style, I hasten to add, I had told the Fir Park board I would be leaving. I had warned them earlier that this could be the case. I had my sights set firmly on the United States and I thought that was where my future lay. I thought it was only fair to let them know my decision as soon as possible. I could have waited, of course, until everything was put in place Stateside, but I didn't believe that was fair to the club. If I left at the end of the campaign it would give the board plenty of time to get a new man in place well in time for the forthcoming season. He would have time, a priceless commodity in football, to look at his squad of players and possibly bring in new faces to strengthen the team for the rigours and challenges that lay ahead.

I had met a guy while on a family holiday in Florida and he assured me he was about to pour a pile of dollars into building a sports complex in Sarasota. I knew he was the real deal and I was flattered when he informed me he wanted to put me in charge of the operation. I would have overall authority and would also run a special coaching clinic for youngsters. I discussed the project with Catherine and daughters Allison and Caroline. It seemed to be too good to be true. It didn't take too long for us to realise our future lay in America and we agreed to taking the plunge and making the move. We were all excited about our new life in the States. Naturally, this was not a spur of the moment thing. I had been over earlier to check out the schools, accommodation and suchlike. I was assured there were investors with big money to put into the project. It had always been my dream to work in America and here I was being presented with what I thought would be the ideal job in a perfect setting. So far, so good.

I was informed the complex would open in October, two months into the new domestic football season. I could have hedged my bets and waited to see how things panned out and then left Motherwell. I didn't think that was fair or honourable. I couldn't have justified it to myself. It just wouldn't have been right to go through the pre-season and then leave the team in the lurch after a few games into the new campaign. That wasn't my style. I would take my chances, leave the club and give them the opportunity to get a new manager in place long before the big kick-off. I thought I owed Motherwell that at least. I still have a present which was given to me by Bill Samuel and a letter where he writes, 'To a great manager from a grateful chairman.' I will always appreciate his backing and support all the way through my first steps onto the managerial ladder. Bill was the type of chairman every manager dreams of having behind them. Unfortunately, he was a rare breed; there aren't too many Bill Samuels out there. In the relatively short time we worked together, I trusted the man completely. And yet I believed my future was in the United States. That was my dream.

Can you spot me in this Celtic squad getting ready for season 1967/68? I'm the fresh-faced youth third from the left in the middle row. That's a youthful Kenny Dalglish second from the right in the back row.

That's me running out behind my wee pal Jimmy Johnstone as we come out of the Parkhead tunnel, primed and poised for action.

Some early action with me displaying my versatility by playing centre-half. Billy McNeill's position was never under serious threat!

On the slide? I hope not. Here I am going down the bannister of the first home I bought in Uddingston. The previous day I had scored and Celtic had overcome old rivals Rangers 3-1 in a Scottish Cup tie at Parkhead.

How about this for ball skills? Bobby Lennox and I have a captive audience of two outside Celtic Park.

In action again for Celtic and this time I am playing in the middle of the park.

Typical Old Firm action with me trying to block a cross from Rangers winger Tommy McLean. Team-mates Tommy Callaghan and Jimmy Johnstone look on.

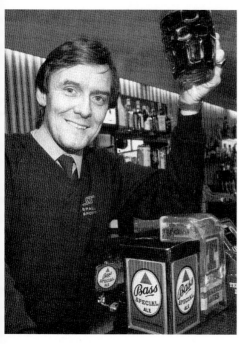

Cheers! Meet mine host of the Davie Hay pub in Paisley. After leaving Motherwell it looked as though this may be my future profession. Thankfully, it didn't turn out like that.

Walking out at Hampden for a match against Wales with Willie Morgan behind me. The opposition player is John Toshack who went on to manage his country.

World Cup woe! How close can you come? I look on in anguish as Billy Bremner misses in the goalless draw against Brazil in West Germany in 1974. The grounded keeper is Emerson Leao, hopelessly beaten, but saved by a wicked bounce.

London calling! I put pen to paper to become a Chelsea player in 1974 with chairman
Brian Mears and manager Dave Sexton looking on.

Crunch! Giving it all for Chelsea with a solid tackle on my Scotland team-mate Willie Morgan,
the Manchester United outside-right.

Just champion! I celebrate with my Motherwell players after we won the First Division title in season 1981/82. Skipper Joe Wark holds aloft the trophy.

Hail! Hail! Me with the Scottish Cup after our thrilling 2-1 comeback triumph over Dundee United at Hampden in 1985.

In the dug-out. I am looking pensive, but I still believe you get a better view from the stand...

Lisbon Lion Bobby Lennox joins me in the dug-out.
I really liked Bobby's presence and he is still a great
Celtic man. He did really well with the reserves while
I was there and won a few trophies. He was a good
man to have around at any time.

Hugs of joy with Tommy Burns after the
Scottish Cup victory over Dundee United.
Tommy was an inspiration to us all.

Flashpoint! I'm letting rip at referee Bob Valentine as I obviously don't agree with one of his decisions.
I'm joined in my protest by Brian McClair, Pat Bonner, Murdo MacLeod and Roy Aitken.

Back in the old routine! Here I am at Celtic with my grandson Vincent for a Legends match against Liverpool who were managed by Kenny Dalglish. How many ex-players can you spot? Back row, left to right: Joe Miller, Murdo MacLeod, Derek Whyte, Pat Bonner, Tommy Boyd, Darren Jackson and Tosh McKinlay. Front: Andy Walker, yours truly, Danny McGrain with his grandson Mitchell, Brian McClair and Peter Grant.

What a trio! Me flanked by two great strikers, Mo Johnston and Brian McClair.

C'mon the Hoops! Catherine and me soak up the sun and the atmosphere before the UEFA Cup Final against Porto in Seville in 2003.

Happiness is... Catherine and I enjoy our wedding day. That's my brother Brian on the left with Catherine's dad Patrick Docherty beside him. New mother-in-law Margaret, bridesmaids Marie and Patsy and flower girl Ann, Catherine's sisters, make up the gathering. The sun even shone!

Walking down the aisle with my daughter Caroline on her big day. Don't we both look just great!

Johnny Depp eat your heart out! This is me in my best pirate's gear along with grandson Vincent in Florida.

Loving it at Livingston! We've just won the CIS Cup and it's smiles all round for me, Catherine and grandchildren Vincent and Scarlett. Others are (left to right): Allison, Caroline's husband Damien, Allison's husband Tomasso, Caroline, nephews Darren and Anton Begley and Catherine's sister Margaret Docherty.

As ever in my life, a hitch appeared when everything seemed to be going so smoothly. I discovered that I couldn't get a work permit. It was going to take even longer than two years before I qualified for the right sort of visa. On top of that, the sports complex ran into problems, too. It was an agonising time in my life, I can tell you. I had been assured time and again there would be no snags. The much-needed Green Card would be in place and I would be working in the sunshine of Sarasota by the time October rolled round. That was the plan, anyway. I flew over in September to see how things were progressing and it was then the full horror hit me. I was told there was no way I was going to get an automatic visa. The authorities had made their decision and it was final. There was no chance I could kick my heels for two years before returning. What on earth would I have done with all that time to kill?

I had given up a great job and I was to regret that decision. No doors in football were opening for me and that was when I bought the pub in Paisley. I reconciled myself to life outside football. And I knew it was my fault. I couldn't point the finger at anyone else. I had been told there would be no problems in the States and I had gone along with that. If I had waited and then discovered the snags that would present themselves I could have just got on with the job at Motherwell with no one being any the wiser. I still don't think that would have been fair to the club. I couldn't have sat through a summer talking to a solid board of directors while knowing I would be on my bike as soon as the sports complex was put together in Sarasota. I had to be up-front and honest. That's why I left. Would I make the same decision today? Probably. I made a wrong call and it looked as though I would pay a fairly hefty price for it.

Again, with hindsight, would I have gone on strike at Celtic before moving to Chelsea in the summer of 1974? No. Would I have walked out on Chelsea after Geoff Hurst took over as manager? No. There's an old joke that goes along the lines of, 'God give me patience – and give me it right NOW!' I was that impetuous human being who could make a decision in the spur of the moment and then reflect on it and say, 'Maybe it would have been better to have taken a step back there.' That's just the sort of bloke I am, though, and I know that will surprise a few who believe my reaction to a crisis would be to merely light a cigar and pour another glass of cold white wine. That's the image, but the real thing is far removed from the public's perception.

You would have thought I had had enough of American dreams, but I tried again in 1992 with Tampa Bay Rowdies in Florida after leaving St Mirren. I invested 50,000 US dollars – about £30,000 back then – in the scheme and my original title was Director of Youth. I coached the team in the final play-off match and was offered the post of General Manager. It was an interesting proposal, but, alas, I couldn't agree terms with the owner. If I was going to make the switch permanent everything would have to be 100 per cent in place. We haggled a bit, but I soon realised I was getting nowhere. It was time to make another major decision. I flew home to Scotland on New Year's Eve 1992 and wondered what the future held in store.

14

BACK HOME

I hesitated for all of a heartbeat before agreeing to become manager of Celtic Football Club in the summer of 1983. I am well aware of a story that continues to do the rounds that I asked for a few days to think over my decision before succeeding Billy McNeill. Not true. I met chairman Desmond White at director Jimmy Farrell's house in Newton Mearns, in Glasgow's south side, and I said yes in an instant. What was there to mull over? I saw it as an honour to even be asked in the first place.

Some folk might have got a bit confused because I did ask for the weekend to get business matters sorted out regarding my pub in Paisley. Believe me, though, there were no second thoughts about accepting the post of what I regarded the best job in football. I loved the club, its magnificent support and I relished the challenges that lay ahead. Davie Hay, Celtic manager. It had a nice ring to it.

I was thirty-five years old when I moved into the office that had once been occupied by the great Jock Stein, the man who had had such an influence on my career. I looked around the place, took a deep breath and then started to get on with the job. Obviously, I am not one to put myself under pressure, so I promised the Celtic fans at least one trophy in my first season or I would resign. I revealed that to a couple of newspaper reporters and the following day there were massive headlines

113

informing everyone, 'Hay will quit if he flops!' I hadn't even been involved in a competitive match as Celtic boss and I was already under awesome strain. Actually, I believed by making that revelation that I would be taking some of the weight off the shoulders of the players. I would become the target, the focal point and they could get on with getting their game in order.

Everyone at Parkhead realised we were in for a long, hard season. There was a lot of work to be done. I knew, too, that the Celtic support would be expecting big things from their new manager. Billy McNeill was – and still is – a legend to those fans. He was going to be exceptionally difficult to replace. For his own reasons, Billy had decided to leave the club and pursue his managerial career in England with Manchester City and then Aston Villa. But I was aware that he was still seen, quite rightly, as a 'Celtic man'. On top of that, there was Europe to contend with and, naturally, expectation levels are always high on this front. Celtic had conquered Europe in 1967 and the supporters saw no reason why we couldn't do that again. There was the ever-present threat from our old foes Rangers. And there was the menace from the two teams who had become known as 'The New Firm' – Aberdeen, bossed by Alex Ferguson, and Dundee United, managed by Jim McLean. I left Celtic nine years earlier when they were wiping the floor with the opposition on their way to nine successive championships. A lot had happened in those nine years and the fortunes of the club had slipped somewhat.

Celtic had won the League Cup, beating Rangers 2-1 in the final with goals from Charlie Nicholas and Murdo MacLeod, in Billy's last crusade, but Dundee United had lifted the title while Aberdeen had ended Celtic's interest in the Scottish Cup at the semi-final stage. Europe didn't last too long, either. The club had a memorable 4-3 aggregate triumph over mighty Ajax – winning 2-1 in Amsterdam – but they went out at the next stage to Spanish side Real Sociedad, losing 3-2 over the two legs. The charismatic Nicholas had followed Billy through the Parkhead exit as he, too, decided to try his luck across the border. Arsenal paid £650,000 for him and, suddenly, the fans found themselves without the manager they adored and the player who was their favourite. Who said it was going to be easy?

I thought about signing a young lad who was making a bit of a name for himself at Partick Thistle, a certain Mo Johnston, but I knew I needed experience up front and I paid £100,000 to Coventry City for Jim Melrose, who had also first come to prominence at Firhill. We kicked off the league campaign against Hibs at Easter Road on 20 August. I looked around the dressing room before the game and I liked what I saw. I witnessed a lot of determination and belief in those players. Pat Bonner, Danny McGrain, my old mate from The Quality Street Gang, Roy Aitken, Murdo MacLeod, Davie Provan, Paul McStay and Tommy Burns were the backbone of the side; every one of them an international. We went into the Edinburgh meeting confident of getting a victory and so it proved with goals from MacLeod and Melrose giving us a 2-0 triumph. The League Cup kicked off four days later with a decidedly dodgy tie up at Glebe Park against Brechin City. Things can go terribly wrong on these occasions, but another goal from Melrose gave us a winning start in that competition. In fact, we won all our opening games in the four tournaments – beating Berwick Rangers 4-0 in the Scottish Cup at Shielfield Park and Danish side Aarhus 1-0 in the UEFA Cup at our place. And we defeated Rangers 2-1 in my Old Firm managerial debut.

We had a 100 per cent record in my first five league games and I could sense the Celtic fans were coming around to my way of thinking. I had always set out my teams to attack and entertain. It was my philosophy that it was better to win a match 5-4 than 1-0 and that thinking would probably upset a lot of the purists out there. Jock Stein had brought me up believing attack was the best form of defence. I was talking to Tommy Gemmell some time ago and we were reminiscing about the both of us playing fullback together at the club for a few years, me on the right and Tommy on the opposite wing. Tommy reminded me that Big Jock would hit the roof if our first move when we received the ball was not to go forward. There was no holding the ball and playing it inside to Big Billy or John Clark in the middle of our defence. There were occasions, obviously, when you were forced to do so, but, in the main, Jock wanted to see you immediately go on the offense. It got to the point that the opposition used to put wingers on Tommy and I, more so my big mate because of his spectacular long-range goalscoring ability. We were being man-marked by our rivals! That being the case, it freed more space for the likes of Jimmy Johnstone, Stevie Chalmers, Willie Wallace and Bobby Lennox to move into.

I agreed with Jock's thinking and I wanted every one of my players to be comfortable on the ball. I wasn't content with it being constantly blootered into the stand by my defenders. Yes, I realise no one has ever scored a goal from Row Z, but such actions break the rhythm of your own side. It means you are not building from the back and the consistency in your team goes to pot. I had Tom McAdam in central defence and he had been converted to that position after starting his career as a striker at Dumbarton and then Dundee United. In fact, he was bought for £60,000 after Kenny Dalglish had moved to Liverpool for £440,000 in 1977. He was never going to be a direct replacement, though, for Kenny. Tom was excellent in the air, strong in the tackle and could pass the ball. And he still popped up every now and again with a goal. What more could I ask?

Our winning start was halted by St Mirren, the team I watched as a kid growing up in Paisley. Brian Whittaker, a player I signed from Partick Thistle, got our goal, but we could only manage a 1-1 draw. I hoped it was just a hiccup. Unfortunately, it wasn't.

We lost 2-1 to a strong Dundee United side at Tannadice and were then held 1-1 by Hearts in Glasgow a week later. Black October continued when we went down 3-1 to Aberdeen at Pittodrie. It's in times like these that you find out a lot about yourself and your players. I rallied the troops. I asked them to take a good look at themselves. They were Celtic players, but they weren't performing like Celtic players. There were no fall-outs, no bust-ups, no tantrums and I wasn't pointing the finger at anyone. As far as I was concerned, we were all in it together. We all had the same goal and that was to make the club successful. We could never waver for a moment from that thought.

Thankfully, we picked up on 29 October with a resounding 5-1 triumph over Hibs at Parkhead and that was a lot more like it. We followed that up with a 2-1 success against Rangers at their place and a 4-0 victory over Motherwell. Three games, three wins and eleven goals scored. I was happy enough. And then my old club St Mirren derailed us at Love Street with a 4-2 triumph. It was back to the drawing board. We then went on a seven-game unbeaten run before losing again to Fergie's mob at Pittodrie. It was a hard-fought encounter and I thought we deserved at least a point, but they edged it 1-0. I wasn't down-hearted by our display although I hasten to admit I hate losing at anything. Show me a good loser and I'll show you a loser.

We regained some pride when we beat Aberdeen 1-0 with a Melrose goal in Glasgow and I realised games against Alex's team were the acid test for Celtic. Dundee United, too. We didn't manage to beat them in our four league games in my first season. They turned us over twice at Tannadice and drew twice at Parkhead. They were an infuriating team to play against. They would leave you with the onus of making all the first moves and then they would pick you off with their counter-attacking play. It wasn't pretty to watch, but it did get results and you couldn't argue with that. It wasn't the way I would ever ask my

Celtic team to perform, though. I thought then – and I still do today – that you have to entertain the fans who have saved up their hard-earned cash to go through the turnstiles on matchday hoping to see something that might bring a little light into their lives.

The title eventually went to Aberdeen. I was disappointed, but I had to accept that Fergie had a settled team and had consistent performers such as Jim Leighton, Alex McLeish, Willie Miller, Eric Black, John Hewitt and Mark McGhee, a player I would later sign for Celtic. They had also lifted the European Cup Winners' Cup by defeating the legendary Real Madrid in the final only a year beforehand. They were a team with a lot of pedigree and I knew they would be the side to beat in the future.

We went all the way in the League Cup and I was delighted to overthrow the Dons in the replay at Hampden with a Mark Reid goal taking us into a showdown meeting with Rangers. That was always going to be a tough game and so it proved as referee Bob Valentine booked six players and awarded three penalty kicks. Unfortunately, two of them were for Rangers. It wasn't a classic confrontation and our opponents appeared to rely on massive kicks down the field from their goalkeeper, Peter McCloy. He hoofed the ball from one end of the pitch to another while completely bypassing his team's midfield. I could hear Jock Wallace yelling from the dugout next to me, 'Get it down the pitch, Peter.' It was a busy afternoon for our central defenders, Roy Aitken and Tom McAdam, as they were bombarded by long, high balls from McCloy.

Ally McCoist was in his element as he ran at the heart of our defence and he claimed a hat-trick. We were two goals down at one stage before Brian McClair clawed one back and then Mark Reid rattled in the equaliser from a spot kick to take the game to extra time. It could have gone either way as the game ebbed and flowed for the next half-hour and Rangers were awarded their second penalty by the ref. McCoist stepped up once more, but his accuracy was lacking as he hit the ball too close to Pat Bonner. Our keeper got down to block the effort, but couldn't hold onto the ball and, as luck would have it, the damn thing rebounded straight back to McCoist who tucked it away.

That left the Scottish Cup as our only hope of achieving a trophy and, of course, I was mindful of my promise to the Celtic supporters at the start of the season. I would like to think I am a man of my word, so you could say I was under extreme pressure when 19 May arrived and we faced Aberdeen in the final on a mild afternoon at Hampden. Rather remarkably, we didn't play a solitary game at Parkhead on our run to the end-of-season showpiece. We opened with a tie at Berwick Rangers on 28 January and a lot was being made of the fact that the date was exactly sixteen years since the Shielfield outfit had knocked out Rangers, then the Cup holders, in one of the biggest sensations in the tournament's history. Was there a repeat on the cards at our expense? We went about our task with a laudable professionalism and coasted to a 4-0 triumph with goals from Brian McClair (2), Frank McGarvey and Jim Melrose.

Next up was a trip to Methil to face East Fife and once again we floored the opposition in a one-sided affair. We won 6-0 and McClair and McGarvey were on target again with Tommy Burns (2), Murdo MacLeod and John Colquhoun, my signing from Stirling Albion, weighing in with the others. Our journey through the national competition took us to Fir Park on 17 March and another overwhelming victory. It was 6-0 again with McClair (2), Burns, McGarvey, MacLeod and Reid on target. Was our name on the trophy? Certainly, the run to the semi-final was fairly impressive with sixteen goals scored and none conceded in three games. St Mirren stood between us and our date with destiny. It still annoyed me that they had taken four goals off us in the league at Love Street and my mood, thankfully, was matched by that of my players. We duly overcame them 2-1 with goals from McClair and Paul McStay. It was looking good and we were in excellent spirits when we turned up at the national stadium for our showdown with Aberdeen on 19 May. Would I be out of a job later that evening? Or would I have won my first piece of silverware as manager of Celtic?

Controversy dogged the encounter, unfortunately, and I was furious when our captain Roy Aitken was sent off by referee Bob Valentine, the match official who had awarded Rangers two penalties in the League Cup Final a couple of months earlier. I was raging at the decision to banish one of our most influential players seven minutes before half-time and I was unhappy at the way it happened. Aitken challenged Mark McGhee and the Dons striker went down. It looked like just another hard tackle in a contact sport. It is a man's game, after all. You take the knocks, get up, dust yourself down and get on with it. I am not implying for one second that the Aberdeen player took a dive or cheated in any way. It was just a fierce challenge and it bowled him over. However, the Dons team, almost to a man, converged on the match official, clamouring for our skipper to be sent off. It was something Aberdeen players did on a regular basis. I don't know if it influenced Valentine, but he ordered off Roy, the first player in over half a century to receive such punishment in a Scottish Cup Final. I thought it was so unfair. It might have been a booking, but nothing more. I looked at our opponents, all smiles as Roy trudged off, shook my head and thought, 'I hope you are proud of yourselves.'

There had been a bit of bad blood between the two teams that season and I recall there were six bookings in a fairly towsy League Cup semi-final. The Scottish Football Association wanted to have peace talks before the Hampden confrontation. They wished to speak to the respective managers and the chairmen. I knocked the idea on the head. Frankly, I didn't see the point of it. What good would have come of it? We would all make the right noises and everything would go straight out the window as soon as the referee blew his whistle for the kick-off. The match official came into our dressing room before the start and was eager to start handing out special warnings to my players. Again, I thought he was overstepping the mark and I didn't think there was any need for it. Who knows what might have happened if I had put up with this ridiculous charade? One thing that was certain was that Valentine, after being surrounded by a posse of Pittodrie players, pointed to the tunnel with indecent haste to banish our skipper.

We were already trailing to a goal from Eric Black, one that looked decidedly offside, when Roy was dismissed. It was always going to be a gargantuan task getting back into the game with eleven men never mind ten. My players showed fabulous courage and spirit throughout the hurly-burly of that contest and we deservedly equalised five minutes from the end through the tireless Paul McStay. I have no doubt whatsoever that we would have gone on to claim the trophy if we still possessed our full complement of staff. The tie went into extra time and, you could have written the script, Mark McGhee got the winner for them. The tackle from Roy must have taken a lot out of him. He even won the sponsor's Mr Superfit award at the end! We had been runners-up in the league, runners-up in the League Cup and now we were runners-up in the Scottish Cup. It was a season of second prizes. That record might appease some managers at clubs where success is not demanded on the same scale as a boss of an Old Firm team. Second is nowhere as far as Celtic and Rangers fans are concerned. It's win or bust.

I had failed to mark my first season as Celtic manager with a trophy. Would I resign? Frankly, there was absolutely no pressure on me from the board or from anyone else for that matter. We had come close, but you don't get a goal if you hit the bar.

I knew it was not good enough. Our support deserved a winning team. We had played some attractive football throughout the campaign and that pleased me. But I didn't need to be told twice that we had still been unsuccessful. I was at Parkhead a couple of days after the Scottish Cup Final and was locking my car door when I heard this voice coming from behind me. 'Davie,' yelled this old chap who was hanging around the entrance, looking for autographs and suchlike. 'You don't have to quit,' he shouted. 'Celtic have won the BP Youth Cup. You did get a trophy!' I had to laugh. My job was safe. For now.

15

SILVER SERVICE AT CELTIC

My first season as Celtic manager had drawn a blank. I didn't need reminding that it was the first season since 1978 that the club had not won a trophy. So, you might assume, correctly, that there was a fair bit of pressure on yours truly on a wet and windy afternoon on 18 May 1985 as we lined up to contest the Scottish Cup with our so-called hoodoo outfit Dundee United at Hampden. I had ninety minutes to turn things around or face another barren campaign. That weighed rather heavily on me although I went out of my way to disguise my emotions. If the players perceive the manager is a nervous wreck or showing signs of being overly stressed it will undoubtedly transfer to them. Outwardly, I was as upbeat as ever. Inwardly, I knew defeat was unthinkable.

We had met the Tannadice outfit nine times over the two seasons I was in charge at Parkhead and won only once, a 3-1 triumph in the league at their place on 20 October 1984. That was our solitary success from eight league head-to-heads. They had beaten us three times and the remaining four matches had ended all-square. There wasn't much between the teams, but they had also knocked us out of the League Cup at the quarter-final stage, winning 2-1 at their place. I felt it was appropriate that we do something about it. It was time for the Celtic support to celebrate again. A crowd of 60,000 turned out to witness the spectacle that was the 100th Scottish Cup Final.

As usual, United sat back and allowed us to come at them while they went through their cat-and-mouse routine. They would suck you in and then hit on the break. We had encountered it nine times in two seasons and here we were at Hampden going through it all again. I warned my team about keeping their wits about them at all times. 'Take your eye off this lot and they will punish you,' was one of the last things I said to my players in the dressing room. It was goalless at the interval and I was reasonably satisfied with what I had seen from my team. Sure enough, Jim McLean had set out his tactics as he had done so many times before. They were trying to lure us upfield and then explode behind us with their pace. About ten minutes into the second-half we were a goal down. They had done it again. I couldn't believe it. Our defence was left exposed, Roy Aitken had to try to match Stuart Beedie for speed and the United frontman got through to squeeze the ball low past Pat Bonner.

That's the way it stood with around fifteen minutes to go. Managers are paid good money to think on their feet and I made two momentous decisions that could have backfired spectacularly. I took off Paul McStay and Tommy Burns and put on Pierce O'Leary and Brian McClair. Tommy was far from happy about being removed from the action. He muttered something as he walked past me on the touchline and I said, 'Just shut up and sit on your backside.' The tension was beginning to tell. It was all or nothing now. I put O'Leary into the middle of the defence alongside Tom McAdam and freed Aitken to get forward on the right. I thought his running power might unsettle the United back-lot. The switches worked a treat, I am happy – and relieved – to tell you.

Davie Provan curled an exquisite twenty-five yard free kick high past United keeper Hamish McAlpine for the equaliser. Game on! We wouldn't be denied and we weren't about to play out time to take the game into an extra half-hour. We could sense victory was ours and, with the clock ticking down, we struck a deadly blow. Six minutes remained when Aitken went on a lung-bursting run down the right before thumping over a ferocious cross to the near post. Frank McGarvey made contact with his head, powered the blurred object beyond a helpless McAlpine and the trophy was ours. The first guy to congratulate me immediately after the final whistle was Tommy Burns. He wasn't one to bear a grudge. By the way, that Cup winner was to be McGarvey's last goal for the club and I have often been asked why I transferred him to St Mirren that summer.

I read in the newspapers not that long ago that Frank revealed that his goal had saved me from the sack. I saved myself from getting a P45, Frank. Actually, I think he should have thanked me for allowing him to stay on the Hampden pitch that afternoon. I made HIM a hero. While I was mulling over my substitutions, I admit I did think of taking off McGarvey. Even he might admit he wasn't playing particularly well against United. But something popped into my head that my old Motherwell gaffer Ally MacLeod used to say. 'Don't take off a goalscorer,' Ally would repeat over and over. 'When you need a goal, keep on your goalscorer.' That stuck with me and, boy, did we need a goal against Jim McLean's team that day.

Frank was coming out of contract that summer and I decided to offer him an extension. I duly did so and I presented him with a deal that was identical to the one that was about to expire. I could see he was distinctly underwhelmed by my gesture. Frank believed he was worth more and I disagreed. I thought he was on reasonable money and I told him so. I asked him to go away and think about it. However, I detected more than just a slight rumbling of discontent from my player. Like Jock Stein eleven years beforehand in my own situation, I didn't want a dissatisfied player in my dressing room. I already had Mo Johnston, signed for £400,000 from Watford in October that season, and

Brian McClair to lead the attack. I was already planning in making them my regular partnership up front in the new term. Brian had completed the season with twenty-four goals and Mo chipped in with nineteen. I had also signed Alan McInally for £100,000 from Ayr United and the bustling hit man, nicknamed Rambo by the fans, was scoring on a regular basis, too. Frank, Cup hero or not, was expendable. I actually accepted a reduced transfer fee from St Mirren for the player to enable him to get a more lucrative signing-on fee. I'm still waiting for him to say thanks.

Actually, reaching the Scottish Cup Final was a bit of a slog for us. We made heavy weather of dismissing Hamilton in the opening round. We edged through 2-1 with goals from McGarvey. At least he started as he meant to carry on in this competition. We sauntered to a 6-0 win over Inverness Athletic, as they were called back then, with a hat-trick from Paul McStay and singles from MacLeod, Johnston and, you've guessed it, McGarvey. We were held to a 1-1 draw by Dundee at Dens Park, but we managed to beat them 2-1 at our place with goals from Johnston and, yes, McGarvey. The semi-final was scheduled for 13 April and Motherwell battled out a goalless draw before collapsing 3-0 in the replay a few days later with Johnston (2) and Aitken doing the damage. Then it was the turn of Dundee United to be added to our hit list.

We had finished second in the league to Aberdeen again and I was more than ever determined to bring that title to Celtic Park. That was my main target when season 1985/86 kicked off. What lay ahead of us was a roller coaster of emotions that left everyone breathless following a scintillating climax to the programme. We were victorious in the championship chase in the most dramatic of all run-ins. For months Hearts had remained at the pinnacle and kept racking up wins on a weekly basis. The doubters were expecting them to fall off their perch, but they maintained an astonishing run that had them clear favourites for the title at one stage. They went twenty-seven games without defeat and I had to admit I thought that was awesome. Cynics had written us off and that was a huge mistake for anyone to make. To be utterly honest, though, I could see their logic.

We lost 3-0 at home to Dundee United on 26 October and the X-certificate stuff continued into November where Frank McDougall claimed all four goals as Aberdeen hammered us 4-1 at Pittodrie and that was swiftly followed by a 3-0 loss to Rangers at Ibrox. Three games, three defeats and ten goals conceded. Two weeks after the Old Firm match we were held 1-1 at home by Hibs. We followed that up with another 1-1 stalemate against Hearts at Tynecastle and then slumped to a 1-0 defeat from Dundee United at Tannadice a couple of days before Christmas. We met them again twelve days later at their place and this time we toppled to a 4-2 defeat. A week later and we had to settle for a 1-1 draw with Aberdeen at Parkhead and seven days later we had a 2-2 draw with Hibs at Easter Road. We beat Dundee 2-1 at Dens Park and then we had four consecutive draws against St Mirren (1-1), Hearts (1-1), Dundee United (1-1) and, the most remarkable of the lot, the 4-4 deadlock with Rangers at Ibrox. I have to admit that it didn't look like Championship-winning form.

Somehow, though, I had a good feeling about my team and my spirits were uplifted by the mood of the players in the dressing room and training. I realised they fancied their chances. I was aware their determination was on a par with my own. We were zeroing in on the league. We had gone out of the League Cup at the third-round stage after drawing 4-4 with Hibs at Easter Road. It went to penalty kicks after extra time and, unfortunately, Pierce O'Leary thumped his effort into the crowd and that was that. We went to Edinburgh to again face Hibs in the third round of the Scottish Cup and we scored three through Brian McClair (2) and Mark McGhee. Alas, someone left the back door open and Peter Latchford conceded four. Europe didn't last long, either, as we went out 3-2 on aggregate to Atletico Madrid.

So, it was the league title or nothing. After that memorable eight-goal encounter at Ibrox, we had eight games left to play. We had thirty-four points and Hearts sat on forty-two at that stage, but I told my players, 'We can take the championship if we win all our remaining games.'

I reasoned, 'Hearts will surely slip up somewhere along the line.' My prediction turned out to be accurate, but, my goodness, did they leave it late. McClair, with a hat-trick, and others from Burns and McInally gave us a 5-0 victory over Clydebank at Kilbowie as we embarked on our exciting excursion to the flag. Johnston and Burns were the men who brought in the points in a 2-1 triumph over Dundee and it was tight in the next game, too, as we overturned St Mirren by the same scoreline, Macleod and McStay on the mark. Three down and five to go. Johnston got the winner against reigning champions Aberdeen at Pittodrie on 12 April. On the same day Hearts beat Dundee United 3-0 in convincing fashion. Were they ever going to trip up?

A week later we got our revenge on our double Cup conquerors Hibs by winning 2-0 at Parkhead with goals from McClair and Owen Archdeacon. Then all eyes were on Tynecastle the following day for a live televised game. Aberdeen were Hearts' visitors that afternoon and I also knew Alex Ferguson, even with his team out of the running for the league, would never allow his players to give anything less than 100 per cent endeavour and effort in any game. Naturally enough, I was delighted when the Dons drew 1-1 in Edinburgh. That dropped point – you only got two for a win back then – would prove fatal. The strain was beginning to tell on our rivals. We had three games to play and Hearts, two points ahead, only had two. They were in the driver's seat. We beat Dundee 2-0 with goals from McClair and Johnston in Glasgow on 26 April while Alex MacDonald's outfit came so close to faltering against Clydebank, who finished bottom of the table. It was tied at 0-0 at Tynecastle with only a handful of minutes remaining when Gary Mackay rifled a drive high into the net from the edge of the box. We had a midweek fixture against Motherwell at Fir Park to look forward to as things got extremely sweaty. McClair, who started his career at Well, flashed in two superb goals in a 2-0 triumph and now it was all down to us and Hearts on the Saturday.

The situation was simple. All they needed to do was avoid defeat against Dundee at Dens Park and the championship was theirs. They were also four goals better off on goal difference. We had to beat St Mirren at Love Street by at least three clear goals, taking into the equation that Hearts would have to concede at least one to lose in Dundee. We also had to hope for a miracle. And, as my mother always insisted, miracles can happen.

As I said, a nation waited with baited breath at the grand finale to an enthralling season, but Celtic went a long way to clinching that title on the FIRST day of the campaign. It's funny how people can so often overlook the obvious. We were losing 1-0 to Hearts at Parkhead on day one after my former player John Colquhoun put them ahead. Obviously, we couldn't have even guessed at how important events would eventually unfold if we didn't get something from this match. We pulverised their defence as we searched for the equaliser. It didn't look as though it was going to be our day, though. The referee was glancing at his watch when a ball was squared from the right and Paul McStay, racing towards the penalty box, struck his shot with devastating power and wonderful accuracy. Henry Smith had been a giant in goal for the Edinburgh men that August day and I realised it was going to take something extra special to beat him. Paul came up with that required ingredient with only seconds to go and we got our leveller in a 1-1 draw. We were to discover just how absolutely vital that gem from our gifted midfielder was when we lined up in Paisley thirty-five games and nine months later.

There are defining moments in football and in life when you realise the gods are smiling on you. One such occasion arrived on the afternoon of 3 May 1986 at the city of my birth. I had watched a sports programme the night before and I was left with the impression that the trophy was as good as already in the Tynecastle trophy cabinet. I was well up for the challenge. I told my players before the game, 'It can be done. We can win this title.' As rallying speeches go, it wasn't quite Churchillian, but it got the message through to my guys. They nodded and, once again, I detected a ruthless determination in my players. There wasn't a quitter in sight. We were five goals ahead against St Mirren before the hour mark and I was standing on the touch-line in awe of my own team. Everyone remembers Brazil's fourth goal against Italy in the mesmerising World Cup Final in Mexico in 1970. I'm talking about the one where it seems every Brazilian player gets at least three touches of the ball before Pele nonchalantly rolls a pass across to the right where the rampaging Carlos Alberto comes thundering in to first-time an almighty effort low past the bewildered and beaten Enrico Albertosi, the Italian goalkeeper. It was a fitting end to a glorious and memorable World Cup.

Take it from me, Celtic scored a goal against St Mirren that was every bit as good and it was just a pity that the planet wasn't tuned in to witness it. Danny McGrain, a truly world-class right back, started it on the edge of his own penalty area. He moved the ball to Murdo MacLeod who gave it back to Danny as we were swiftly building a move down our right-hand side. Danny shifted it inside to Paul McStay who switched it to Roy Aitken and once again the ball landed at Danny's feet. He touched it on to Brian McClair and he flashed a ball across the face of the

Saints goal. Mo Johnston, lurking in the danger zone as usual, came sliding in at the back post to nudge the ball into the net. It was all done at bewildering speed and it is right up there with any goal I have ever seen scored by any side. It was enough to win the title on its own. However, it all looked as though it was going to be to no avail. Johnston (2), McClair (2) and McStay had us 5-0 ahead after fifty-four minutes, but Hearts were hanging on at Dens Park. It had been goalless at the interval and we were in the dark about what was happening in the second-half. We didn't have a radio in the dugout as I didn't want any distractions and, of course, these were also the days before mobile phones.

After eighty-three minutes at Love Street, we were coasting to what might have been an impressive, but ultimately meaningless, victory. Then something quite amazing happened. I remember their keeper, Jim Stewart, had the ball in his hands and was about to launch it downfield when a huge roar came up from the terracings. He looked startled for a moment. Our fans were going doolally. We all knew what had happened – Dundee had scored. I knew there were two players named Kidd on the pitch that afternoon, Hearts' Walter and Dundee's Albert. I was told Kidd had scored and, by the reactions of our support, I didn't have to enquire which one. There was unconfined joy as the fans danced jigs everywhere and then there was another massive cheer. Dundee had scored again. The title was ours! Albert Kidd had netted a second and that was that. Hearts had slipped up, but, all credit to them, they made it one helluva championship run-in. I always liked Albert Kidd, by the way. He was signed by Ally MacLeod from Arbroath and played for me at Motherwell. I could never have guessed the landmark role he was to play in my career. Do you know I never got the opportunity to thank Albert for his contribution to our success? Albert, if you are reading this, get in touch and the drinks are on me!

I must state here and now that we were not lucky in being crowned Premier League kings. The league race, as is so often claimed, is a marathon and not a sprint. The best team over thirty-six games deserves to be the winners. It was tight, but we were the champions on merit. We were the league's top scorers with sixty-seven goals. We were locked on fifty points with Hearts, but, in goal difference terms, we were plus twenty-nine and they were plus twenty-six. That was the winning margin. After we celebrated our momentous triumph, I could look forward to my summer break and I was ready to come back for the new season reinvigorated and ready to build on our league success. I had already pinpointed some players I wanted and I realised our defence would need strengthening. We were scoring goals, but we were leaking them, too. I was already preparing for another exciting campaign.

A year later I was out of a job.

1 6

A FATEFUL DAY IN MAY

I spent most of the morning at Celtic Park on a fateful day on 20 May in 1987 tidying up a few things, looking at contracts and informing the players that the club's proposed summer tour of Australia had been cancelled. I talked to chief scout John Kelman and we discussed a few players we might go for in the summer. I wanted to get us straight back into harness after relinquishing our league championship to Rangers. That was sore and it would be fair to say that I was not happy with the Celtic board at the time when they refused to release transfer cash to strengthen the team while Rangers were buying the likes of England internationals Terry Butcher, Chris Woods and Graham Roberts. On some occasions, it seemed as though I was in the boxing ring with both my hands tied behind my back and any chance of success was a complete impossibility.

But I was still eager to get things in place for the new campaign. I had at last persuaded the board to loosen the purse strings and they allowed me to buy Republic of Ireland centre half Mick McCarthy from Manchester City for a club record fee of £450,000. I met Mick at a hotel in Carlisle and the entire deal was done and dusted inside half an hour. Off my own bat, I offered the player £1,000 per week as his basic wage. I didn't feel the need to run it by the directors because that was the going rate and Rangers were only too happy and willing to sign players on similar or enhanced terms. I decided Celtic had to move with the times and we needed to shore up a defence that was conceding too easily and too often for my liking. Even Hamilton Accies, later to be relegated from the Premier Division, scored three against us. Mind you, we netted eight at the other end and our defensive deficiencies were overlooked by many, but not by me.

A week after the win over Hamilton we lost another three in a defeat against Dundee United at Tannadice. Dundee also scored four against us in another loss on Tayside and I was aware the league was slipping away with Rangers going from strength to strength. We lost 2-1 in the League Cup Final to Graeme Souness's outfit and a goal from John Robertson, a shot that took a wicked deflection off Paul McStay, ended our interest in the Scottish Cup at Tynecastle. We went out of the European Cup in the second round to a strong and multi-talented Dinamo Kiev side, 4-2 on aggregate.

So, I saw my main task during that pre-season to regroup and regenerate fresh optimism within the club. I never got the opportunity. After returning home from my morning's duties at Celtic Park, I received a call from Jack McGinn's secretary asking me to return to the ground for a meeting with the chairman. No one had said a thing to me earlier in the day. I hadn't an inkling of what was to come as I drove back to the east end of Glasgow. I had been having contract talks with Mo Johnston, Brian McClair and Alan McInally who were coming to the end of their deals. Possibly, I thought, something had happened on that front. I got to the park and Jack McGinn was there to meet me. The chairman looked ashen-faced, but I still didn't have a clue as to what was around the corner. Jack looked at me and said, 'We have decided that we must get rid of you as manager of the club. You can either resign or you can be sacked, but we would like you to resign. There will be compensation from the club.'

Thirty-eight little words that saw my world cave in on top of me. My immediate emotion was that of disbelief. Why had nothing been said in the morning? Why hadn't there even been a hint of such action? Disbelief gave way to a feeling of being let down by a board I had gone out of my way to protect when the going got tough and the supporters were demanding answers about the lack of new signings and investment. Eventually bitterness set in. I couldn't help it. I looked at the chairman and he was obviously uncomfortable with what he had just said. I had been very publicly betrayed. I had lost the job I loved.

Celtic prided themselves in never having sacked a manager in their history and they didn't want to do so with their centenary year in 1988 coming up fast. They wanted me to quietly walk away and let everyone think I had quit. I stared back at the chairman and said, 'No chance. If you want me out you will have to fire me.' There was a long silence and I added, 'Who's got my job? Who are you going to replace me with?' Jack was now looking distinctly ill at ease. He didn't want to answer that one. I wasn't about to drop to my knees and plead for my job. They had made a decision and, only a year after winning the championship, I was no longer the Celtic manager. Could you blame me for feeling bitter? I said at the time that it was like a death in the family. That, of course, was a gross exaggeration. I was hurt, though; badly hurt and humiliated by a board I had continually warned to look at the bigger picture and see what Rangers were doing across the city. Our age-old rivals were investing heavily in their playing resources and were bringing in quality from England.

No one could ever accuse me of lacking ambition and there was no one at Celtic Park more single-minded than me when it came to keeping Celtic at the pinnacle. However, when I needed the board to back me, they back-stabbed me instead. It's changed days now, of course, and millions have been spent in recent times in bringing in the likes of Chris Sutton, Neil Lennon, John Hartson,

Scott Brown, Shunsuke Nakamura and Jan Vennegoor of Hesselink. The club have also been successful in signing players that were on Rangers' radar such as Paul Hartley and Scott McDonald. The present board are willing to back their managers. I wasn't afforded that luxury by some directors who scoffed at the Ibrox side and believed money couldn't buy success. In football, proper investments will bring their reward. Liverpool won back-to-back European Cups in 1977 and 1978 with players such as Kenny Dalglish, Kevin Keegan, Graeme Souness, Alan Hansen and Ray Clemence in their line-ups. Hardly anyone came through their youth or reserve teams. I am a great advocate of nurturing your own talent and building for the future, but there are other times when you need a quick fix and you can only do that through sound purchases in the transfer market.

I should have known what was coming when I went to Upton Park on a Wednesday night to see West Ham playing Chelsea. Once again, I had informed the board that I believed we needed urgent strengthening. In fact, I had made my plea after we had won the title the previous season. I was far from satisfied with the depth of our squad. I repeated this throughout that summer, but, alas, no one was listening. Initially, I travelled to London to have a look at outside right Pat Nevin and centre half Joe McLaughlin, who were doing well for my old Stamford Bridge club and two players I believed would be excellent acquisitions for Celtic. We were lacking a player who could perform wide on the right after losing Davie Provan to illness. Paul McGugan was tried in the middle of the rearguard, but he lacked experience and the authority much needed in that central defensive position. Nevin and McLaughlin would have filled those voids at Celtic and, with them in place, I believe we could have retained our championship. I also wanted St Mirren right back Steve Clarke around that time, but once more the directors didn't stump up the cash and he went to Chelsea, instead. We finished second to Rangers, but there wasn't a lot in it. Money spent on new players would have made all the difference.

I was saddened when I returned from London and picked up my newspaper a day later and Jack McGinn was quoted as saying, 'If Davie Hay wants to bring those players to Celtic then he will have to pay for them himself.' I thought it was a remarkably silly thing to say. I couldn't imagine Celtic fans being enamoured by those words while Graeme Souness continued to splash the cash at Ibrox and his club were promising to continue doing so throughout the summer. We were very much the poor relations at the time and it wasn't a position I was comfortable with. Far from it. I didn't talk to Jack for about a fortnight afterwards and, upon reflection, I know that was wrong. Relations were strained, to say the least, and that cannot be right. A manager and a chairman should always have dialogue. We were singing from the same hymn sheet, after all.

On that May day, however, I realised my four-year stint as Celtic manager was over. Once I had taken it all in I asked the chairman about compensation. He told me the board hadn't worked that out yet, but he would get in touch. I reaffirmed that I would not resign and I left Parkhead in a bit of a daze. Remember, this is the same board of directors who allowed me to spend a record £450,000 on a player just one week beforehand while also giving me a wage increase from £33,000 per year to £40,000 during the season. Those decisions suggested they had not lost faith in me. None of it made a lot of sense.

I drove home and broke the news to my wife Catherine and she was clearly distraught. We talked things over with daughters Allison and Caroline and I think we were all emotionally drained. I was in the public eye and I was out of work. At first, I didn't want to leave the house. In those sort of circumstances, you don't want to meet anyone because there is nothing more to be said. You care, too, about the children and what is being said at school. My sacking was completely unexpected and, even now, I don't think too many of that particular board of directors could be proud of the way it was handled.

After discussing the events with Catherine, she asked, 'Who's going to get your job?' It was the same question I had posed to Jack McGinn. 'I don't know,' I replied. Later on that evening, I was watching the news on television and it was then and only then that I discovered Billy McNeill would be returning to Celtic as manager. I stared at the screen in disbelief. I was out, Billy was in and it all seemed to be done in a matter of hours. Everything seemed to be handled so badly and I think I deserved to be treated in a fairer manner. I had nothing against my old teammate Billy. He was unemployed after being dismissed by Aston Villa and was available. Actually, I have to admit that I maybe played an unwitting role in being removed from my job and being replaced by Billy.

At the end of the season my good friend Peter Rafferty, the president of the Celtic Supporters' Affiliation, had arranged for a twentieth-anniversary celebration of the Lisbon Lions at the Normandy Hotel in Renfrew. Billy, as captain of that wonderful team, was invited, of course. I was absent, though. Previously, I had agreed to go to London for the same weekend before I knew anything about the Lions' anniversary. I went with Catherine to see Michael Crawford in the hit musical 'Phantom of the Opera' in the west end. The following evening we visited a nightclub called Silks and mixed with the likes of Joan Collins and co. All was well with the world.

I don't know if the topic of returning to Celtic was ever brought up with Billy at the Lisbon Lions anniversary. If it had been in anyone's mind at the club it would surely have been too good an opportunity to pass up. Afterwards it emerged that Billy had met Jack McGinn at a supermarket car park in Clydebank to discuss the possibility of becoming manager of the team again.

It was all very hurtful, but I didn't blame Billy. Far from it. If I had been in an identical situation I'm not too sure that I wouldn't have done the same. The lure of Celtic is fairly powerful. Who knows?

I had to wait a few months before I eventually received my compensation cheque from Celtic. If I remember correctly, it was around £50,000 before tax. As far as the money went, there wasn't enough cash printed to take away the pain I felt of being fired by the club that was imbedded in my soul. I even received a message from Cardinal Winning, a well-known Celtic supporter. It simply said, 'Time is a great healer.' I realise now that the sentiment is 100 per cent correct, but try telling that to me back then. I went at least six months before I could even start to push the memory of that wretched afternoon to the back of my mind. I realise it will never be completely wiped from my memory banks. However, as time goes by, you learn to cope with the hurt. There is an old saying that states you should 'spit out the bitter pill'. I've done that.

And I also left a lasting legacy – I introduced the players' lounge! Amazingly, the club did not have a place inside the ground where players' families and friends could meet before and after games. Catherine was allowed in because she was the manager's wife, but the players' wives, girlfriends, children, relatives and pals had to wait outside in the car park beforehand, irrespective of the weather. There was nowhere else for them to go. At Chelsea, they had a fairly swish players' lounge and it seemed an awful lot more civilised and sophisticated than having folk milling around outside while the players got showered and changed. Sometimes you had to hold them back to have what is euphemistically known as 'a quiet word'. Our chief scout John Kelman had a fair-sized office, but, obviously, it wasn't used at the weekend. I utilised it on Saturdays and John got his office back on Monday. Why had no one thought of this before?

I watched events unfold at Celtic that summer just like any fan. The club, champions of their country a mere twelve months beforehand, appeared to be imploding. Mo Johnston went to French outfit Nantes for a bargain £350,000, Brian McClair agreed an £850,000 tribunal deal with Manchester United, Alan McInally moved to Aston Villa for around £250,000 and a similar fee took Murdo MacLeod to Borussia Dortmund. Davie Provan was forced to retire far too soon and there was a sentimental parting of the ways for Danny McGrain, who, at thirty-seven years old, had been given a free transfer and went to Hamilton. It looked as though the club was starting afresh.

By the way, I don't think I am the first manager to be shown the door at Celtic. I came across an old newspaper clipping not so long ago. It read, 'I can only assume the chairman and his board of directors felt that a change of managership might bring a change in the team's fortunes. I want to wish my successor every possible good fortune. At the same time, I must confess I was deeply hurt over the whole thing. No hint of a change had been given to me as I prepared to leave for a fortnight's holiday. You can imagine my feelings when, a few days later, I picked up a newspaper and read that I was likely to lose my job. It was obviously not just a rumour and when I returned I called on the chairman who asked me to hand in my resignation. I did so, of course, but the whole affair has caused me much unjustified embarrassment.' Sound familiar? The words belong to Jimmy McStay, the Celtic manager who was replaced by Jimmy McGrory in July 1945.

Forty-two years later I could have penned something similar.

17

EUROPEAN NIGHTS –
THE WONDERFUL AND THE WOEFUL

Doctor Jozef Venglos was in the dugout to witness one of the truly memorable European nights in Celtic's history on the evening of 2 November 1983. Unfortunately, he was with the opposition as Parkhead positively rocked with the club, 2-0 down from the first leg, running amok against Venglos's Sporting Lisbon side and soaring to a resounding, rollicking, riveting 5-0 triumph in a truly epic UEFA Cup confrontation.

It was one of those special evenings in the east end of Glasgow that left you transfixed and enthralled by the beautiful game. A European night at a packed Celtic Park was a sheer adventure into another glorious level of football. They could be nerve-shredding encounters. They could also be confrontations that saw your players respond to a different sort of challenge and prove their mettle. When things clicked into place, the excitement was raw, the tension was high and the entertainment was awesome. It was Ripping Yarns meets Raiders of the Lost Ark! It could also be X-certificate.

The whirlwind evening against Sporting Lisbon is one that will never be removed from my memory bank. That encounter encapsulated everything that is good about Celtic Football Club. The world and its auntie knew we were a team that played the proper way. We set out to attack and entertain and we combined both those qualities in admirable fashion against Dr Jo's team.

They were a very good side and deserved their two-goal advantage from the first leg. They had a big leggy striker in a bloke called Jordao and I told my defence to pay particular attention to him. He was scoring goals for fun in the Portuguese League and I marked him down as the main threat. I'm not too sure if my players were listening – he scored two goals on a night when we did little right.

Dr Jo and co. must have thought they had done enough to ease their way through to the next stage. Celtic, though, can react like a wounded animal in such circumstances. My players realised full well they had not done themselves justice – in Lisbon of all places! Sporting wore their green-and-white hoops against us and we were in our all-green change strip in the return. At some times it looked as though we were playing against ourselves. I had urged the players to get a quick goal before our opponents settled into their passing game. It was important that we unnerved them as swiftly as possible. In only seventeen minutes we had pulled one back when Frank McGarvey launched over a cross from the right and Tommy Burns, so adept with the ball at his feet, demonstrated he was no slouch in the air, either, as he rose at the back post to nod the ball beyond the keeper.

Half-time was fast approaching as we searched for the second goal to level the tie on aggregate. Two minutes from the interval there was pandemonium in their penalty box as they tried desperately to clear a cross from Davie Provan. Tom McAdam barged in, killed the ball on his chest and then hammered an unstoppable effort through a ruck of players into the net. It got even better. Right on the stroke of half-time Brian McClair burst into their box and finished with his normal aplomb. We were a goal ahead with the second-half still to play. It's in moments like these that you have a huge decision to make. I had set out my team to go for Sporting and it had worked a treat. However, there was still the nagging thought that one goal from our opposition would put them through on the goals away rule. I decided to keep going for the jugular.

Murdo MacLeod rattled in the fourth and Burns set up McGarvey for No.5. It was a night where we could do no wrong. It was as good a display of attacking football as you could have seen anywhere, even if I do say so myself. Sporting were no mugs, either. They were doing exceptionally well in their domestic league, but they had no answer to the green tornado that swept them out of Europe that November evening in 1983. Fifteen years later the affable Dr Jo returned to Celtic Park for a European tie – this time as Celtic manager! He was back at the ground where he had suffered such a humiliating loss and he was in the dugout I once occupied. He was in charge for the Champions League-tie against Irish outfit St Patrick's Athletic on 22 July 1998 and he still didn't see his team score a goal! It was score-less although Celtic did win 2-0 in the second leg. Funny old game, eh?

After annihilating Sporting we were drawn against Brian Clough's Nottingham Forest. 'The ego has landed,' was the head-line in one newspaper and I fancied pitting my wits against this unique character. He had conquered Europe in 1979 and 1980 with Forest and now had his sights set on the UEFA Cup. We travelled to their place for the first leg on 23 November on a cold and frosty evening. Conditions underfoot were treacherous, but we played some excellent football and should have scored right at the end with the game balanced at 0-0. Paul McStay got a clear sight of goal and struck a venomous right-foot effort from just inside the box. Unfortunately, the ball swept over the crossbar and the chance was gone. Paul was such a clean striker of the ball that I have no doubt that he would have hit the target if the ground conditions had been better. I met Brian Clough on the morning of the match as we checked out the pitch. We met prior to the kick-off where he was very courteous to Catherine and

her mother. Some people insisted he was an abrasive personality, but I didn't see that side of him. Afterwards, he praised
the way Celtic had played and even agreed his team had been
most fortunate to get a draw. I know he meant every word.

It was back to our place for the second leg on 7 December
and a crowd of 67,000 was in attendance to see if we could put
this outlandish individual in his place. Cloughie, as you might
expect, arrived in fine style. Forest pitched their HQ in Ayrshire
and, as they drove to their destination, this extrovert character
actually ordered the team bus to stop at my pub in Paisley. The
players disembarked and their boss ordered up a round of
drinks for the entire party. The first one was on the house, but
he dug into his own pocket to pay for the second one. That
was Cloughie, though – a complete one-off. Actually, we both
had something in common – our football playing careers were
over before we were thirty. Mine ended at twenty-eight, of
course, and Cloughie, a prolific goalscorer at Middlesbrough
and Sunderland, was finished at twenty-seven after a serious
injury.

As we prepared for the game in Glasgow, I stressed to my
players to watch Forest on the break. Like Dundee United, that
was their favoured tactic. It was the usual frustrating cat-and-
mouse stuff and we couldn't go at them hell for leather as we
had done in the previous round against Sporting Lisbon. We had
no choice but to swarm all over the Portuguese as we went in
to that encounter two goals adrift. This was different. We had
done the hard work away from home against a very accomplished team. We had to continue in that manner in Glasgow.
Of course, that is all easier said than done. You can't blame the
players for getting caught up in the atmosphere with a sold-out
Parkhead shuddering in its foundations with the passionate
support urging you to go forward at all times. However, I went
over and over the need for us to play with a little extra caution.

Unfortunately, the players lost a little of the discipline that had served us so well at the City Ground.

It was said the foxes took to the hills when Cloughie was in town. He was as cunning and crafty a manager as I had ever confronted. It was goalless at the interval and my players were going about their job in a very professional manner. We were wary of their counter-attacking and our tactics looked solid. Nine minutes into the second-half and we were undone. It was a typical break from defence into attack by Forest and Steve Hodge raced through to tuck the ball behind Pat Bonner. We had the bulk of the play and possession and suddenly we were a goal down. Did I detect a wry smile on the face of my opposite number in the Forest dugout? He was certainly smiling twenty minutes later when they staged an action replay and Colin Walsh netted their second. We now required three goals in about fifteen minutes. It wasn't going to happen. Murdo MacLeod scored a consolation goal for us near the end. Cloughie was expansive in his praise of Celtic afterwards, but he still went home with a quarter-final spot to look forward to while we had zilch. It was a hard lesson to learn.

We had kicked off the competition on 14 September 1983 with a 1-0 home win over Danish outfit Aarhus. Roy Aitken netted the only goal and I realised we were in a delicate tightrope situation for the return. So, what did I do? I dropped Brian McClair who had scored four goals in a 6-2 victory over Dundee the previous Saturday. I was Rafa Benitez before Rafa Benitez! I think Brian was more than slightly stunned, but I went for experience in Denmark and it paid off with a handsome 4-1 triumph. Aitken, again, MacLeod, McGarvey and Provan were the goalscorers. I was vindicated. And I put on Brian as a second-half substitute just to keep him happy.

I made my playing debut in the European arena in fairly unremarkable circumstances when I lined up in Switzerland against

Basle on 17 September 1969. It ended goalless and the Swiss actually defended against us. Our forward play earned us a fearsome reputation and our opponents played it safe right from the start. Goals from Tommy Gemmell and Harry Hood gave us a 2-0 triumph a fortnight later in Glasgow. I was on the substitutes' bench for the next two breathtaking games against Benfica when we let slip a three-goal advantage before drawing 3-3 on aggregate following extra time in Lisbon. It went to a toss of a coin back then and Billy McNeill called it right. I was back in place for the next round and we overwhelmed Italian champions Fiorentina 3-0 with Bertie Auld putting on a master class while also scoring a fabulous goal. We lost 1-0 in Florence and that got us through to meet Leeds United. I've already talked about those two absorbing encounters in a previous chapter and also the debacle in Italy in the final against Feyenoord.

The following year we were in the European Cup again and we dismissed Finnish outfit Kokkola 14-0 on aggregate. I played right back on both occasions, but I returned to midfield for the next games against Waterford. We thumped the Irish side 7-0 at Parkhead and 3-2 at their place. That got us a spot in the quarter-final against the mighty Ajax and it was a tussle everyone was looking forward to with some relish. That was a magnificent Dutch outfit with the likes of Johan Cruyff, Johan Neeskens, Ruud Krol and Piet Kiezer strutting their stuff. The first leg was in Amsterdam and we were more than holding our own with about fifteen minutes left to play. Then the roof fell in on us. We were left gasping as our opponents claimed three goals, with Cruyff getting one. We travelled home in silence; beaten emphatically 3-0 and we hadn't known what had hit us. A goal from Jimmy Johnstone gave us a win in Glasgow, but it was the Dutch who got through and they went all the way to the final where they beat Greek side Panathinaikos 2-0 at Wembley. This special team were to retain the trophy for another two years. They were the cream of Europe at that stage, no doubt about it. And we had the scars to prove it.

We reached the European Cup semi-final in 1971/72 and literally came within inches of reaching the final. Unfortunately, I was out through injury and was in the stand as we fought out two goalless draws against the ultra-cautious Inter Milan before it went to penalty kicks. Dixie Deans took our first effort and lashed it just over the bar. An inch or so downwards and it would have been perfect. If only. The Italians had obviously been practising their spot kicks and they scored with all five. We went out 5-4 on penalties and that was sore after my teammates had dominated for much of the three and a half hours of actual play.

A couple of years later we were involved in the infamous brawl with the odious thugs who masqueraded as footballers in the name of Atletico Madrid. They arrived in Glasgow for the first leg of the European Cup semi-final and right from the start they showed they had not come for a game of football. That was way down their list of priorities. They started kicking Jimmy Johnstone all over the place straight from the off. Some of the tackles were simple assaults. If they had been committed out on the street the offender would have been jailed. It was farcical. The Turkish referee hadn't a clue how to deal with these 'animals', as Wee Jinky labelled them forever afterwards. They were managed by an Argentine called Juan Carlos Lorenzo and Jock Stein had come up against him in 1967 when this loathsome individual was in charge of the ruthless Racing Club in the three World Club Cup games. The last of those descended into outright warfare as battles erupted all over the pitch with the Celtic players, unfortunately, losing their cool under extreme provocation. Lorenzo was facing Big Jock again and, sadly, his mindset was still the same. He sent out his players to hack at everything in sight. Jinky was their No.1 target, but I was getting kicked, too. Everyone was getting kicked.

Three Atletico Madrid players – Ayala, Diaz and Quique – were sent off and nine were booked by a harassed match official in a night of shame. If Atletico had performed like that today I have no doubt whatsoever that they would be booted out of Europe by UEFA. Unfortunately, television coverage isn't what it is today and the cameras missed a lot of what was going on off the ball. As it was, they did receive a small fine and a warning about their future conduct. Big deal. It was a brutal evening when football took a back seat as far as the Spaniards were concerned. This collection of hooligans with blood on their studs actually managed to keep the game scoreless. In fact, it was a non-game. We had been well warned by Big Jock not to get involved. Actually, I think we treated our opponents too well.

A crowd of 74,000 watched in horror that evening and couldn't believe or take in what they were witnessing. Jinky was kicked black and blue and he was also their target at the final whistle. No one was going to be shaking hands with this lot as we made our way to the tunnel. Then I saw Jinky being walloped again by one of their players. Deep in the tunnel, away from prying eyes, I decided to exact some retribution for my wee pal. I got 'involved', for the want of a better word, with a couple of their players and punches were thrown. I could hear one of them squealing and by the time I reached the dressing room I had a clump of someone's hair in my fist. I wonder how that got there!

Now we had the little matter of the return leg in Madrid to cope with. Their fans discovered which hotel we were staying in and they kept up a steady drumbeat for hours throughout the night. They also got a hold of the telephone number in the room Jinky was sharing with Bobby Lennox. Apparently, Jinky's face went chalk white when he answered a call in the early hours of the morning. 'Bobby,' he shouted, putting on the bedside lamp. 'Bobby, they're going to shoot me!' Someone had threatened to kill him. Now, Jinky was as brave as anyone I have ever met, but he was more than just a little perturbed that he had just received a death threat. Who could blame him?

He went to Big Jock to relay the news and our manager smiled and said, 'Aye, they've threatened to shoot me, too. At least you can go out there and run about. I'm a sitting target in the dugout!' The whole pathetic Atletico Madrid episode is one that is better forgotten. We were subject to abuse everywhere we went in Spain. Normally, the players will go out sightseeing and suchlike. We would have needed an armed guard to leave our hotel such was the hostility shown toward us.

The actual ninety minutes passed in a calmer atmosphere at the Vicente Calderon Stadium. We were doing reasonably well considering the circumstances and were drawing 0-0, but, as luck would have it, they scored two late goals and got through to the final where they would meet Bayern Munich. And this bunch of louts and cowards came within a minute or so of winning the trophy. How unjust would that have been? Football would have been the loser. However, they were a goal ahead in the fading moments when the West Germans were awarded a free kick. Their giant defender Georg Schwarzenbeck strode forward and blasted an unsaveable effort into the roof of the net. I cheered as loudly as I would have done a goal from Celtic. There is a happy ending – Bayern won 4-0 in the replay with two goals apiece from Gerd Muller and Uli Hoeness.

What is it about European competition that can transform apparently normal, sane individuals into a bunch of lying, cheating scumbags? I will never in my life be able to recover from the recollection of the outrageous antics of Rapid Vienna when they played at Parkhead in the second leg of our European Cup-Winners' Cup second round tie back on 24 October 1984. Who could forget that night? The warning signs were flashing in the first game in Vienna two weeks beforehand. They had a particularly vicious midfielder called Reinhard Kienast and he was doing his best to get sent off with his wild lunges. McGarvey and McInally took a couple of dull ones, but the referee, a Bulgarian named Yordan Zhezkov, didn't want to know. McGarvey, in fact, went off injured after another reckless lunge from Kienast. Shortly after the restart they went ahead, but McClair equalised. Then they got another before their most famous player, Hans Krankl, completed the scoring three minutes from time. In between those goals, McInally was ordered off for a challenge that was nowhere near any of the continual assaults perpetrated by the Viennese throughout the game. Would they resort to these underhand tactics in front of a packed house in Glasgow? It got even worse.

We were 2-0 up by the interval with goals from McClair and MacLeod and were coasting. Krankl was never far from the Swedish match official, Kjell Johansson, during most of the game, moaning about this, that and the next thing. He did not enhance his reputation as a world-class striker in the eyes of anyone who witnessed this prima donna performance. We got a third goal when their keeper fumbled a shot from McGarvey and Tommy Burns slid in to toe-poke the ball over the line. The shotstopper rolled around in 'agony' while his teammates went through their routine of having a go at the ref. The goal was perfectly good and, of course, it stood. At last justice caught up with Kienast when he was spotted punching Tommy on the back of the head and off he went. Not before time.

It was real powder-keg stuff now and the mood of the Austrians didn't get better when we were awarded a penalty kick after poor Tommy was booted by their keeper. Rapid Vienna's version of the Elephant Walk, led by Krankl, descended once more on the beleaguered official. They surrounded him and pleaded with him to consult his linesman. Johansson, probably fed up with the constant bickering from their players, booked Krankl before agreeing to go over to the touchline beside the old Jungle, the area that housed the more boisterous among the Celtic support. There was the usual pushing, shoving and jostling and, in the midst of all this, one of their players, a substitute called Rudi Weinhofer, suddenly collapsed to the ground holding his head. He lay prone on the turf for almost ten minutes. He was holding his head and eventually he came off, swathed in bandages, claiming to have been struck by a bottle. It was all nonsense, of course. The game restarted with the penalty kick being given and Peter Grant smashed it past the post! Television pictures later showed that Weinhofer hadn't been hit by a bottle or anything else for that matter. It was all a phoney act in an effort to get the game abandoned.

At one stage it looked as though Krankl was going to lead his players off the pitch which would have brought automatic expulsion by UEFA from the competition. He thought better of it and played on. Unfortunately, someone in the crowd had thrown a bottle, but it was at least twenty yards away from Weinhofer or any other Austrian player. UEFA's official observer was a West German named Dr Hubert Claessen and he said in his report that he had seen a bottle come on to the pitch, but it had not hit any of the Rapid Vienna players. I didn't believe for a second that would be the end of the matter. I was proved right. Celtic were fined £4,000 and the Austrians £5,000. Kienast was suspended for four games and their vociferous coach, Otto Baric, was banned from the touchline for three matches. Rapid Vienna immediately appealed, changing their story to say that Weinhofer had been struck by a coin and not a bottle. By the way, the Austrian was examined by an ambulance man in Glasgow and, needless to say, there were no signs of a cut.

The committee that sat on the appeal didn't check any television evidence for reasons known only to themselves. They doubled Rapid Vienna's fine, but, in a remarkable U-turn that suspended belief, they ordered a replay which had to be 100 kilometres away from Celtic Park. How they reached such a diabolical decision is anyone's guess. Rapid were delighted, as you might expect. They had been fined a total of £10,000 and they would receive half the gate receipts when the match took place at Manchester United's Old Trafford. They would actually be 'punished' by making a profit.

We were angry at being ordered to play that third game. We had won fair and square only to have it binned because some moron threw a missile onto the pitch. I was interviewed on TV later that night and I tried to play down the entire situation. I said, 'That might turn out to be the most expensive half-bottle of vodka in history.' I didn't realise how apt those words would turn out to be. We made our way to Manchester on 12 December and I think we had 40,000 fans inside the ground long before the kick-off. The mood was grim. The supporters, like everyone at the club, were convinced they had been robbed. I was angry, too, for we had played very well against Vienna Rapid, almost as good as the 5-0 romp against Sporting Lisbon the previous year. We never did get the praise we deserved for overturning the Austrians.

The Celtic party stayed at a hotel at Haydock near the race-course as we didn't want to get caught up with the emotions of our huge following in Manchester city centre. Old Trafford was heaving with seething Celtic fans by the time the kick-off arrived. There was a lot of venom and poison about. It was an extremely tense occasion, a highly-charged evening, to say the least. We were not fated to book our place in the quarter-final that season. We came out the traps at a fair old toot and we were so unlucky when Roy Aitken struck the post in the seventeenth minute. We had been attacking en masse and they hit us with a classic sucker punch. They raced straight upfield with my team disorganised and their centre forward, Peter Pacult, swept an effort wide of Pat Bonner.

We were now 4-1 down on aggregate and we would have to claim three goals to push the game into extra time. We tried. Oh, how we tried, but it wasn't to be. It ended 1-0 for them and cheats had been allowed to prosper. There were another couple of incidents as two fans wearing Celtic colours got on the pitch and one of them got involved in a tangle with their goalkeeper. The other had a go at their goalscorer Pacult as he overdid the celebrations at the final whistle. The police lifted them both and I knew we would be in line for some more punitive action from Europe's governing body. The offenders were both from England, but they had turned up to support us. We had no jurisdiction over them, but once more we were in the firing line. We travelled home in silence and I bought the first edition of the *Daily Record*. The back page headline screamed, 'No Justice!' That just about summed up the entire sad episode.

UEFA acted once again to put the boot into us. We were ordered to play our home European Cup Winners' Cup first round tie in 1985 against Atletico Madrid behind closed doors. We got an excellent 1-1 draw in Madrid with Mo Johnston scoring with a typical header, but the second game on 2 October was simply surreal. As you might have gathered by now, I believe Celtic Park is built for big European occasions. An empty Celtic Park is fairly freakish. We also had to kick off in the afternoon and it all had the element of a training session kickabout. Officials of both clubs and UEFA, journalists, stewards, ambulance men and some ballboys – with our own Derek Whyte among them! – were the only people allowed in the ground at the kick-off. It was an impossible task to lift the spirits of the players in such eerie surroundings. It was a bit different from the last time Atletico Madrid were in town in 1974! We just couldn't adapt to an empty Celtic Park. Whoever said silence is golden certainly got that wrong! We could not galvanise ourselves and it was bizarre to hear the players talking to each other. The Spaniards relished the thought of not having to face our marvellous and eardrum-rattling support and they reacted in such a manner. Murdo MacLeod hit their bar and they ran up the park to open the scoring. You'll have to take my word for it! They scored a second before Roy Aitken pulled one back, but Europe was a dead end for another year.

We were in the European Cup the following 1986/87 season and we eased through the first round with a 3-0 aggregate win over Irish outfit Shamrock Rovers with Johnston (2) and MacLeod getting our goals over the two legs. Dinamo Kiev were next up and we couldn't have asked for a stiffer challenge. They had beaten our European conquerors Atletico Madrid 3-0 to lift the Cup-Winners' Cup in fine style in Lyon. They were a crack outfit, no doubt about it. Naturally, we would have preferred the first leg away in Kiev as that gives you home advantage in a situation where you know exactly what you have to do to progress. They had the wonderful Oleg Blokhin, a former European Footballer of the Year, in their line-up and I think the Russian international team at the time was just about made up exclusively with Kiev players. As we kicked off on a typically cold, slightly foggy evening in the east end of Glasgow on 22 October I didn't realise it would be my last European match as manager of Celtic at Parkhead.

A goal from Mo Johnston gave us a 1-1 draw and we were just about written off by everyone before the return at the City Stadium which was a 100,000 sell-out. Not one of my players, though, was conceding defeat. Nor was I, of course. Far from it. Celtic had met and overcome massive hurdles in their history and this was another mountain to climb. Once again, I sensed the mood in the camp was good. There were no chins on chests. They were an admirable collection of characters. Thousands of Ukrainians were not about to knock us out of our stride. As Big Jock was often fond of saying, 'No one in the crowd ever scored a goal.' We took the lead through Mark McGhee and that silenced the masses on a freezing evening in Kiev. We played well, but this was class opposition and they got their act together to eventually beat us 3-1. However, they had to fight every inch of the way. Their manager, the respected Valeri Lobonovski, hailed my players and said it was the best performance he had seen from a foreign side on Russian soil for twenty-one years. Praise indeed. Nice words to treasure because I never managed the club at that level again.

I've been in charge of Dunfermline and Livingston in Europe since, of course, but, with no disrespect to anyone, there is nothing quite like being the Celtic boss on a super-charged European Cup evening and the ground is shaking with emotion. I have been very fortunate to sample that rarefied atmosphere as a player and a manager. There have been incredible highs; there have been insufferable lows. Memories, a mixture of glad, sad and mad, are made of this. However, my biggest regret will always remain the European Cup Final defeat from Feyenoord at the San Siro Stadium in 1970. That was the one that got away.

18

WEE JINKY AND ME

Jimmy Johnstone, at a mere 5ft 4in, always stood out in a crowd. He was a mesmerising mix of magic and mischief and you couldn't take your eyes off him when he was embroidering his uncanny skills into the pattern of a football game. The Wee Man was a genius, a sorcerer, a maestro, a crowd-pleaser and, at times, a match-winner. He was blessed with an extraordinary talent. He was also my good friend.

Jinky, of course, will be forever remembered for some of his off-the-field exploits, too, and, as you might expect, some of these tales have grown arms and legs over the years. Why let facts get in the way of a good story? Yes, he could be a wee scamp at times. And, yes, he could be temperamental; it must have had something to do with that mop of brilliant red hair he sported as a youngster. But he was a bubbly, effervescent character more often than not. Jinky's widow Agnes is a cousin of my wife Catherine and we were always close. I've heard it said I was often his unofficial minder on international business and we did room a lot. I thoroughly enjoyed his company and he always had an outrageous anecdote to tell.

He was funny guy, too. John Clark may have been a Lisbon Lion and immortalised in Celtic history, but he still accepted that he had to be Jinky's chauffeur at times. John would pick me up at Uddingston Cross and then we would travel on to Jinky's house. Jock Stein had a thing about always being punctual and he let you know how displeased he was if you turned up late for training without a good excuse. John would peep the horn of his car outside Jinky's front door and, on a regular basis, Agnes would appear to tell us our teammate would be with us as soon as possible. A lot of the time he was still in bed! John and I would listen to the car radio as we awaited the presence of the Wee Man. 'Watch this,' said John. 'I bet you he turns off the radio when he gets in.' Sure enough, Jinky would glide into the passenger seat beside John and, without a word, he would switch off the music. He never said a thing. There was no explanation. This went on for ages.

One day there was no sign of Jinky or Agnes as John and I pulled up and honked the horn, as usual. A couple of minutes went by. Another toot. Still nothing stirred in the Johnstone household. John and I were now getting a bit anxious as training was due to start in about ten minutes' time. 'I'll go and see what's keeping him,' I ventured. I walked up the pathway to the front door and pressed the bell. The chimes rang out, but still no sign of Jinky. I motioned to John, 'I'll go round the back and see if he's in the kitchen.' As I opened a gate at the side of the house I was confronted by this gigantic Alsatian dog. It was a Hound of the Baskervilles job and it looked as though it fancied a large slice of yours truly for breakfast. It snorted and barked and raced in my direction. I slammed the gate shut, turned on my heels and ran back to the car. 'Let's get out of here,' I gasped. Jinky had bought the ferocious-looking beast for protection. The only snag being that he had forgotten to tell anyone.

There was another time when both Jinky and I missed our lift from John. We couldn't find a taxi and there was no sign of public transport. 'We're going to be in trouble with Big Jock,' I needlessly informed my companion who, of course, had a bit of previous with our gaffer on this front. Then I had a brainwave. Tunnock's, the confectionary giant, had a yard in Uddingston which was just across the road from where I lived. I sprinted to the yard and was delighted to find a friendly Celtic supporter who agreed to give me a lift, pick up Jinky and squeeze us both into his delivery van and get us to Parkhead in time to save us from a certain rollicking from our boss. It worked a treat.

When I was breaking into the team in 1969 I played mainly at right back and from that position I could see how good Jinky was as he was performing in front of me. He was an absolute dream. I loved bombing up and down that right wing, especially when we were playing in front of the fans in The Jungle. Those were the sort of punters who weren't interested in the comfy seats in the stand; The Jungle was their place. That's where they stood week in, week out and those were the guys to impress. I knew they were knowledgeable about the game and I was also only too aware that they would give any player their full support and backing if they believed you were giving your all for the club. I was never known as a slacker and it was music to my young ears as Jinky took the ball for a walk inside and I got the opportunity to hare down the touchline with those fans urging me all the way. Sometimes I got a pass and, on other occasions, the Wee Man decided to go solo. Either way, it was an exhilarating experience playing alongside Jinky.

Big Jock had to change our training routines to ensure we were all involved. Jinky's dribbling skills were phenomenal and there were occasions when he was simply waltzing past everyone at will. 'That's enough of that, Johnstone,' our boss would bellow from the touchline. Jinky, as usual, paid no heed. An exasperated Stein then introduced two-touch football to curb the Wee Man's enthusiasm. You would gather the ball in one instant and move it on at speed in the next. Jinky could no longer keep it all to himself. Well, something had to be done to allow the rest of us to get a kick at the ball because there was little or no chance of us getting it off our colleague by fair means!

There are so many lovely stories about Jinky, laced with a lot of humour. His legend transcended mere football. Hollywood actor Robert Duvall, of *Godfather* fame, was watching footage of Celtic in action in the sixties as he prepared to make a football movie in Scotland called *A Shot At Glory*. Duvall was transfixed by Jinky dodging in and out of befuddled defences while generally creating mayhem. The actor paid our player the highest accolade; he named his dog Jinky!

Jinky and I and a few of the other lads enjoyed a social life away from football. There was no bevvying in the countdown to a game, it didn't matter if it was the European Cup or a friendly. That was a no-no. However, on a Saturday night the lads were allowed to wind down, normally at the Redstones Hotel in Uddingston. We would usually be joined by George Connelly, who lived in Blantyre, and Bobby Murdoch and John Hughes, who were both based in nearby Bothwell. The Redstones looked after us and gave us our own little area away from most of the punters. We would start off with a couple of beers. Then another couple. Beer would then be dropped for a couple of Barcardi and Cokes. Then another couple. As I recall, there were a few ruined meals in the Hay household back then. It didn't help, either, that there was usually an irate wife waiting to have a Saturday night out. Thankfully, Catherine didn't possess a rolling-pin!

I was more than a little dismayed when there seemed to be no future in football for Jinky when he eventually hung up his boots. He had graced the game and, at his best, was undoubtedly world-class and Scotland didn't produce too many of his kind. When I went back to Celtic as manager I contacted the Wee Man. I had an idea he still had something to contribute to Celtic's cause. I realised the youngsters at the club still saw him as a superstar. Just mixing in his exalted company seemed to gee them up and give them a boost. Jinky, for all the praise he received from around the world, was a genuine down-to-earth character. He had been winding down his career by playing for Shelbourne in Ireland, Elgin City in the Highlands and then Blantyre Celtic in the Juniors where it had all kicked off nineteen years earlier. I don't mean this in a nasty way, but my wee pal should not have been mixing in that company.

I had a word with Bobby Lennox who was doing a great job running the reserve team at the time. I knew Bobby and Jinky were the very best of buddies and I mentioned to our second-team coach that I had been thinking about getting a Youth post for Jinky. 'Great idea, Davie,' enthused Bobby. So I brought in the Wee Man and he took over the newly-formed Under-18 team. By the way, Bobby's reserves won the league and the Cup that season and everything looked good for the future. Sadly, though, Jinky possessed a self-destruct button. He could be a complex personality if he perceived there was an injustice being done to him. It could be real or imagined, but you could always detect that Jinky was fretting about something.

The young players, as I said, loved being in Jinky's company. They appreciated what he meant to Celtic. Jinky would take training, but still wanted to display all his tricks and flicks. The kids were hardly getting a touch of the ball as Jinky went through his tantalising routines. He was taking a trip down memory lane. I had to remind him on a few occasions that he was supposed to be supervising training and not participating in it. He was still like a wee boy with his first ball. You would have to take it off him at gunpoint. A lot of people had warned me about employing Jinky. I was told he would let me down. They were quick to throw that back in my face when things didn't work out. Simply put, Jinky was a free spirit. He was a performer and, of course, that is what he excelled at throughout his glittering career. He won nine League Championships, five League Cups and four Scottish Cups. There was the little matter, too, of the European Cup breakthrough in 1967.

Jinky is right up there with Johan Cruyff as one of the all-time greats in my opinion. The Dutchman was the real deal. I played against him at club and country level and I'm still waiting to get near him. Like Jinky, his bravery was immense. He took the knocks and came back for more. He also possessed perfect poise and uncanny balance. You could see frustrated opponents trying to barge him off the ball, but he would resist their crude challenges, change angles, accelerate and make them look leaden-footed. He was good in the air, had fabulous vision and could score goals. Did I also mention he had a great game awareness and was an outstanding team man? That guy had everything and you have to wonder what he and Jinky could have conjured up between them if they had ever played in the same team.

Jinky, of course, is no longer with us, a victim of motor neurone disease. The illness was diagnosed in 2001 and he died on 13 March 2006 at his home in Uddingston. He was only sixty-one years old. I visited him not often enough before he passed away. Sadly, his body had been ravaged by the disease. But on my last visit he was still the charismatic, genuine Wee Man I had known for so long. His bravery was immense, even inspirational. And his sense of humour had remained intact. He was still laughing and cracking jokes throughout my stay.

The supporters voted him The Greatest-Ever Celtic player in 2002. I have always insisted those supporters knew their football.

19

MO AND THE SECRET DRUGS TEST

Mo Johnston took very little persuading before becoming a Celtic player in October 1984. I got the impression that he might have happily paid the transfer cash out of his own pocket to join his boyhood idols. And then he signed for Rangers five years later! I would have given you any odds you cared to ask for against that ever happening, especially on the day he could hardly contain himself at the thought of performing in those famous green-and-white hoops.

I liked Mo and I always reckoned he was more of a rascal than a rogue. He trained hard and you could never ask for anything more from him during a match. Celtic got him for £400,000 after he had scored twenty-three goals in a season and a half at Watford. He also helped them to the 1984 FA Cup Final where they lost 2-0 to Everton, another club he would sign for on his soccer travels. Actually, Jim McLean, Dundee United's manager at the time, is due a large thanks in helping Celtic land Johnston.

I didn't think we could afford Mo and I was looking around elsewhere for someone who may be more in our price range. Davie Dodds, an experienced striker at the Tannadice club, was discussed, but McLean was looking for far too much so I went shopping elsewhere. I had missed out on Johnston in 1983 when I signed the more experienced Jim Melrose and once again Mo appeared on my radar. I knew he was Celtic crazy and I also realised he would do a great job for us. After a few meetings with the board, I was given the go-ahead to try to get the deal sealed. I travelled to London with Jack McGinn, who was vice-chairman at the time.

The agreed fee was a club record and, as manager, I did the negotiating on the player's personal terms. Changed days! We were in Langan's Brasserie, the top eatery in London back then, and Jack and I sat down with Johnston, his agent Frank Boyd and a lawyer from Watford. Of course, there was a bit of toing and froing as there can be with transfer deals, but I had the distinct feeling there would be no hitches. I told the agent, 'That's our final offer. Take it or leave it.' Thankfully, Boyd was satisfied with what was on the table and the deal was done. We set about demolishing the menu after that. I recall golfer Nick Faldo was at a table next to us and it really made Mo's day when a glamorous kissogram girl came in. He looked a bit miffed, though, when he realised she hadn't been sent for him! The bill duly arrived and Boyd picked it up, made a face and handed it onto Jack. He stifled a gasp as he looked at the bottom figure. He passed it back to the agent. This went on for about five minutes until Boyd decided, 'Why don't we toss a coin for it, Jack?'

Our vice-chairman hesitated for a moment before agreeing. The coin was flipped and Jack got lumbered with the bill. He almost fainted! Mo was our player and he contributed massively to Celtic winning the championship the following season. He was fearless, liked to get in about it, rummel up rearguards and try to unsettle defenders. He had extraordinary positional sense and he also possessed lightning reflexes. If a goalkeeper fumbled anything when Mo was around, the ball invariably ended in the back of the net. He rattled in fifty-five goals in three years and formed a lethal partnership with Brian McClair. They were the perfect foil for each other.

I would rate Mo Johnston as my best-ever signing. Yes, I know that might rankle with some of the Celtic support who were far from happy that he decided to move to Rangers in July 1989, especially when he had already been paraded as a Celtic 'signing' a few weeks beforehand. Mo had changed his agent from Frank Boyd to Bill McMurdo and it is now clear that the transfer from French side Nantes to Parkhead had never been rubber-stamped. That information somehow found its way across Glasgow to Rangers. That was most unfortunate on someone's behalf at Celtic although I must say I don't believe any of the blame could be put at Billy McNeill's door. I had done the deal to sign Mo in that extremely expensive restaurant in 1983, but club directors and accountants were taking more and more to do with the financial side of things five years later.

Mo, of course, was no stranger to controversy and he could be a source of a major headache or two. I believe, though, that he was more than just a little persecuted during his three years at the club. He was hounded around Glasgow and I'm convinced there were more than a few smear campaigns going on to blacken his character. He figured on the front pages of the newspapers too often for comfort, but, always remember, Glasgow is a gold-fish bowl. I lost count of the amount of characters who would drop snippets of information in my ear about Mo. It would start, 'I think you should know this . . .' Then another outlandish tale would unfold. I was more than aware that a lot of them were put around by mischief makers with nothing better to do. If Mo had been up to half of what he was supposed to be involved in then he would never have been fit to play on a Saturday.

One story that would not go away was the allegation that Mo was taking drugs. Let me state for the record here and now that I did not believe these suggestions for one moment. However, they were like the snowball that rolls down the hill and becomes an avalanche. The stories just wouldn't go away. Eventually, I decided to act and put everyone's mind at ease, especially mine. Brian Scott was the Celtic physiotherapist at the time and I hatched a plan with him that would get Mo into hospital for special checks. Mo, of course, was kept in the dark. We informed him he had to undergo an exhaustive medical check. The doctors, though, had arranged tests that would once and for all ascertain if there were any traces of any kind of drugs in the player's system. Stimulants would have been detected immediately. Only a handful of people knew about these examinations and Mo was not one of them. The press would have had a field day if that had leaked out. 'Celtic Drug Test For Johnston'. Perish the thought. His character would have been blackened forever. So, there was a strict code of secrecy surrounding the entire episode.

Shortly afterwards, we received the results of the tests and they told me what I had known all along – Mo Johnston was clean. At last, I had the evidence, but it was a shame that we were all put in that position in the first place. Before I was sacked as manager in 1987 I had tried hard to get Mo to extend his deal with the club. He and Brian McClair were a marvellous double-act up front and played so well alongside each other. As I have said in a previous chapter, Brian, too, was coming out of contract at the same time as his front-line partner. I had hopes of persuading Brian to stay, but I knew Mo would be on his way. I believed he had had enough of Glasgow. He told me he thought there was an orchestrated hate campaign being waged against him. He gave me the impression that he was at the end of his tether and needed to get away from his native city. I wasn't surprised he agreed to go to France and join Nantes that summer. That's why the mind boggles that he made the momentous decision to return to Glasgow to sign for Rangers, of all teams, in 1989. Maybe it was just a bit too quiet for Mo in France!

Some transfers, of course, don't work out for one reason or another. Playing for the Old Firm takes you to another level and the demand for good results is unrelenting. I bought Brian Whittaker from Partick Thistle for £65,000 and was convinced he had all the makings of a decent left back. He was not a big, bruising defender, but a guy who looked quite composed on the ball. Having played in the fullback position, I knew what was expected in that particular berth. Big Jock had taught me all those years ago that you must think positively at all times and your first touch must be to get forward. I expected a lot from Whittaker, possibly too much, and he played only ten games for us before I sold him to Hearts. I had to make a quick decision in his case and it came down against the player. He wasn't cutting it at Celtic and when I heard Hearts were interested I cashed in immediately.

The fullback position was one I relished and this will probably surprise you, but I actually preferred to play at right or left back rather than in midfield. I think a lot of people believed my natural role in the team was in the middle of the park, but I saw myself as more of a fullback, mainly on the right. I was fortunate enough to possess a good engine and I had a fair turn of speed, too. Supporting the frontmen down the flanks was enjoyable. Big Jock would mix it up, of course, and give me a place in the midfield when he thought we were coming up against opposition who were known to try to intimidate their opponents in that vital area of the park. I relished that challenge, too, and I always kept in mind that if you were going to clatter into someone and let them know you meant business it was always best to do it around the halfway line. No one was going to score a direct free kick from that range!

20

BIG JOCK v FERGIE

Silence. You could hear the proverbial pin drop. Seconds before a Celtic Supporters' Club charity event at a hall in Cardonald was in full swing, the place packed to the rafters. It was one of those question-and-answer events and I was in the firing line. It was all good-natured stuff, of course, until I was asked a simple question, 'Who do you rate as the greatest-ever manager?' The inquisitor believed he already had the answer to his own query. 'Sir Alex Ferguson,' I responded. Silence descended very quickly. Some of the supporters spluttered, put down their pints and looked at each other. 'Did he say Ferguson?' seemed to be the question on everyone's lips. 'Not Jock Stein? Did we hear right?'

The question was posed again just in case I had misunderstood or had misheard the original. 'Davie, I asked who do you think is the best-ever manager?' I replied again, 'Sir Alex Ferguson.' The look of incredulity on the faces of the people in front of me took me slightly aback. I had been posed a question and I had answered it truthfully. I was beginning to wonder if I would get out of Cardonald alive! This revelation was made in 1999, so I can't be accused of jumping on the bandwagon in recent times.

Actually, you might as well compare Michelangelo to Leonardo da Vinci when you match up Big Jock and Sir Alex. They have both had a huge input in the game. Both were inspirational in their own ways and both had massive influences in the development of football. It's interesting to note that Sir Alex himself believes the best boss of all time is Jock. However, I happen to believe what Fergie has achieved will never be surpassed. What he has done at Manchester United is nothing short of phenomenal. He won't see his 60th birthday again, but his incredible enthusiasm has never wavered or waned. By the end of season 2007/08 he had won the Champions League twice amid a veritable avalanche of silverware on the domestic front.

He had to show true grit to weather the storm when he first arrived at Old Trafford after his successes at Aberdeen. He had picked up the European Cup Winners' Cup, beating the legendary Real Madrid in 1983, and was used to triumphs. However, remarkably, he went four years at United before picking up his first trophy. That was a testing time, but he had the courage to see it through and it was important, too, that he got solid support from his chairman at the time, Martin Edwards. Yes, there were calls for Fergie's head – ridiculous when you think of it today – but Edwards remained in his corner. The chairman obviously had immense faith in his manager and, by God, was he repaid big-style when Fergie's machine got moving. Chairmen of that status are pure gold for a team boss, but, unfortunately, they are not exactly thick on the ground. Goodness knows how things would have panned out for Fergie if Edwards had listened to impatient fans and pulled the plug. I shudder to think. I bet the Manchester United support does, as well!

It's ironic that a young Alex Ferguson used to sit in with Big Jock and his assistant Sean Fallon when they were out for a meal near their homes in the south side of Glasgow at a restaurant called The Beechwood which is virtually in the shadow of Hampden Park. Fergie thought about going into the cooking business when he eventually quit playing and he spent a few evenings picking up tricks of the trade in the kitchen. You never know, if his career hadn't taken a remarkable path, he could have been the first Gordon Ramsay! When Jock and Sean arrived that was the end of the culinary exercises for the evening for a young man willing to listen and learn. There was a genuine friendship between Jock and Fergie. They had both come from basically working-class backgrounds, Jock from the mining village of Bellshill, and Fergie from Govan, with the shipyards providing much-needed employment for the citizens of the area.

Both were no-nonsense, self-motivating individuals and if anyone crossed either of them it was tantamount to soccer suicide. There was a ruthless streak in both of them and success for their teams was everything to them. They both liked to win with a bit of a swagger and adventure. Jock and Fergie were class acts and, ultimately, football has been the winner.

It was surely ironic that Fergie should be sitting beside Jock on the bench that fateful night in Cardiff on 10 September 1985 when the Scotland manager collapsed at the end of a 1-1 World Cup draw with Wales. Sadly, they could not resuscitate Jock and he passed away in the dressing room. I watched as the drama unfolded on my television at home in Giffnock. Images were a bit sketchy and no one seemed to be too certain what exactly was happening. It looked as though Jock had fallen over. You instinctively fear a worst case scenario and the dreadful news came out minutes later. I immediately thought of his wife Jean.

By a strange quirk of timing, Alex and his Aberdeen team were due to play Celtic at Parkhead four days later in a league game. It was obvious we were all in shock and it didn't seem to matter that we won 2-1. Big Jock dominated everyone's thoughts that day. Afterwards I drove Fergie to the Albany Hotel in Glasgow for a function. The Aberdeen entourage had left to go home without their manager. The Hay team were in the car, as usual. Fergie tried to lighten the mood by turning round to talk to my daughters Alison and Caroline. He said, 'Do you know your dad was a dirty so-and-so when he was a player? Do you want me to show the bruises I've got after he put me up in the air at Parkhead?' Actually, I could remember that particular 'tackle' and, yes, he did go spiralling skywards! Nothing wrong with Fergie's memory, then. Mind you, I'm sure he'll admit he could put it about himself. If you had taken off his elbows he wouldn't have been able to play at all.

Actually, I had the chance to become a scout for Manchester United shortly after I was sacked as Celtic boss in 1987. Journalist Jim Rodger got in touch to see if I was interested in such a post. I guess the invite would have come from Fergie, but, to be honest, I still saw myself staying in football as a manager. It was a much-appreciated gesture, though. At times like that it's good to know you are still remembered and the world hasn't turned its back on you. I still hadn't turned forty and I believed I had something to offer as a boss. I will always insist that Celtic sacked a better manager than the one they hired four years earlier. Those four years in charge at Parkhead taught me an awful lot.

In my short spell at Motherwell, Big Jock tried to get me involved in the Scotland international set-up. I remember going with the Under-21s to Italy for a game while Rikki MacFarlane, who bossed St Mirren, was in charge. It was nice of Jock to think of me, but I didn't pursue that side of things simply because I was too busy at Fir Park. They were my employers and they deserved my complete commitment. So, the international scene wasn't big on my agenda back then.

Although I had my differences with Big Jock on occasion, I still genuinely liked the man. He did have a sense of humour and I recall a morning I got a telephone call from him before I turned up for training. Harry Hood, Lou Macari, George Connelly and myself were roped in to doing some fashion modelling for the clothes store C&A. The photographer took us to the Art

Galleries at Kelvinhall and we went through all sorts of routines, modelling jackets, trousers, shoes etc. It was all a bit of a laugh and I recall we didn't get a fee for our afternoon's work. Instead, the shop told us we could keep what we modelled. I got a jacket that wasn't even real leather. I think they called it leatherette and it turned into a form of seaweed in the rain! Anyway, the lads and I did our stint and the photographs duly appeared in the following day's newspapers. My phone rang at home and on came the unmistakeable tones of our manager. 'What are you thinking about? You're a footballer not a model. You big Jessy!' My modelling career ended there and then.

I have nothing but the utmost admiration for Big Jock. The way he introduced myself and the likes of Kenny Dalglish, Danny McGrain, George Connelly, Lou Macari and so many others to first team football was nothing short of phenomenal. He would look ahead, pick a game he thought you could do well in and then give you your opportunity. He cared for his footballers, but you crossed him at your peril. I've never actually been on the receiving end of the so-called 'hairdryer treatment' from Fergie, but you just know it exists. I don't think for a fleeting moment that the Manchester United boss does it for effect. I think if you are the object of his attentions then there is every chance you deserve it.

Jock and Fergie have given so much to football. Both will be remembered for all time with the greatest of affection by grateful football supporters. It's the very least these two sporting giants deserve.

2 1

THE QUIET ASSASSIN

The Quiet Assassin teamed up with Ron 'Chopper' Harris when I joined Chelsea in 1974. Two rather terrifying and intimidating nicknames, I think you'll agree. Do you know neither of us were ever sent off in our senior careers? There is a world of a difference between hard men and hatchet men in soccer. Sometimes it could be borderline, but I knew neither Chopper nor myself were dirty players. Neither of us would knowingly injure another professional. Sure, if the ball was there to be won we would go into the challenge with every ounce of power, strength and energy we had at our disposal.

Actually, I have to admit I was ordered off once in a reserve game and I was raging as I trudged towards the dressing room, realising I had let down my teammates with a foolish action. It was in a match against Rangers at Ibrox and I was involved in a little tangle with Alex Miller, later to become manager of Hibs, St Mirren, Aberdeen and Morton before having a back-room stint at Liverpool. It was no big deal, but we squared up to each other and I motioned my head towards my opponent. Wrong thing to do, but hardly life-threatening. Miller went down like he had been hit by a wrecking ball. I looked at him as he writhed around on the turf and immediately realised I had made a huge mistake and I was in big trouble. The referee was completely taken in and I was dismissed.

I was extremely remorseful in the dressing room as my colleagues played on with a man short. It didn't matter that it was only a reserve team fixture. It would have hurt me just as much if it had been a World Cup-tie. We eventually lost 4-0 and I learned a harsh lesson there and then. It was one that would stay with me throughout the remainder of my career. Afterwards, I brightened up a little when our manager, Sean Fallon, an Irishman who was as tough as teak, came in at the end of the game, told me off for my stupidity and then said, 'If you are going to go off, make sure he goes with you!'

I didn't like what the Rangers player did that evening. It would never occur to me to do such a thing to an opponent. I recall playing for Celtic against Hearts at Tynecastle one day and I had a bit of a skirmish with one of their midfield men, Jim Townsend. He wasn't happy with me and, while the referee wasn't looking, he headbutted me in the face. There was no way whatsoever I was going down. I stood my ground, stared back at him and said, 'Is that the best you've got?' He never came near me for the rest of the game. Wise choice, Jim.

It was Tommy Docherty, of course, who gave me my formidable moniker when we were both together with Scotland. The Doc was a colourful, flamboyant sort of character and must have reckoned the name Davie Hay was a bit mundane. The Quiet Assassin was then brought into play. Ron Harris never chopped down anyone when I was around. Like I say, we were both committed professionals, dedicated to the cause. Ron was no Peter Osgood and I was no Jinky Johnstone, so we played to our strengths and that, mainly, was winning the ball off our opponents and setting up moves. I don't think anyone should ever have taken these name tags too literally. I'm fairly certain England and Leeds United defender Norman Hunter never actually lived up to his 'Bites Yer Legs' nickname. I hope not, anyway. Liverpool's Tommy Smith wasn't made of iron and I don't believe

for a moment that the Spanish international with the unpro-
nounceable name was, in fact, the Butcher of Bilbao.

I might be quiet, but, to my certain knowledge, I have never
assassinated anyone. I would have been the worst hitman in the
world, anyway, with my wonky right eye. On the subject of nicknames I do have a particular favourite, the one given to Crystal
Palace player Fitz Hall. His mates have christened him 'One
Size'. That's class!

Football, as I have insisted throughout my career, is a man's
game. It's physical and you will get your share of hard knocks
along the way. Let's face it, the fans relish a bone-rattling
challenge, don't they? A player is out there performing for
them and giving his all for their team. They may not be blessed
with a superabundance of skill, but they are part of a unit and
they are a vital cog in the system. The Brazilian team that
captured the imagination of football supporters everywhere
on their way to lifting the World Cup in Mexico in 1970 was
one of the finest collections of individual talents you are ever
likely to witness.

They paraded the likes of Pele, Gerson, Alberto, Jairzinho and
Rivelino, each the possessor of spellbinding, sublime skills. But
they also had players such as Brito, an uncompromising central
defender, Clodoaldo, a hard-working midfielder, and Tostao, an
energetic frontman whose continual running and probing opened
up space for Pele. It's all a question of getting the mix spot on.
Celtic's European Cup winning team of 1967 had Jimmy
Johnstone, Bertie Auld, Tommy Gemmell and Bobby Murdoch.
They also had John Clark, an unfussy defender who tidied up
behind everyone. Manchester United conquered Europe a year
later and, of course, they had Bobby Charlton, George Best and
Denis Law in the ranks around that era although, of course, The
Lawman missed their European success through injury. They also
had Nobby Stiles to keep an eye on things in midfield and at

the back. Ruud Gullit, Marco van Basten and Frank Rijkaard at AC Milan and Franco Baresi in defence. Need I go on?

You can have all the splendour that is pleasing on the eye, but you still need that little element of steel to hold and knit everything together. You must ally panache with power, talent with tenacity. Jock Stein used to call some players 'serviceable' and we knew where he was coming from. One of his great strengths was utilising a player to the utmost of his ability. He never got confused about that. He zeroed in on your main asset and played on it endlessly. No one was ever asked to attempt to carry out a task that was outwith his ability. We were all different parts of a jigsaw and we all had our clearly-defined parts to play.

It never bothered me coming up against a hardman. I had a few fierce confrontations in my playing days and one of the guys who could dish it out was Brazil's central defender Luis Periera in the 1974 World Cup Finals. He was a colossus of a man and he would launch himself at anything that was within range. He clattered me a few times when we played them and, just for good measure, I replied with a couple of dull ones as well. He gave it and he took it. That to me, was what it was all about. I couldn't stand crybabies. Pereira was anything but that. I remember him being sent off against Holland when goals from the majestic Johan Cruyff and Johan Neeskens gave the Dutch a 2-0 triumph. It was the last game in Group A and the winners knew they would get through to the final. That was the set-up in 1974. They both went into the game on four points. I've seen the game and the Dutch were by far the better team. It should also be said that they were not slow to throw an elbow around if they thought it was necessary. They were not a team to be intimidated.

The red mist must have descended on Pereira and he hurtled into a mighty challenge against Neeskens. The Dutch midfielder was sent spinning and the referee immediately brandished the red card. The towering South American made his way slowly to the tunnel. It appeared that there was about half of Amsterdam in Dortmund that night and the raging Dutch fans were making all sorts of gestures to the Brazilian. Another player might have headed for the safety of the dressing room at the speed of light, but not big Luis. He stopped at the touchline and started making gestures of his own. In Glasgow parlance, it looked as though he wanted to have 'a square go' with the Holland supporters. There were 54,000 in the Dortmund Stadium and I don't think you'd need an honours degree in geography to work out that most would have come from just across the border. That didn't faze Luis. He stood his ground before some brave policemen, about ten, I think, persuaded him to move on.

In that same World Cup, we came up against Zaire, of course. My goodness, were these guys tough. They were solid. You kicked them and then hobbled around with a sore toe for a minute or two. They didn't even blink. When people talk about hardmen they normally associate the term with big, raw defenders who thunder into tackles. That's not always the case. Denis Law, my particular favourite, was never one to run for cover when the going got tough. There wasn't much of Denis, but he was afraid of no one. Same goes for Jimmy Johnstone. He would spend some games more often in the air than on the ground, but he still came back for more.

Within the game, players always respected their opponents if they were hard but fair. You could spend ninety minutes kicking hell out of each other and go for a drink afterwards. Fans of the opposing sides would never have believed it. There are some things that are unacceptable, though, and have absolutely nothing to do with sport. I'm talking about spitting and it's not easy to walk away when someone has just gobbed in your face. Atletico Madrid in 1974 were those sort of brainless louts. Not all of them, but a fair percentage who thought nothing of participating in this vile act. When I was at Livingston we had an Argentine player called Sergio Berti. He arrived in August and was back in Buenos Aires a few days later. He spat on a teammate during a friendly! I was told about his unsavoury actions and, once the evidence was looked at, we sent him packing. The thing is he didn't seem to think he had done anything particularly wrong. Spitting appeared to be acceptable where he came from. What to you and me would be an utterly despicable antisocial act appeared to be merely a slight character defect to the Argentine. Adios, Sergio, close the door behind you!

Hardmen, genuine tough guys, would never have resorted to that.

22

THE MEN IN BLACK

John Gordon didn't know who or what had hit him. It was me. He was lying face down in the mud at Parkhead, arms and legs akimbo, a fairly undignified sight as he slumped in a heap following my rather vigorous shoulder charge. I could have been in big trouble because John Gordon was, in fact, the referee. To give him his full title, he was JPR Gordon, of Newport-on-Tay, and, frankly, I had had enough of his ropey decisions that particular day.

It's not something I would recommend to any budding footballers out there and, as we all know, we should never attempt to take the law into our own hands. There are occasions, though, when the little red devil on your left shoulder possesses a lot more persuasive powers than the little white angel on the right. The wee guy with the trident won the argument on this occasion. I was running past the match official when I saw my opportunity. I sort of lost my footing, careered to the right and caught Gordon totally unawares. He collapsed like a sack of spuds. I'll never forget the look on his face as he turned around after hitting the deck with an almighty thud. He was clearly puzzled. Had I taken leave of my senses? 'Sorry, ref,' I said. 'I slipped.'

He couldn't do a thing. How could he prove it wasn't an accident? And, as I recall, the ground conditions that day were dodgy. He got up, wiped some mud off his kit, glowered for a moment and then got on with the game. Of course, he would have had his suspicions, but he had no proof. These were the days when there were only one or two television cameras at the game unlike today when there seems to be one attached to every blade of grass. The TV people had, of course, been following play, so no one, apart from a few supporters in the ground perhaps, saw my impromptu act of retribution. I was very careful with the rest of my challenges during that match. Somehow I got the impression that JPR would have been only too delighted to get my name in his little black book for any reason.

Yes, I have had my ups and downs with referees over the years. As a player and a manager I have always been passionate about my sport. I always wanted to be a winner and I make no apology for that. As you will no doubt have discovered by now, my laid-back public image isn't quite 100 per cent accurate. The ninety minutes on match day were the most important in life to me. But only for ninety minutes. Those could be anxiety-provoking minutes where emotions wouldn't be so much running high as heading for orbit. You had prepared all week for the game and had gone into every detail with minute precision. When the referee blew for the kick-off the next ninety minutes were the sole focus of your attention; the most important minutes in life. But, I repeat, only for ninety minutes. At the final whistle, you could be transformed back to a normal and rational human being again. Well, most of us!

Referees, though, had the ability to wreck your concentration. They could wipe out a week's hard work at a stroke with a crazy decision. And that's when people can go up like a Roman torch. In my playing days, Bobby Davidson of Airdrie was, in my opinion, by far the worst referee to take charge of Celtic games. I am not saying he was biased, but I would need the rest of this book to catalogue the decisions he made against Celtic that can be filed under C for controversial. He was a constant irritant and when you saw he had been designated by the SFA to take charge of one of your games your heart sank. What will he conjure up today? How can he upset thousands of Celtic fans? Somehow he always seemed to find a way.

He was the match official for the 1970 Scottish Cup Final when Aberdeen were our opponents. It was only ten days after we had beaten Leeds United 1-0 in the European Cup semi-final at Elland Road and we would meet them again four days after the Dons game. Naturally, the players and fans were still in a state of euphoria when Davidson blew to start the contest. The ref's display at Hampden that afternoon was disgraceful. I knew there was never any love lost between Jock Stein and Davidson and you have got to hope that personal feelings wouldn't come into play to settle old scores during a game of football. Celtic were massive favourites that afternoon – I believe you could get odds of 7/1 against Aberdeen – and we were confident without being complacent. Davidson first stepped into the spotlight when he awarded our opponents a penalty kick after the ball struck Bobby Murdoch in the midriff. The ref signalled handball and would be not be dissuaded even after Bobby went to him and showed him the mud on his jersey where the ball had hit him. Davidson was having none of it – a penalty it was. Joe Harper sent Evan Williams the wrong way with the award.

It was still early enough for us to get back into the final. We knocked the ball around in our usual fashion, probing and looking for an opening. Bobby Lennox, as he usually did, harassed their keeper Bobby Clark when he was kicking the ball from hand. There was no six-second rule in those days for keepers to release the ball. Some goalies used to waltz around their area for what seemed eternities, especially if you were losing, before deciding to put the ball back into play. On this occasion, Clark flipped the ball up, but before he could kick it, Bobby, with those aston- ishing reflexes, flashed in a foot, nicked it from him and, as the keeper watched open-mouthed, ran round him and plonked it in the net. It wasn't dangerous play because Bobby made his challenge from the side, so it wasn't studs up right in front of Clark. Once the ball has been released, it is up for grabs. Bobby did what he was perfectly entitled to do and won it fairly and squarely. Not according to Davidson, though. He stifled the cheers from our support by immediately awarding the Dons a free kick. I think he motioned that our player had kicked the ball out of the keeper's hands. That wasn't the case. It's just a pity that all the slow-motions replays we are treated to these days weren't available in 1970. Both of the referee's big decisions would have been seen to have been abominably wrong.

Big Jock was seething on the touchline and the players were sharing that emotion on the pitch. Derek McKay netted a second for them in a breakaway and we were beginning to get the notion this might not be our day. Bobby Lennox pulled one back near the end and, as we piled forward in an attempt to snatch an equaliser, they sneaked up the pitch once more and McKay knocked in a third after a low cross from the right had eluded our keeper. The outcome of the Scottish Cup had hinged on refereeing decisions and they had gone against us and had gone for our opponents. It was a difficult defeat to accept.

Bob Valentine, too, had his moments when he was in charge of Celtic games. In fact, I asked the authorities to ban him from handling any further Celtic matches in my last season. Of course, he had been the referee when we lost the League Cup Final against Rangers and the Scottish Cup Final to the Dons in my first season as Celtic manager. I had been unhappy with his handling of both of those games and, in fact, was hauled before the SFA Disciplinary Committee after remarks I made following the Scottish Cup Final. I had been asked by the press for my thoughts on Valentine's display and, as you might expect, I had strong opinions on his sending off of Roy Aitken. I said so and that led to me being fined by the SFA bosses. So much for free speech. As a player, despite the hardman tag, I was rarely in trouble with the authorities. I picked up a booking or two, but nothing serious. As a manager, I seemed to be continually getting involved and that fine was the first of several I would be hit with during my four-year spell as Parkhead boss.

I realise it was irrational and completely out of character for me to request the SFA to remove Bob Valentine from officiating at Celtic matches. Like that was going to happen. After a particular game, I had had enough. That's when I made my plea to the SFA, but, if I had stepped back and been a bit more patient, I would have realised I was merely wasting my time. This will surprise you, but I actually thought Bob Valentine wasn't a bad referee. And there is no way I am accusing him of being biased one way or another. It was just we didn't seem to get too many breaks when he was around. Tiny Wharton was another official who seemed to get up the nose of the Celtic support. He sent off Jimmy Johnstone on two occasions and, sorry Wee Man, the ref got both those decisions right! One was for taking a lunge at Rangers midfielder Therolf Beck, a fairly unassuming Icelandic player who rarely courted trouble, and the other was for a touch-line fight with Partick Thistle's Ian Cowan. In the case of Beck, I think Jinky was heading down the Ibrox tunnel even before Wharton could tell him he was off and his fight with Cowan was always an accident waiting to happen. The Thistle lad, like Jinky, had bright red hair and when these two came face-to-face it was like nitro meeting glycerine. Tiny – who was about 6ft 4in – was a referee I liked although I believe I might have been in the minority of one in the Parkhead dressing room with that train of thinking.

As you've probably gathered by now, I was never one for taking a step back and biting my tongue if I thought an injustice had been done. That wasn't my style. If I had something to

say I went ahead and aired my views. I cracked up with Davie
Syme after our 2-1 League Cup Final defeat against Rangers in
1986. I've covered that explosive encounter in a previous chapter,
but I think the referee simply lost the plot. He ordered off Mo
Johnston. Then he awarded our opponents a ridiculous penalty
kick and Davie Cooper scored the winner minutes from the end.
Ironically, I only saw footage of that spot kick recently when I
was doing an interview for Celtic TV. It was worse than I thought
first time around!

The match official also did something in that confrontation I
have never witnessed before – he ordered off a player and allowed
him to come back onto the pitch. Remarkable. Syme dismissed
Tony Shepherd, who had done absolutely nothing. It appeared
the ref thought my player had struck him from behind. No such
thing happened. Syme seemed to have a glazed look in his eyes
as his linesman persuaded him to allow Tony to return to the
action. 'I've made a mistake,' he said to me as I stood on the
touchline. I replied, 'You're a mistake!'

I made my feelings known after the game. Yes, I was bitter,
but I believed every single word I uttered at the press confer-
ence. Privately, the Celtic directors agreed with my criticisms.
Publicly, they body-swerved any controversy and toed the party
line. Celtic put out a statement that inferred that disciplinary
measures would be taken within the club. Syme booked seven
Celtic players that day – Mo Johnston, who was also sent off, of
course, Pat Bonner, Roy Aitken, Alan McInally, Derek Whyte,
Peter Grant and Owen Archdeacon. I still felt a grievance and I
told the board everyone had been punished enough. I talked
them out of taking any further action if, indeed, they had planned
to do so in the first place.

I used to believe foreign referees should take charge of the
biggest games in our country. They couldn't possibly be accused
of bias toward any Scottish team if they came from Italy, Spain,

Germany or any country you care to mention. I don't think there would have been a communication problem, either. The rules of the game are the same wherever football is played. It would have removed any lingering doubts about a match official's questionable decision-making. However, I am not of that opinion these days for one very good reason – new technology. Big Brother is watching and that can be no bad thing. Surely match officials would welcome and embrace anything that can only help them when it comes to calling it right. It's all in the spirit of fair play, after all. The paying customer, the guy who turns out every week in all sorts of weather conditions, shouldn't be short-changed, either.

Or maybe we should just accept the obvious – a lot of referees may know the laws of the game, but do they actually know football?

23

JUST CHAMPION IN NORWAY

I came home from Norway after season 1988/89 with a league and a cup; the league I won with Lillestrom and the cup was a parting gift from the players. It was such a wonderful gesture after we had enjoyed a thoroughly good campaign. At the end of it, though, I knew it was time, once again, to move on. I was offered an extension which I declined because of family reasons.

As I prepared to say my farewells, the players surprised me when they congregated in the dressing room and then presented me with a silver trophy as their way of saying thanks to me. It was a bit overwhelming; a genuine gesture that was greatly appreciated. I looked around the place and I knew my work was done. Hopefully, I had left them in good hands and they had a stint to look forward to in the European Cup. I learned a lot during my spell at Lillestrom and it was a welcome addition to my CV. Basically, I had gone in cold and had to learn fast what football in that country was all about. Certainly, I found they did things differently in Norway.

I'll give you a quick example. We were battling away for the championship when we reached the mid-season break. When I returned I took the players as usual for training. It was imperative we kept our momentum going in the charge for the title. At Lillestrom, I was not the manager but head coach. That meant I was in total charge of the team selection, preparation, fitness levels, tactics and the rest. However, the board of directors dealt with all the finances and contracts. Fair enough. On this particular day I was looking around for our star striker, Jan Age Fjortoft. He was our main goalscorer and a key member of the team. 'Where's Jan?' I asked innocently. A director was close by and called over, 'Oh, we've sold him to Rapid Vienna.' Just like that. I hadn't been consulted about any possible transfer and, of course, was just a shade perplexed. The club had received what they thought was a suitable bid for Jan from the Austrian outfit and the deal was done without my knowledge. But, as far as they were concerned, they had done nothing behind my back. I soon found this was normal in Norway, if more than a little frustrating and annoying.

I had to accept that was the way they operated and the board believed they were doing their best for the club. It was their job to look after the finances and, as coach, it was my duty to look after all the matters concerning the team. The board never once stuck their oar in on this front. That was my domain and they never even thought of interfering. Bliss! We won the league, they banked the transfer cash and everyone was happy after a very interesting and eventful campaign. I found the Norwegians to be an extremely polite race and an absolute joy to work with – even if they sold your main goalscorer from under your nose! When I joined the club they were going through a transitional period and, basically, I had to start afresh. They didn't even have a recognised team captain and I happen to believe this is a vital component in any club. I don't think he is just the guy who runs out in front of the team and gets involved in the toss of the coin before the start of the game. I always saw it as very important in a team's thinking and the captain was the man who should epitomise everything you are trying to achieve.

Maybe I was spoiled at Celtic when I started and Billy McNeill was skipper. You couldn't have asked for a guy with better leadership qualities and I learned a lot from Big Billy. I took my time at Lillestrom before eventually giving the nod to the player who had done most to impress me. He was a good, solid and honest performer. I used to jot down the line-up on a piece of paper and pin my selection to the noticeboard on the dressing room wall. The players could see who was in and who was out and we could discuss the selection. This went on throughout the season without any problems. Then, on the last day of the season, the bloke I had selected as skipper came to me and said, 'Mr Hay, thank you for the honour of captaining the team. I should point out, though, that my name is Dyrstad and not Drystad as you have written on the team sheet. I thought I might point that out if it is OK.' It took the guy the entire season before he picked me up in my error. Now that is polite.

By the way, while I was in Norway I heard the news that Mo Johnston had signed again for Celtic. I telephoned to congratulate him on his return, but I immediately sensed all was not well when he said, 'Davie, the deal's not done yet. I haven't signed anything.' I was left wondering what was going on with my old player. I didn't have to wait too long to find out!

When it became widely known that I would be leaving Lillestrom after our title success I received a call from an agent in Sweden called Lenny Norgren. 'Do you fancy becoming boss at Gothenburg?' I was asked. They were one of the biggest – if not THE biggest – clubs in their country and they had been impressed by the way I handled things at Lillestrom. However, I had made up my mind to return to the UK and I politely declined their advances. Lenny was an agent I trusted completely and he was instrumental in my next move to Watford. He had arranged a Scandinavian trip for Mo's old club, and their manager, Colin Lee, mentioned he was looking for an assistant while his team were in Sweden preparing for the 1990/91 season. Lenny put my name forward, Colin got in touch and we had a wee natter about the prospect of me continuing my career at Vicarage Road. I agreed to join as Colin's No.2, but, unfortunately, we couldn't stack up the results and he left about four months later. Watford brought in Steve Perryman as his replacement and I decided it was better that I moved on, too.

So, it was back up the road again to see what might open up for me in Scotland. Before I had gone to Lillestrom I had been in touch with my hometown club St Mirren as my career took a new path and I became a fully licensed agent with FIFA. People scoffed all those years ago that agents would be a flash in the pan, but I insisted they were here to stay. I thought I would give it a try. My first client was Love Street player Ian Ferguson. He was in the middle of a long drawn-out transfer wrangle between the Saints and Rangers with Manchester United also showing an interest. Ian had started at Aberdeen, but had been allowed to go because they thought he was too small. He then worked as a hospital porter while playing part-time with Clyde. He joined St Mirren, scored the winner for the Paisley side in the 1987 Scottish Cup Final against Dundee United and, suddenly, was hot property. There were all sorts of stories flying around about his inevitable departure from Paisley. He kicked off the 1987/88 season as a St Mirren player, but it didn't look likely he would still be in place by the end of the campaign. And so it proved in February 1988.

I thought Ian needed assistance and I offered my services. We met and had a chat and he asked me to act on his behalf. I believe Rangers originally offered something in the region of £500,000 for the midfielder, but that had been rejected out of hand. The player was unsettled by everything that was going on, rumour and counter-rumour, until the clubs eventually agreed on a figure of £800,000. All we needed now was to sit down and agree personal terms and I would like to think I helped Ian in that capacity. Once we had fine-tuned everything in the contract it was time for the player to pose for the usual photograph, pen in hand, the so-called contract on the desk while flanked by the Rangers managerial double act of Graeme Souness and Walter Smith. Chairman David Holmes and secretary Campbell Ogilvie were also in attendance.

As ever, there was a small snag and I hope Ian doesn't mind me disclosing this. He was required to wear a tie with his new club jacket. We found a tie no problem, but Ian then had to admit to me he didn't know how to tie a knot! Obviously, I wasn't thinking straight because the simple thing to do would have been to put the tie round my neck, do up the knot, loosen it and then place it around Ian's neck. That would, indeed, have been the simple thing. So, what I did was to try to sort out the tie while standing in front of Ian. Have you ever tried to carry out this exercise when everything seems back to front and upside down? Impossible. The newspaper photographers were getting impatient as Ian and I tried all sorts of complex ways of getting this useless piece of apparel in place. Eventually, I stood behind Ian, stretched over his shoulders and tied the knot the way I would have done for myself. Only without someone standing in front of me.

Ian was ready for the snappers at last. The pictures were taken, everyone was happy and I went off for a bite to eat with my now-sartorially correct client, Graeme and Walter. I duly got my cheque from Rangers for my role in the deal. Would you believe it? My first agent's fee was paid by Rangers! I should have had it framed. Ian went on to play in Rangers' nine-in-a-row title sequence and made 336 appearances for the club. I would hasten to add to Celtic fans – I was never on the payroll at Ibrox. Anyway, over a very convivial meal, I realised it might not be the most appropriate time to remind Graeme that he had helped to get me the sack from Celtic the previous year!

24

WANTED MAN

It has always been a source of amazement to me that I never became manager of Hibs. I can now reveal that I had at least two opportunities to become boss of the Easter Road side. The first came in 1986 and the second was four years later. The initial offer came after Celtic had won the league championship and I can admit I was sorely tempted. Kenny Waugh, who was the millionaire chairman of the Edinburgh outfit at the time, was prepared to just about double my salary at Parkhead in his genuine bid to get me to join his club.

I had been involved in yet another money wrangle with the old Celtic board and I pointed out that I had not had a wage increase in the three years I had been manager of the team. I had started on £30,000 per year and, since we had won nothing in my first year as boss, I didn't think it was right to ask for a pay rise. However, we had lifted the Scottish Cup the following year and then, of course, the league title the season after that. I thought I was worth more money and I told the Celtic directors of my feelings. I realised Graeme Souness was earning more than me at Rangers and the word on the grapevine was that Alex Ferguson, at Aberdeen, and Jim McLean, at Dundee United, were also picking up higher salaries than me. In fact, a very good source informed me both Fergie and Jim were earning 'substantially' more. I could possibly accept that Graeme might get extra because Rangers were throwing money around at the time, but I believed it was unacceptable that clubs such as Aberdeen and Dundee United, without anything like the fan base of Celtic, could afford to shell out more cash to their managers. I wasn't having that and I told the board. My argument was that the manager of Celtic should be one of the highest earners in the Scottish game because of the status of the club.

I had gone into my fourth season as Celtic manager and had been rewarded in the summer with a pay hike of ten per cent to take my salary to £33,000. As usual, it was a bit of a wrangle to get extra cash. To be fair, there had been a bit of turmoil in the boardroom with Desmond White, a chairman I liked and who would always listen to you, passing away shortly after our Scottish Cup win while he was on holiday in Crete. Tom Devlin had succeeded him, but he, too, was in poor health. Everything had to be taken into consideration.

Kenny Waugh, who had the controlling interest at Hibs, might have heard about some friction between the board and me at the time. Although everything is done behind locked doors and marked 'confidential' it doesn't take long for things to get into the public domain. Waugh had been impressed by the way Celtic had won the championship, although I can tell you there was one director at Parkhead who didn't quite think along similar lines. When I was looking for a pay rise he informed me, 'Remember, Davie, you weren't manager of a title-winning team until seven minutes of the season to go.' That's when Dundee scored their two late goals against Hearts, of course, while we were beating St Mirren 5-0 to take the championship on goal difference. Was he inferring I got lucky? I could never be bothered arguing with someone with such an absurd outlook. The best team won the league. Start and end of.

There was contact from journalist Jim Rodger who had been the go-between in my strike action at Celtic in 1973. The Hibs financial package was put to me. Not only was the basic salary well in excess of what I was getting at Celtic, but there was also a huge signing-on fee. The deal would have made me a wealthy man. I might even have been awarded a written contract, something I didn't have at Celtic! The generosity of Kenny Waugh was close to overwhelming me. I had been impressed by his ambitions and he had given me something to think about. I didn't go back to Celtic to see if they could match what was now on offer at a rival club. Would they even be interested in trying to equal the Hibs deal? I remained silent. I didn't think it would have been ethical to use Kenny Waugh and Hibs as a lever in this manner. I admit I was tempted to move to Edinburgh. I looked at the figures in front of me in black and white and I genuinely wondered about what to do next.

As ever, I discussed everything with Catherine and the family. In the end, though, they knew it would be my decision. Loyalty to Celtic ultimately won out. I got word to Kenny Waugh to tell him I had been sincerely flattered by his wonderful offer, but I couldn't leave Celtic. He was the perfect gentleman, accepted my decision and I received his best wishes. Then something rather startling happened at Parkhead – I received another wage increase. This time the board slapped another £7,000 on my salary taking it to £40,000. That was a bit of a shock because, seven months earlier, they were pleading poverty and insisting there was no extra cash. Then, in a short space of time, they had added another £10,000. It was a strange way to do things, but I wasn't complaining. I wondered if anyone had leaked the news that Hibs were prepared to offer me an awful lot of money to quit Celtic and take over at Easter Road. Obviously, that would have been a massive slap in the face for Celtic to lose their boss to a so-called provincial club in Scotland. At the end of the day, I was satisfied. Mind you, my loyalty went for nothing at the end of the season when I was sacked!

The next time Hibs got in touch it was all cloak-and-dagger stuff. The club used a middleman to relay a message that they were interested in offering me the manager's job. Would I be interested? The quick answer was 'yes'. I was assistant to Colin Lee at Watford at the time, but would have been only too happy to come back across the border and be my own man again. It would have been ideal because Colin was sacked shortly afterwards and replaced by Steve Perryman who would bring in Peter Shreeve as his No.2. I quit when I heard Colin had been fired. So, before all that happened, I was intrigued in what Hibs had to say. There was one snag, though: they already had a manager, Alex Miller. I was aware of rumblings of discontent among the Hibs supporters at the time and that was when contact was made. I can't name the individuals who were pushing to get me on board for fear of embarrassing them. Take my word for it, though, they were men with power. I admit I had a meeting with one of them and, again, I was impressed by their ambition.

However, I told him, 'Come back to me when you don't have a manager and then we will discuss things fully. I am not about to back-stab anyone.' The individual might even have been taken aback that I was willing to take this stance. That's the way I am and I don't play by anyone else's rules. I've got my yardstick and I will always abide by it. A week or so went past and the Hibs guys were still insisting they wanted me to take over. I didn't put anyone under any pressure; if it happened, it happened. I'll tell you this – I would have loved that job. Hibs had always been an attractive proposition and they were a team that had a history of playing football the way I like it to be played. However, I wasn't about to compromise my beliefs – even if Alex Miller once got me sent off in a reserve match!

But, as is the way in this game, Alex Miller got to hear about what was going on. He demanded a face-to-face with a couple of people and they backed down. I was informed the deal was off. I merely shrugged my shoulders and accepted the situation. Possibly, if I had forced things events would have turned out differently, but I am not that sort of guy. What you see is what you get. As far as I was concerned, the possibility of a move to Edinburgh was off the table. Fair enough, let's move on. Remarkably, there was another nibble later in my career. I was doing well at Livingston and, of course, we had beaten Hibs in the League Cup Final around that time. Someone rolled the thought by me, but it went nowhere. I wonder if they might try again. It's probably too late!

25

HOME SWEET HOME?

It seemed inevitable that I would manage my hometown club St Mirren one day and that's precisely what happened when I was appointed boss in March 1991. My managerial circuit now included Motherwell, Celtic, Lillestrom, Watford and, at last, the Saints. You could also throw in some youth team coaching at Chelsea for good measure.

I didn't do myself any favours at Paisley four years earlier when I was the agent who helped Saints' best player Ian Ferguson get his £800,000 move to Rangers. Of course, Ian had helped the club win the Scottish Cup in 1987 and, as ever with success, the supporters' expectation levels go up another notch. They sample victory, they like it and they want more of it. Sadly, football doesn't work like that. The scripts may be written, but they are rarely followed.

The following season St Mirren were drawn against Clydebank at Love Street in the first defence of their trophy. The Saints were thumped 3-0 on their own ground and reality once again replaced fantasy. It didn't help, either, that the club also went out of the League Cup at the first hurdle, beaten 1-0 by St Johnstone at home. They also finished ninth in the ten-team Premier League and Tony Fitzpatrick, who had captained the club as a teenager, was named manager in place of Alex Smith. By the time I turned up in 1991 I realised a lot of work lay ahead. Only Merlin ever possessed a magic wand and I certainly didn't have one. The club, to be frank, were in dire straits as far as league results were concerned. The team had won only three of their first twenty-five games before March kicked in. St Mirren finished bottom with nineteen points from a possible seventy-two as it was still two points for a win at that time. Hibs were second bottom, six points better off.

League reconstruction saved the Saints the ignominy of toppling down a division. Two more teams were being introduced to the top league and relegation was suspended for a season. To be fair to the Paisley side, they had underlined their ambition by bringing in the likes of Steve Archibald, Victor Munoz, Tomas Stickroth and Gudmundur Torfason. Archibald and Munoz, of course, had performed at the very highest level with Barcelona, Stickroth was bought from Bundesliga outfit Bayer Uerdingen and Icelandic star Torfason arrived from Belgian side Genk. It hadn't paid off, though. At the end of the season I had to let the two former Barcelona boys move on. I had often heard that Steve Archibald could be a difficult individual, but I have to say he agreed with me that it was best for all concerned that St Mirren get the chance of a fresh start. Hopefully, we parted on good terms. Steve and Munoz had been exemplary professionals during their stay in Paisley and I know they spent a lot of time giving advice and so on to the younger players.

Changes were made, but, like the previous season, it was a struggle throughout. We finished eleventh, one off the bottom, and we went down alongside Dunfermline. It was around that time that I had been thinking of investing in Tampa Bay Rowdies as I have said in a previous chapter. The lure of the States just wouldn't go away. I couldn't see a future with St Mirren, no matter how hard I tried. Director Bob Earlie offered me a three-year deal and it was make-your-mind-up time. While I deliberated, the contract was taken off the table. I thanked the club and flew to Florida. I was back in Scotland by New Year's Eve 1992.

During the summer of 1993 I received a telephone call from my old Celtic pal John Gorman, one of The Quality Street Gang. We had kept in touch and our wives Catherine and Myra were close. He had just taken over as manager of Swindon Town from Glenn Hoddle and he was looking for an assistant. 'Are you interested Davie?' Of course I was, but there was one niggling little doubt. I had found it strange to be No.2 to Colin Lee at Watford although, of course, I gave it my best shot. However, I was more used to standing or falling by my own decisions. John Gorman was a friend, though, and I was certain we could work together. I didn't quite get that right.

Swindon had just been promoted to the top flight and Glenn Hoddle was in demand. He went to Chelsea and I think he expected John to go with him. However, the partnership was broken up when John decided to go solo at the Wiltshire club. He needed an experienced assistant and John turned to me. It was another interesting challenge. I read recently that John admitted he thought the job didn't really suit me and I believe he was right. However, I realised the club had ambitions and even paid a record club fee of £500,000 for Jan-Aage Fjortoft, the player who had been sold from under my nose by the Lillestrom directors.

John and I put in a bit of overtime as we prepared the team for what lay ahead in the top division. As usual, we were being written off by the experts before a ball had been kicked. It looked as though our critics were spot on, too, when the action got underway. Swindon kicked off with a 2-1 defeat at Sheffield United and followed that up with a single goal loss to Oldham at home. Liverpool were our next visitors and they hammered us 5-0. Southampton also took five off us in the next encounter at the old Dell. It took us until the fifth game to get a point in a goalless draw with Norwich City. By the end of September Swindon were bottom of the division.

Some crazy things happened around the club at that time. John was out for a training workout with most of the players in a place called Aldbourne, just outside Swindon. I was putting some others through indoor routines at the ground when I received a rather strange phone call. At first I thought it was an obscene caller when I heard all the panting coming down the line. I was about to hang up until I detected John's voice. He was still out of puff, but managed to say, 'We're in a pub down here. Get the rest of the lads and join us.' I knew the pub he was referring to and I told the players we were finishing training early to go for a drink. They thought I was joking, but we eventually caught up with John and the rest of the squad and, sure enough, they were standing there at the bar, still dripping sweat in their training gear and having a beer or two. 'John, what's going on?' I asked reasonably. 'It can't do any harm, Davie,' wheezed John. 'I've got to try something different, haven't I?' It seemed a bit extreme to me, but fair enough. We were due to play Queens Park Rangers in two days' time!

John then thought it would be a good idea to bring forward Christmas by a month or so. He knew Dave Bassett, then the Sheffield United manager, had done the same thing in switching his club's annual party to the start of a season because he believed his team played better in the second half of the campaign. It seemed to work, too, as they beat Manchester United 2-1 in the opening day of the season. John decided this was what we needed, as well. He had a word with a rather puzzled landlord who agreed to put together an Xmas party, with turkey and all the trimmings, for Swindon Town the next day. We turned up and there were decorations everywhere and, sure enough, it really had a festive feel to it. With a game just twenty-four hours away this time booze was banned. The players really seemed to enjoy themselves and we were in good spirits the following day when Queens Park Rangers rolled into Wiltshire.

Swindon were still looking for their first league win and John had prepared in a rather unusual way to see if we could turn the corner. Our quest wasn't aided by the fact we had Luc Nijholt, the former Motherwell defender, sent off inside ten minutes for a strong challenge. However, we went in a goal to the good when Keith Scott headed in from a corner-kick. It was all QPR after the break, but we held out for that first elusive triumph. What is it pop band Wizzard always regale us with every December: 'I wish it could be Christmas every day'? Swindon would have won the Premiership if that had been the case! There was a bit of a fall out between John and I when I tried to take some of the load off his shoulders. I had a go at the players one day, really ripping into them. Afterwards, John said I shouldn't have done that – they were HIS players.

I left at the end of the season and Swindon, as you might have expected, were relegated. John moved out about five months later. I'm glad we kissed and made up because we got some terrible news from John early in 2006. He telephoned to say his wife Myra had passed away after a long battle against cancer. Things like that tend to put football into sharp perspective.

26

HOORAY HENRIK

The Henrik Larsson deal was on the brink of collapse. I realised something would have to be done within the next crucial twenty-four hours if Celtic were to sign the Swedish international from Dutch side Feyenoord. If we did not act with the utmost speed there would be no transfer. I had travelled to Gouda, in Holland, where I was to meet Henrik's agent Rob Jansen and try to put the finishing details on the contract. Wim Jansen had just taken over as Celtic manager in the summer of 1997 and we struck up an immediate rapport. I had worked the previous three years with Tommy Burns, who had brought me back to Celtic in June 1994.

Wim, who had been in the Feyenoord team that had beaten Celtic in the European Cup Final in Milan in 1970, remembered me from our playing days and we had a chat about the way ahead for the club. I might not have been there at all because I was close to quitting after Tommy and Billy Stark left. I was in a quandary because Tommy, Billy and I were a team behind the team. However, Celtic wanted me to stay on and, after a lot of soul-searching, I agreed. What would be the point of us all being out of a job? I decided to remain and discuss things with Wim. I'm glad I did. He was an impressive bloke and his ambition was obvious a couple of minutes into our wee natter. He wasn't in Scotland to top up his pension. He was here to do a job for what he called 'one of the most famous football clubs in the world.'

Wim trusted my judgement completely and I appreciated that. He would listen to my views on a player and would give me the thumbs up or down on whether or not we should proceed. He listened to advice and always kept an open mind. Naturally enough, he wasn't quite up to speed with some of the Scottish players around at the time, but he had an extensive knowledge of the continent. And, with his Feyenoord background, he knew all about a bloke called Henrik Larsson. 'I want him, Davie,' he said. 'He will do well for this club. I know it.' He had made Henrik one of his essential targets that summer and, armed with that knowledge, I flew to Holland to meet the player's agent. I had done business with Rob Jansen before and I liked him. He dealt in quality players and Henrik Larsson certainly came into that category. When I met up with Rob in his office, Henrik, his wife Magdalena and baby son Jordan were there, too. The fee had been set at a mere £650,000. It was more of a steal than a deal. There was a clause in the player's contract that would allow him to move on if Feyenoord received such an offer.

It was obvious that Wim knew the ins and outs of Henrik's contract and the Swede was as eager to come to Celtic as we were to have him. I had seen him play as an out-and-out left-winger for the Swedish international side and had always quite liked the look of him. He had a fair turn of pace and excellent ball control. I didn't realise then what a place he would take in Celtic history and the part he would play in revitalising the club. As Henrik, Magdalena and Jordan sat in the corner, Rob suddenly became very serious. He was a businessman, after all, and, while wanting his best for his client, he wanted a good deal for himself. That seemed fair. Rob asked for something in the region of £140,000 for his part in the transfer. It was hardly an extravagant amount. I telephoned Jock Brown, the general manager, and relayed the message. Now, unless you have been living on the moon for the last decade or so, it was well known that Fergus McCann, the club's owner, was never going to become famous for throwing his money around. 'Not one more slim dime,' was one of his oft-used phrases and you knew he meant it. He could be stubborn when it came to loosening those purse strings.

I know Jock would have had to go to Fergus to run the sum by him. Nothing was paid for at Celtic without the say-so of Fergus. I could hear him asking, 'Can we bring the agent's fee down a bit?' That was his style. I reassured Jock that Rob's fee was not excessive, especially as we were getting a special talent in Henrik for £650,000, which was buttons in the market at that time. I was asked to see if Rob would modify his cash demands. He proved to be every bit as stubborn as Fergus. It was going to be £140,000 or there was every likelihood that the player would be moving elsewhere. Can you get your head round that thought? Now, as I said, I had a good relationship with the agent and we had worked together before when I helped to bring Pierre van Hooijdonk to Celtic in 1995. Rob, rightly or wrongly, didn't think he received a proper percentage of that million-pound move. He was going to get his money's worth on this occasion. I realised he was not bluffing. I telephoned Jock again and emphasised that we should pay the £140,000 without a quibble. There was no room for manoeuvre. I reasoned that Celtic were getting a world-class player for well under £1million and that figure seemed to be the starting point in transfer bids for distinctly average players around that time. I said, 'Make it happen.'

Rob agreed to wait for one more day and, thankfully, Jock didn't hesitate. He was sent over, completed the negotiations and, on 27 July 1997, the club had a rock-solid contract signed, sealed and delivered. Celtic had just landed a legend for £650,000. It must still rate as one of the greatest transfer deals in the history of football. I think you could say the club got their money's worth from the Swede! Even Fergus agreed. In fact, not even the most outrageous optimist could have foreseen what Larsson would bring to Celtic over the next seven years. Remember, Rangers had just completed their sequence of nine successive titles and that matched Celtic's effort that started in 1966 and carried through to 1974. They were going for ten in a row and that could not be allowed to happen. Henrik Larsson played an awesome role in derailing the Ibrox juggernaut in his first year at Parkhead.

I wonder how he would have fitted in with the Three Amigos – Pierre van Hooijdonk, Paolo di Canio and Jorge Cadette? They had all departed the scene by the time Henrik arrived, but it would have been highly interesting to see how they could have fitted in together. It was Fergus, of course, who gave that trio their nickname and there always seemed to be something going on in the background with the club's owner and these three colourful, charismatic and controversial characters.

Thanks to Tommy Burns, I was involved in bringing that talented trio to Parkhead, starting with big Pierre. I had travelled to Holland a few times around that period because Dutch football was at a very good standard and there were players who could be bought for reasonable fees. I took in an NAC Breda game one afternoon and Pierre was outstanding. You couldn't possibly miss him because he was about 6ft 5in, but he was very skilful on the ground with the ball at his feet. Normally, extremely tall guys are like a giraffe on ice when they are asked to do anything on the deck, but Van Hooijdonk ticked all the boxes.

I was looking at another Dutch striker at Twente Enschede at the time. His name? Michael Mols who, of course, did eventually come to Glasgow – to sign for Rangers. At that time, though, Celtic had the choice between these players. I made another trip to see Pierre in action against Heerenveen and that helped me make up my mind. I had noted in previous games that he never wasted a direct free kick. He may not always have scored, but he always hit the target. It was an extra in his weaponry and I was impressed. I advised Tommy Burns to sign him and we duly did. It's ironic to think our giant Dutchman scored the goal that gave Tommy his only silverware as manager of Celtic. Who could forget Pierre's soaring header against Airdrie on a sun-kissed afternoon at Hampden on 27 May 1995 that delivered the Scottish Cup?

The setting was far removed from the Arctic temperatures the fans had to endure on the same ground when they got their first glimpse of Pierre. Celtic, of course, were playing all their fixtures at the national stadium that season with multi-million pound reconstruction work being carried out at Parkhead. It was 11 January when our latest signing took his bow in front of the Celtic support against Hearts. It didn't take him long to win them over. He elegantly pulled down a high ball, killed it in an instant and turned to thunder an unstoppable drive high into the net. The Edinburgh side eventually got a point in the 1-1 draw, but I think everyone went home more than happy at the first appearance of Van Hooijdonk in the Hoops.

Next to join us was Portuguese international striker Jorge Cadete and if Pierre thought he had made an instant hit with the support he had nothing on Jorge. He came on as a second-half substitute against Aberdeen in a league game on 1 April 1996 and scored after only FIFTEEN seconds. He took a pass in his stride before knocking it past the outrushing goalkeeper. Welcome to Glasgow, Jorge! Celtic won 5-0 that evening with Pierre and Simon Donnelly chipping in with two apiece. The football that was played that night was what was associated with Celtic. It was entertainment all the way and Tommy Burns and Billy Stark deserve massive credit for that. It is just a pity that they could not convert style into silverware.

Agent Raymond Sparkes delivered a video of Cadete in action.

He had been in dispute with Sporting Lisbon and could be had at a reasonable fee. I had seen him before, of course, and I recall him scoring two goals against Scotland in a European Championship game in Lisbon in 1993. I knew he was electric in the box and would score goals in any company. He was the sort of class finisher defenders hated facing. He played right on their shoulder and it was dodgy to try to play offside against this guy. One slip in concentration and he had the lethal ability to punish you. I telephoned Sir Bobby Robson, the former England international boss who had been Cadete's gaffer for a spell at Sporting Lisbon, to get my card marked. Bobby didn't hesitate in recommending the player. 'He's a top quality striker,' said Bobby and that was fair enough testimony for me.

Paolo di Canio arrived in the summer of 1996 for a cut-price £1million from AC Milan and I had taken the trip to watch him in the flesh in a European tie against Bordeaux in France. Milan, with players such as Franco Baresi, George Weah and Paolo Maldini in the team, were 2-0 up after the first leg at the San Siro. Di Canio came into the team for the return and the French, with Zinidine Zidane orchestrating everything, fought back to win 3-2 on aggregate! You would be forgiven for thinking that might have put me off the Italian, but, in fact, it had the opposite effect. His teammates thought they were coasting, but his attitude was absolutely right. He displayed a lot of determination and ability. He was cajoling his colleagues throughout, but, alas for Paolo, they were not responding. His attitude won me over. I would be recommending we sign him. I sat in the stand that night alongside Bruce Rioch, who was Arsenal manager at the time. We were chatting and he asked me when I was going home. I told him I would be staying overnight and making my way back to Scotland the following day. He casually informed me he was jetting back to Heathrow in a private plane. How the other half lived!

Paolo duly arrived and, as I anticipated, the Celtic support took to him immediately. He was a Celtic-type player, no doubt about it. It was never dull with Paolo around and he made up the complete set of the Three Amigos. Van Hooijdonk was the first to go after more behind-the-scenes aggro. He didn't seem interested any more and made it plain he wanted to try English football. He got his wish when the club sold him to Nottingham Forest for £4.5million in March 1997. A month later di Canio was voted Player of the Year by his fellow professionals, but, unfortunately, a Scottish Cup semi-final replay defeat from Falkirk signalled the end for Tommy Burns as manager. The temperamental Italian wasn't going to be far behind. He claimed Fergus McCann had reneged on a contractual promise and walked out in July. A month later he moved to Sheffield Wednesday for £4million with Celtic receiving Dutch winger Regi Blinker as part of the deal. Celtic fans, understandably, were not happy. They had taken Paolo di Canio to their hearts and they believed more should have been done to keep him at the club.

Jock Brown had reassured the support di Canio would not be transferred just weeks beforehand. When the deal was done, Jock informed the followers that he had not been sold, but 'traded'. That cut no ice with the fans who felt as though they had been let down. It was also only a matter of time before the third amigo, Jorge Cadete, left the building. He had refused to return from Portugal for pre-season training and, reluctantly, he was sold to Spanish outfit Celta Vigo for £3.5million. I know the club did go out of their way to try to entice this exciting talent back to the east end of Glasgow, but he wasn't interested. It was around this time he revealed he had a parrot at home called Fergus. I wonder who that was named after! Cadete did return to Glasgow a few years later for a short spell with Partick Thistle. He was a mere shadow of the striker who had terrorised defences in a brief but memorable stint with Celtic.

By the way, there was another Dutch player who had caught my eye while I was tracking big Pierre. He was a no-nonsense and uncompromising centre half who was with a team called Willem II. He was tall, athletic, virtually unbeatable in the air and extremely fast on the deck. He could use the ball, too. I put his name forward because I knew the Dutch side would accept £800,000 for him. We did not have enough money for both Van Hooijdonk and this player, so we had to drop our interest in the defender. He later signed for PSV Eindhoven for the fee I had been quoted, but he cost considerably more when he joined Manchester United. It was Jaap Stam and Sir Alex Ferguson didn't hesitate in splashing £15million for him after impressive displays for Holland during the 1998 World Cup Finals. Celtic could have got him for £14.2 million less!

Wim Jansen had joined the club in July 1997 and Murdo MacLeod, who had been dismissed as manager of Partick Thistle the previous season, came in shortly afterwards as his assistant. It was around this time that I realised Wim could be good for the club. He was a bit of an unknown and his job prior to joining Celtic was in Japan with Hiroshima. The fans waited to see how the club would react to being turned upside down. Wim and I were busy in the summer as the team went through a massive shake-up. July was a bit hectic on the transfer front. Striker Darren Jackson arrived from Hibs for £1.5million, Scottish international midfielder Craig Burley cost £2.5million from Chelsea, French left back Stephane Mahe joined from Rennes for £500,000 and goalkeeper Jonathan Gould was a £200,000 snip from Bradford City. Henrik Larsson, of course, was already in place.

All eyes were on the kick-off against Hibs at Easter Road on 3 August 1997 for the opening day of the league season and, hopefully, the beginning of a glorious new era for the club. Wim sent out this team: Gordon Marshall; Tommy Boyd, Malky Mackay, Alan Stubbs and Tosh McKinlay; Jackie McNamara,

Simon Donnelly, Craig Burley and Andreas Thom; Darren Jackson and Tommy Johnson. Henrik Larsson was on the substitutes' bench, but he would play a major role in the outcome of the game. It was deadlocked at 1-1 when Wim introduced Henrik to the expectant Celtic fans. The Swede set up the winner with an inch-perfect pass, but, alas, the ball went straight to my former St Mirren player Chic Charnley. Everyone knew Chic had a sweet left foot and he didn't hesitate to use it as he ran onto the loose ball and first-timed a ferocious 20-yarder low past Marshall. That was the winning goal. It wasn't quite the start we were looking for from Henrik or from Celtic, for that matter.

How would Wim react? He immediately displayed a ruthless streak and axed keeper Marshall and he never played for the club again. Jonathan Gould got the nod and he made his debut in front of over 45,000 fans at Celtic Park the following week. Wim showed great faith in Henrik and played him in the No.7 shirt that afternoon. Unfortunately, the result was identical to the previous week with the Fifers going home with the points. A rather unkind headline emerged in a newspaper that had a former player stating Wim had been the worst thing to hit Hiroshima since the atomic bomb. No one was laughing, especially our manager who would not be sidetracked from the task at hand. His determination was more than commendable. You only get one chance to make a first impression and two successive defeats didn't please the Celtic support.

Thankfully, there were signs of things to come the following week when Henrik scored his first goal for the club in a 2-0 victory over St Johnstone in Perth. As usual, the Swede did things in style with a flying header that almost ripped a hole in the net. Darren Jackson got his first goal, too, and we were on the board. The signings continued with Danish international centre back Marc Rieper arriving in a £1.8million deal from West Ham in September. He made his debut only days afterwards in a close-fought 3-2 triumph over Motherwell at Fir Park where Craig Burley claimed two, his first league goals for the club. It was early days, but it looked as though Wim's jigsaw puzzle was coming together. He was still looking for a bit of extra quality in the middle of the park and that was provided by Paul Lambert when he joined for £2million from Bundesliga outfit Borussia Dortmund in November. He had helped the Germans win the Champions League the previous season, beating Juventus 3-1, and he was a first-class acquisition. Again, like Mo Johnston all those years before him, he didn't take a lot of persuading to put pen to paper.

Following the home defeat from Dunfermline in the second game of the campaign, Celtic had racked up eight successive victories. That came to a halt at Ibrox on 8 November when Paul Lambert made his Celtic debut as a substitute. The team played well, but couldn't convert their chances and were undone by a Richard Gough goal. A crowd of 47,464 turned out for the following game at Parkhead against Motherwell and were as baffled as anyone as the Fir Park side emerged with a 2-0 victory. That wasn't in the script. Four days later 49,427 were in attendance in the east end of Glasgow to see a late header from Alan Stubbs give Celtic a 1-1 draw with Rangers. That was to turn out to be an extremely vital point at the end of the day.

Three games and no wins. Were the cracks beginning to show? How would Wim cope with the strain? I used to have a cup of tea with Wim in his office most mornings and I have to say I was hugely impressed by his single-minded attitude. He was utterly convinced that things would come together. We had to keep our focus. The fans were certainly showing their support for the Dutchman. Next up at Parkhead were Dundee United and 48,200 rolled in for the third consecutive home game. A total of 145,091 had turned out over that period. The supporters were backing the revolution. Henrik hit two against the Tannadice men to take his league tally to double figures. He was emerging as a formidable frontman with the happy knack of putting the ball in the opposition's net. That was down to a change in his role by Wim. He could see he would be more effective inside and his days of playing on the wing were over.

That was demonstrated once again the following Sunday, 30 November, when the Swede was on target again as Celtic lifted the League Cup – then under the guise of the Coca-Cola Cup – by defeating Dundee United for the second successive game. This time it was 3-0 at Ibrox and Marc Rieper and Craig Burley were the other goalscorers while a crowd of 49,035 watched the enthralling action. It was the first time the club had won this trophy in fifteen long years. It was a bit of a breakthrough for Wim because, after only three months in charge, he had given the supporters some tangible success. He put out this team: Jonathan Gould; Tommy Boyd, Marc Rieper, Alan Stubbs and Stephane Mahe; Jackie McNamara, Craig Burley, Morten Wieghorst and Regi Blinker; Andreas Thom and Henrik Larsson. Enrico Annoni, bought from Roma by Tommy Burns the previous season, Simon Donnelly and Paul Lambert came on as second-half substitutes with McNamara, Thom and Blinker making way. Wim was doing his best to keep everyone involved. Exciting – and dramatic – months were ahead. They were certainly dramatic for me!

Around this time I was told of a Norwegian striker who was making a bit of a name for himself, Harald Brattbakk. He played for Rosenborg and I decided to have a look at him. I had seen footage of him playing against Real Madrid in a Champions League match and I was impressed. However, it is always good to check out the players in the flesh. Agents were unlikely to provide you with a video of their clients skying the ball over the bar from two yards, were they? All the good bits were on tape and the rest were left on the cutting room floor. So, off I went to see Harald in action for myself. I detected he liked to come in from the left and hit right-foot shots at goal. He got a lot of goals in this manner and I reckoned he could provide an X-factor at Celtic. He was something different, not a big hit man who would put himself about. He was actually quite slight and, off the pitch, wearing his spectacles, he looked like an accountant. I decided he was worth a chance and the club prepared to shell out £2million for him to become the eighth player signed that season. Ironically, I lost my job a week or so before the signing was complete.

The fans continued to follow in their thousands and Brattbakk admitted he was 'blown away' by the atmosphere when he made his first appearance as a substitute in front of 49,806 fans in the 1-0 win over Hearts on 13 December. Craig Burley, beginning to strike up a nice partnership with Paul Lambert in the middle of the park, was the goalscorer. The fact that Burley and Lambert were beginning to be a perfect foil for each other was emphasised three games later when they both scored the important goals that saw Rangers defeated 2-0 at Parkhead – the first time we had won the New Year fixture in ten years. Craig got the opener with a neat angled shot low past the stranded Andy Goram and Lambert's second effort was Goal of the Century material. Goram pulled off a magnificent save from a rasping Darren Jackson drive, but the ball was worked back to the inrushing Lambert who connected perfectly from about twenty-five yards and his unstoppable first-timer raged high into the net.

There was now a genuine belief about the place that Celtic could win their first league title in a decade. What a difference to the glum, dismal outlook at the start of the campaign when the first two games were lost to Hibs and Dunfermline. It was just a pity I would not be around at the end to participate in the championship celebrations.

27

CELTIC'S FIRST TITLE IN A DECADE – AND SACKED AGAIN!

Celtic went into the last league game of season 1997/98 knowing exactly what they had to do to clinch their first championship in a decade and, in doing so, prevent Rangers from achieving an astonishing ten-in-a-row winning sequence. Wim Jansen's men had to beat St Johnstone at Parkhead by any margin and the title party could begin in earnest. Rangers were due to face Dundee United at Tannadice, but their destiny was out of their hands. Celtic had seventy-one points going into their last league encounter while Rangers had two fewer.

I had started the season as the club's assistant general manager, but on this crucial day I was with Livingston in a consultancy role. I had been shown the door by Celtic for a third time. I felt I should have been involved in the east end of Glasgow, but, instead, I found myself watching Livi lose 2-1 to Inverness Caley Thistle in front of 2,812 fans at Almondvale.

You would have expected everything to be rosy in the background at Parkhead in a season where the club was so close to glory. You would have been wrong. Wim Jansen, who had won the League Cup and was within ninety minutes of delivering the league title in his first campaign as Celtic manager, was clearly unhappy and there had been leaks of a rift between the Dutchman and Jock Brown, the general manager. If I had found out anything about Wim Jansen in the months I had worked with him it was that he was very much his own man. He didn't accept interference or meddling. If he thought he was being overruled or bypassed he would show his displeasure.

Remarkably, Wim left the club two days after bringing home the Premier League title following ten years in the wilderness. His assistant Murdo MacLeod followed shortly afterwards. I beat them both through the exit after my relationship with Brown became somewhat strained. It reached breaking point around halfway through the season and I have to say I was resentful at the way I had been treated. I had actually been interim general manager for a spell and had an interview for the top job. Apparently, I was found by my interviewers to be 'unsuitable'. Now, I know a lot of people in the game believed the job was as good as mine and any interview would be a mere formality. Managing director Fergus McCann obviously didn't agree with those views.

Fergus, who had taken over the club in fairly dramatic fashion, felt the position should go to someone with a professional background. Jock Brown, whom I had once employed as my lawyer, had no previous Celtic connections and was also in the running. Of course, he got the nod. I was massively disappointed, to say the least. So, there was a degree of friction between us from the very start. The Celtic support appeared to be dumbfounded that a guy who doubled as a lawyer and a match commentator could get such an important post. Despite any animosity, Jock and I knew we had to work together for the good of the club in an extremely important campaign. Let me admit straight away there were faults on both sides. As time progressed, I thought Jock was veering away from the actual football side of his role and becoming more involved in the finances. I told him this at the time. I tried to get it across that the supporters were more interested in watching a good football team than pouring over a balance sheet. I said so forcibly at times. I also realised Wim

Jansen and Jock didn't gel and a division was becoming obvious off the park. In addition, I thought I deserved an enhanced contract from the club, but I never got any support from Jock. Something had to give. It came to a head and Fergus had to make a choice. Once more I found I was expendable. It didn't stop me continuing to support the club, though, and I watched the title run-in with a fair degree of fascination. I really wanted Wim Jansen to complete his mission. I wanted Celtic to be crowned champions.

All the aggro had been bubbling under the surface as the season came to a conclusion. Nerves were evident in the third last game of the season against Hibs in Glasgow on 25 April. A crowd of 49,619 turned out to cheer on their favourites with the championship very much in sight. Hibs, after beating Celtic on the opening day of the season, were heading for relegation. Rangers had to travel to Edinburgh that afternoon to take on a dangerous Hearts side, who still had ambitions of overtaking their Ibrox rivals and achieving second place. A defeat at Tynecastle for Walter Smith's men would have had the champagne being put on ice in Celtic supporters' households everywhere. Including mine! It had been a long time since the bubbly had flowed in celebration of a title triumph. Far too long.

Rangers had hammered Hibs 3-0 at the start of the month, but Celtic were prepared to accept any winning margin against a team that was virtually doomed. Hibs hadn't kept a solitary clean sheet on their travels all season and had conceded five at the same venue on their last visit just before Christmas Day with Craig Burley (2), Jackie McNamara, Morten Wieghorst and Henrik Larsson getting the goals. Could they hope to hold out Larsson and co. this time around? Remarkably, that's exactly what they did. Veteran goalkeeper Bryan Gunn wasn't exactly overworked as the game limped to a tame goalless scoreline. How did Rangers fare in the capital? News came back that they had won rather easily by 3-0 with goals from Rino Gattuso (2) and Jorg Albertz.

Rangers now had sixty-nine points, one behind Celtic. It was getting too close for comfort.

The Ibrox side had the opportunity to go top of the Premier Division when they met Kilmarnock in Glasgow on Saturday, 3 May with Celtic playing Dunfermline at East End Park twenty-four hours later. If the tension was showing on Celtic, it was also getting through to their oldest rivals. They blew their opportunity and lost 1-0 to an Ally Mitchell goal. Wim Jansen took his troops to Fife in the realisation that a victory would mean the long, anxious wait for the title was over. Celtic would be crowned kings of Scotland for the first time since 1988. Would you believe I travelled through to Fife with the Davie Hay (Paisley) Celtic Supporters Club, which is run by my good friend Peter Rafferty? I had missed out ten years ago as I had left the previous summer, but I was ready to give it pelters now. I felt like quiz master Magnus Magnusson on *Mastermind*, 'I've started so I'll finish!'

I could just about taste the champagne as Simon Donnelly fired Celtic ahead. I was in the stand with the fans and we waited for a second. And we waited. Nerve ends were jangling everywhere, on the park and on the terracings where 12,719 crammed into a ground whose official all-seater capacity was 12,509. It wasn't much of a spectacle, truth be told, but no one would have minded if the referee had just blown for time-up and allowed the festivities to kick off in real. The clock was ticking down when disaster struck. Dunfermline had rarely threatened all afternoon, but, with only minutes remaining, they equalised with a header from substitute Craig Falconbridge. No one could believe it. We travelled home in silence.

So, it was going all the way down to the wire. There was no hiding place in the countdown to Saturday, 9 May, an afternoon that would define who would get the winners' medals. This was it. Celtic had won twenty-one of their previous thirty-five league games, drawn eight and lost six. Rangers, over the same period, had won twenty, drawn nine and lost six. Mathematicians were hard at work with all the permutations. Wim, I knew, was not interested. He demanded a victory. All the off-the-field difficulties were pushed firmly into the background as Wim refused to be distracted as he prepared his players for that last determined assault on the trophy.

As I said at the start, I was at Livingston on the big day. They were paying my wages as a consultant to the club and that had to be respected. My head was elsewhere, though. And my heart, too. I saw film of the game later on in the Hay household. I could imagine Wim telling the players, 'Now is the time for heroes.' St Johnstone were in town on judgement day and Wim sent out this team: Jonathan Gould; Tommy Boyd, Marc Rieper, Alan Stubbs and Enrico Annoni; Jackie McNamara, Paul Lambert, Craig Burley and Phil O'Donnell; Simon Donnelly and Henrik Larsson. It was a good-looking line-up with a lot of attacking options.

The contest had barely started when Henrik Larsson picked up the ball on the left of midfield about thirty-five yards out. He had one thing on his mind as he sped towards the Saints danger zone. Henrik possessed that wonderful ability to wrap his foot around a ball and belt in one of those mind-boggling efforts that look as though they are going wide until they start to bend viciously and zero in on target. That's exactly what Henrik produced against the Saints and although their keeper, Alan Main, threw himself flat out to his left there was no way he was going to keep the ball out of the net. Another special delivery from Celtic's very own Special One, long before anyone had ever heard of a certain Jose Mourinho!

It was clear to me, even watching on the small screen and knowing the result, that Celtic needed that second goal to calm themselves down. Jock Stein, all those years before Wim, made the same point over and over to his team if they had a slender half-time lead. 'Away out and finish the business,' he would say. 'Then you can all enjoy yourselves.' In games against certain opposition, Big Jock would insist, 'There will be no need for recriminations if you just keep scoring goals. No one has any answer to the ball being put in their net.' You would have to accept some dodgy refereeing decisions, of course, and Jock some-times likened it to a boxer being in the ring against an Italian opponent in Italy. He would joke, 'You've got to knock him out to get a draw!'

Wim had left out Harald Brattbakk from his starting line-up and I have to confess I wasn't too surprised. What did intrigue me, though, was his startling lack of consistency in front of goal since his £2million arrival from Rosenborg where he had been a prolific scorer in the Norwegian league. It had taken him nine league games to get on the scoresheet at Celtic – and on that occasion he scored all four in a 4-0 romp against Kilmarnock at Parkhead on 21 February. Four days later he added another two in a 5-1 victory over Dunfermline. Six goals in two games. That was a bit more like the player I had watched in Norway. Had the floodgates opened? Amazingly, he then went another seven matches without a goal. Harald blew hot and cold, no doubt about it. I must have watched him during one of his hot streaks.

But Wim still believed in the player and knew he could be a vital substitute to have around against St Johnstone. Once more my little Dutch friend was proved right. Just as the tension was going into overload, Wim sent on Harald and it's history now that the Norwegian did deliver that killer goal. When he knocked that ball over the line from close range there was a collective sigh of relief from the players and the 48,701 fans. How I wished I had been among them. Rangers beat Dundee United 2-1, but that didn't matter, though. The title was back where it belonged and ten years of pain and hurt were wiped away at a stroke. Celtic beat St Johnstone 2-0 and finished with seventy-four points while Rangers had seventy-two. Henrik Larsson, the bargain £650,000 purchase from Feyenoord in the summer, played in thirty-five of the thirty-six leagues games throughout the campaign and netted sixteen goals. Those were his first steps on his way to becoming a Celtic legend.

The Celtic support, euphoric on the Saturday, were enraged on Monday as Wim's departure became public. It was all rather bizarre. Celtic had appointed Wim to come in, buy eight new players while overhauling the personnel, and, hopefully, bringing in a trophy or two. Wim had delivered on all fronts, but he still felt he had to quit the club. The fans were baffled and no one could blame them.

Intrigued, I watched from the outside. The supporters were not happy and, sadly, that was obvious at the start to the following season when they actually booed during the unfurling of the league flag before the opening game against Dunfermline. There were 59,377 in the ground that day and a fair percentage of them took the opportunity to let the management know precisely how they felt about Wim Jansen leaving. The same Wim Jansen who had become Celtic's first championship-winning manager since Billy McNeill ten years beforehand. Doctor Jozef Venglos, who had taken over from Wim, must have wondered what he had let himself in for!

For my own part, I decided to take the club to court to sue for breach of contract. I shouldn't have bothered. I lost and I have to say it was all a colossal waste of time. Celtic parted company with Jock Brown on the morning of 7 November that season – the same day the club hammered Dundee 6-1 later on in the afternoon.

After winning the league the previous season, the team manager, his assistant, the general manager and the assistant general manager had all left the club. As they say in America, go figure!

28

CHEERS AND CHEERIO
AT LIVINGSTON

I believe winning the League Cup with Livingston in 2004 was by far my greatest achievement in football as a manager. Yes, even more so than lifting the league championship at Celtic in 1986. Even better than the Scottish Cup Final triumph in 1985. You are expected to be successful at the Old Firm. Trophies are regarded as second nature and should, all going well, roll in on a consistent basis. If not, it's a crisis and it's time for another inquest and a sacking or two. That's not the way it was at Livingston. They are a provincial club and they should not be allowed to take one of the major pieces of silverware up for grabs.

I was not in charge the night we kicked off our trek towards a place in the history books at Hampden. I was, though, when we ended it at the same ground. No one was tipping dear old Livi as potential winners of the tournament when we arrived at the national stadium for our second round tie against Queen's Park on 23 September 2003. Exactly 1,011 fans were in attendance that Tuesday evening. Our 3-1 victory over our amateur opponents didn't quite make the headlines. Two goals from Lee Makel and one from Quino ensured the club a few column inches in the newspapers the following day. We caused more of a stir in the next round, though.

We travelled to Tannadice to take on Dundee United on

23 October and we remained in the competition after their goal-keeper, Paul Gallacher, was adjudged to have pushed the ball in his own net. It was a good, disciplined performance from my team and anything but lucky. We were through to the quarter-finals on merit and we got another tough one in Aberdeen at Pittodrie. Surely these Livi upstarts would be put in their place now. That seemed to be the thinking from a lot of people. It was a typically cold and windy evening in the Granite City on 2 December and the fans were treated to a gem of a contest. Both teams went at it right from the kick-off and we were deadlocked at 2-2 after ninety minutes with Derek Lilley and Fernando Pasquinelli on target for us. I talked to the lads on the pitch before the start of the extra half-hour and I sensed we could settle this one. Lee Makel rattled in the winner and, suddenly and unexpectedly to more than a few of our critics, we were through to the semi-finals. Significantly, Hibs knocked out Celtic that night, winning 2-1 in Edinburgh.

We were drawn against Dundee in the last four and the encounter was scheduled for Easter Road on Tuesday, 3 February 2004. That was the evening when I am convinced my back-room staff of Allan Preston, Billy Kirkwood and Paul Hegarty believed I had blown a gasket. I made a decision that baffled them, but it was one of those occasions when you have to back your own judgement. You have to stand alone at times when you are a manager and you have to have faith in your own convictions. We hadn't played well in a goalless first-half. Dundee had control of the midfield and were dominating proceedings. It wasn't going to get better in the second-half and I realised a drastic rethink was required. That was when I announced I was taking off skipper Oscar Rubio, our central defender, and putting on another forward, Fernando Pasquinelli. My back-room trio clearly thought I had lost my marbles. Rubio, who was on Real Madrid's books at one stage in his career, was a key man in our set-up. He was a good leader, too, but he was sacrificed that night. He looked a little puzzled, too, but, being a good professional, he accepted my decision. Our rejigged formation started to click and we were heading for Hampden when Derek Lilley got a last-minute winner. I wonder if Preston, Kirkwood and Hegarty rated me a genius after that tactical switch?

The other half of the Old Firm, Rangers, were also dumped from the competition the same evening as they lost 4-3 on penalty kicks to Hibs after the game had finished 1-1 following extra time. So, it was Hibs v Livingston on Sunday, 14 March to contest the silverware. We were used to being written off by this stage. The Easter Road side were seen as a glamorous outfit with some of the best emerging talent in the game. They had the likes of Scott Brown, Gary Caldwell, Derek Riordan, Garry O'Connor and Kevin Thomson in their ranks. Scott Brown, alone, was worth more than my entire Livi team! In fact, one of their substitutes was Steven Whittaker and he cost Rangers £2million. He didn't even get a game. There are times, though, that being the underdog can suit you. It can fire up your players and really inspire them. No one gave us an earthly; we were to be cannon fodder for Hibs. It may have been that our opponents were a bit too over-confident when the teams took the field that day. Possibly, they underestimated us. Why not? A lot of teams did – to their cost!

I thought long and hard about my line-up. Everyone had played a major role in getting the club to within ninety minutes of the biggest prize in their history. With due consideration I announced my side. The team lined up: Roddy McKenzie; David McNamee, Oscar Rubio, Marvin Andrews, Jamie McAllister; Emanuel Dorado, Lee Makel, Burton O'Brien; Stuart Lovell, David Fernandez and Derek Lilley. Scott McLaughlin, Fernando Pasquinelli and Jon Paul McGovern would eventually join the action as substitutes, replacing McNamee, O'Brien and Fernandez. Those were the lads entrusted with bringing one of Scottish soccer's top trophies back to Almondvale. Just over 1,000 saw us embark on our great adventure back at Hampden six months earlier. This time there were 45,443 fans in the ground and I must congratulate the Hibs support. They came through to Glasgow in their thousands and created a carnival atmosphere. However, I think it inspired my troops more than their favourites!

We kept it tight and it was scoreless at the interval. I was getting the impression that the Hibs players were becoming more than just a little frustrated as the second-half wore on. This was not turning into the procession that was anticipated by so many. They had dismissed Celtic and Rangers, the previous season's finalists in the competition, but Livi were refusing to roll over. Hibs were getting a bit more anxious and that was down to my side working hard all over the pitch and battling for each other. We were suffocating Hibs and then, bang, we were a goal ahead through Derek Lilley. Amazing! Our opponents tried to come back with an instant reply, but we were in no mood to let our grasp slip from the trophy. Jamie McAlister hit the second and that's how it finished. Livingston's name was on the League Cup and that was an incredible feat. I was so proud. Some of the older supporters could remember when Livi were a mere works team called Ferranti Thistle before the remarkable transformation that had seen them victorious at the national stadium.

Have you seen that movie *Mike Bassett, England Manager* with Ricky Tomlinson in the title role? There's a bit in the film where he is dancing on tables and I thought, 'If it's good enough for him, it's good enough for me.' At the club's celebrations I was photographed on top of a table and it appeared in several newspapers the following morning. I didn't care a jot. I was letting off some steam after an extremely demanding season that had got off to a rather bizarre start. Jim Leishman had left the club for Dunfermline and I expected to be given the managerial job outright. Jim and I were seen as co-managers, anyway, so it seemed the natural progression. Well, that's what you might have thought. Someone at the club must have had a brainstorm and they appointed a Brazilian by the name of Marcio Maximo Barcellos whose main claim to fame was that he had discovered Ronaldo – the Brazilian not the Portuguese Ronaldo at Real Madrid. Aye, and half that vast continent also spotted the potential in the player at the same time. Oh, and he had also managed the Cayman Islands. I've been there on holiday and it's a nice place, but I didn't even know they had a football team. Putting it bluntly, it was a sure-fire recipe for disaster.

I decided to take a back seat and let the circus take centre stage. There was no way I was going to give up my contract to move aside for an unknown incomer. I had worked hard for that deal. I was beside Jim in the dugout all the way through the 2001/02 season when, after winning promotion the previous year, we finished in third place in the Premier League behind winners Celtic and Rangers. That was a fairly impressive achievement. It also brought European football to Livingston for the first time and we got through our debut appearance in this arena, overwhelming Liechtenstein part-timers Vaduz on the away goal rule after 1-1 on aggregate. The glamour of it all! We scored six goals over the two legs against experienced Austrians Sturm Graz in the next stage, but we also contrived to concede seven and went out. It was nice while it lasted.

I was more than slightly taken aback, then, when I was given the news in June 2003 that a big-name South American was taking over the running of the team. I don't know about big name, but it was certainly long! Anyway, he had some interesting thoughts on how football should be played. They might just have worked on the Copacabana beach on a gorgeous sunny afternoon, but would they click at Parkhead, Ibrox, Pittodrie, Tannadice or anywhere else during one of our typical winters? It took only nine games for us to get our answer. The Brazilian left as quickly as he had arrived and I took over as manager on 23 October 2003. I was beginning to expect the unexpected at Livingston and, after the club had dropped into administration, we were taken over by an Irish businessman, Pearse Flynn, who, I was told, was a Celtic fan. For whatever reason, one of the first things he did was to inform me that there would be a shake-up at managerial level. I had guided the team to a League Cup triumph just two months beforehand, but that didn't appear to be enough.

My assistant Allan Preston was appointed football manager and Flynn took me aside to say, 'There will still be a role for you at this club, Davie.' I looked at him and replied, 'What, like making the tea?' I left immediately and was appointed manager of Dunfermline a week or so later.

Of course, I returned in a back-room capacity during the ill-fated 2008/09 season when an Italian consortium bought over the club. It was all well intentioned, but it ended in ignominy and controversy. I knew the chairman Angelo Massone, but I have to say I was not privy to what was going on at boardroom level. The finances and running of the club had nothing to do with me. I was there in a purely footballing capacity and, sadly, had to quit in the summer of 2009 to look after my own business interests. Livi will always have a special place in my heart.

29

FALL OUT IN FIFE

Dunfermline sacked me with only three games remaining in the 2004/05 season. It was the right decision. The board had to take drastic action to save the club from dropping out of the Premier League and they did so by handing me my P45. If a change of manager meant the team being galvanised then it worked. Believe it or not, I was happy for them. They have decent people at that club and it couldn't have been easy for them to fire me. That wouldn't have been their preferred course of action. However, Dunfermline came first and I can well understand that.

Mind you, I wasn't quite so philosophical on a Saturday afternoon on 30 April when we were playing Livingston, of all teams, at Almondvale. The pressure was on in the drop zone and ourselves, Livingston and the two Dundee teams were all embroiled in an end-of-season scramble for safety. The day I took the team to my old stomping ground in West Lothian I realised how important victory would be. Three points were essential. I took my place in the stand, but it was only at the interval that I discovered Jim Leishman, the club's director of football, had also gone into the crowd and sat among the travelling Fife fans in the stand. I wondered about his motives.

Jim, I realised, had always been a hero to the Dunfermline support. So, what was he doing in their midst this particular afternoon? I thought it was all big-time stuff, showing he was one of the lads. I was far from happy with Jim's antics. We had come a long way together with Livingston and so on and I would always expect loyalty from a so-called ally. I didn't feel I got it that day. Livi, managed by Richard Gough, beat us 2-0 with goals from Burton O'Brien and James McPake. Dunfermline were now anchored at the foot of the table. I didn't get a chance to speak to Jim immediately afterwards, but when I did eventually catch up with him I let him know exactly how I felt. I was sacked two days later and, as expected, Jim took over as manager. I spoke to him again after I left the club and, to be fair, Jim apologised. We have since smoked the pipe of peace and I'm glad to say Jim and I are friends today.

However, that was a sore one back then. It was agony watching them try to stay among the elite with three games to go. I was pleased when they beat Dundee 5-0 at East End Park to throw themselves a lifeline. Derek Young led the way with a hat-trick. An own goal gave them a 1-0 victory over fellow strugglers Dundee United at Tannadice and it was going to be an interesting last day in the frantic struggle to get away from the dreaded trapdoor leading to the First Division. Suddenly the focus of attention switched to Dundee, especially after their dramatic five-goal collapse against the Fifers. They dropped two points the following week in a 1-1 draw with Inverness Caley Thistle at Dens Park.

Dunfermline could even afford the luxury of a last-day 4-0 defeat at Kilmarnock when Dundee again shed two points in a 1-1 stalemate with Livingston at Almondvale. The Dens Park side were condemned to a place outside the top league after finishing on thirty-three points – one fewer than Dunfermline. Livi completed the programme on thirty-five with Dundee United one better off. A mere three points separated the bottom four teams. Now that is tight! It also highlights how ruthless football can be when you note that the four teams in the fight for survival all parted with their managers through the season. I was fired from Dunfermline, of course, Jim Duffy lost his job at Dundee, Ian McCall was sacked at Dundee United and Allan Preston, who replaced me at Livi, didn't last the campaign, either. Aye, it's ugly in the beautiful game!

I didn't hesitate when I got the opportunity to go to East End Park at the start of the season. I got on well with Jim Leishman at Livingston and, of course, there was the Jock Stein connection. It was at the Fife club in 1960 that the Celtic legend came to prominence as a manager in his own right after working with the reserves at Parkhead. He won the Scottish Cup in 1961, beating Celtic 2-0 in the replay, after leading the club out of the old Second Division. Four years later he would win the Cup again, this time as Celtic boss as they overcame Dunfermline 3-2. Football? Whoever said it was a funny old game?

So, I knew I was going to a club with traditions. Jimmy Calderwood and Jimmy Nicholl had got the team to the Scottish Cup Final where they lost 3-1 to Celtic in May. It was to be their last game as they moved to Aberdeen and I was the choice to take over. I threw myself into the job, as I always do. However, there were problems around the corner that I couldn't have foreseen. I couldn't have got off to a worse start as the club went out of the UEFA Cup in the second qualifying round to Icelandic outfit Hafnarfjordur. We drew 2-2 at their place, but they refused to play on the plastic pitch that had just been laid at East End Park. We were ordered to take the tie elsewhere and we ended up at St Johnstone's McDiarmid Park. It didn't feel much like a home tie to me, but we had to comply with the wishes of our guests. We were winning 1-0 and, late on, looked as though we were coasting. We realised they would have to score two goals to go through. Sickeningly, that's exactly what they did. One minute, we're as good as in the next round; the next, oblivion.

It was a horrible start to a new career and it didn't quite get the fans onside straight from the off. Money problems then became a major issue. The players were being asked to take pay cuts and bonuses were slashed, too. The previous season I believe bonuses were in the four-figure category. If I was looking for a player I could only offer him something like £600 per week and some Junior clubs can pay upwards of that. I don't believe the support realised just how bad it was. Craig Brewster was one of our best players, but he came to me in November and told me he had the chance to go to Inverness Caley Thistle as their player/manager. He was thirty-six-years-old at the time and had given the club more than two good years since arriving from Hibs. I didn't want to step in his way and allowed him to go. I arranged a transfer fee of around £60,000 which included add-ons because I knew every penny counted at the club. In normal circumstances you might give a good servant a free transfer, but these were far from normal circumstances and we had to get a few quid into the bank. Ironically, Craig won the Bank of Scotland Manager of the Month award for March, just before I got the sack.

Some supporters weren't happy that Craig had left, but they really didn't have a clue about what was going on with the finances behind the scenes. We started the league campaign with a creditable 1-1 draw with Dundee United on 7 April at our place. We then fired three successive blanks as we lost to Inverness Caley Thistle (2-0), Aberdeen (1-0) and Kilmarnock (1-0). We steadied the ship with a 1-1 draw with Motherwell and then we gained our first leg win of the season against Hearts with Barry Nicholson scoring the only goal of the game. In hindsight, two of our best results were a 2-1 victory over Dundee at Dens Park on 23 October and the 3-1 triumph over them in the return on New Year's Day. We didn't know it at the time, of course, but they were to prove crucial to the club's survival.

Like the previous season, we were looking for a good run in

the Scottish Cup to help swell our coffers. We negotiated a 3-1 win over East Fife in a replayed third round tie and were then drawn against my old club Celtic. We had home advantage, but it didn't prevent them from romping to a 3-0 success with goals from John Hartson (2) and Chris Sutton – over £12million worth of football talent. How Dunfermline could have done with a fraction of their value. The League Cup lasted as far as the quarter-finals before we lost 3-1 at home to Hearts. So, from February onwards all eyes were on us in the league and making sure we didn't fall off the ladder.

And that took us down to 30 April and the 2-0 defeat from Livingston that saw us look up at the other eleven teams in the SPL. It was not a comfortable place to be. I was sad to go, but I knew Dunfermline's board of directors had to do what they saw as the way of turning things around. That led me to the exit, but there were no bad feelings. Far from it. I knew there were good people in that boardroom and when I shook their hands and wished them all the best for the remaining three games, I meant it. When they responded in kind, I knew they meant it, too. It's never nice to lose your job, but this time it worked for my ex-employers. Relegation would have brought a financial disaster and possible ruin to a proud club. I was delighted Dunfermline would continue in the big-time.

30

TOMMY BURNS: AN INSPIRATION

Tommy Burns approached me at St Joseph's Roman Catholic Church in Clarkston and said in a matter-of-fact manner, 'The cancer's back.' There was no preamble, no warning of the information he was about impart. To passers-by, we could have been two former Celtic managers discussing the previous day's game. How do you react to such shattering news? Tommy, of course, had already been diagnosed with the awful disease and it appeared it had gone into remission. Now, after a chance meeting between us, Tommy had told me the news I didn't want to hear. Sadly, one of our last meetings was at St Cadoc's RC Church in Newton Mearns when we were in attendance for the christening of our grandchildren, Louis and Cole.

When I looked at Tommy I saw before me an extremely courageous human being whose religion had carried him through so many obstacles in the past. Sadly, on 15 May 2008, after a brave battle, Tommy Burns succumbed to the illness. He was taken from us at the age of only fifty-one. He had so much more to contribute to life. Firstly, as a family man, a loving husband to Rosemary, a doting father to Emma, Jenna, Jonathan and Michael and a man who would have been a caring grandfather to Cole. Secondly, to all things Celtic, the club he truly loved. And, thirdly, to all of us as an inspiration.

I liked Tommy a lot and it was a privilege to get to know him so well. He was a decent man and did things with a lot of style and panache. Just look at the way he played. Just recall how Celtic performed when he was manager. Everything was done with a flourish. What about that left foot? He could hit targets from all angles and ranges and it was evident even from a very early age that Tommy Burns was going to be a bit special. I can tell you he was 100 per cent professional when I was his Celtic manager. He had a temper, too, I seem to recall. If he didn't agree with you, he said so. And, like a man, he said it to your face. I've already talked in a previous chapter about taking him off during the 1985 Scottish Cup Final while we were losing 1-0 to Dundee United. He didn't agree with that decision and was swift to let me know as he walked past me to the substitutes' bench.

But he was the first to give me a hug when that final whistle went and we had won 2-1. That was so typical of the man. Tommy had such a lovely demeanour that he made everyone in his company totally relaxed. He had a good sense of humour and possessed a sharp wit, that's for sure. For me, Tommy always epitomised the spirit of Celtic and I count him among my blessings.

I know he rated our 5-0 UEFA Cup triumph over Sporting Lisbon in November 1983 as his favourite European night and I have to say it is one of mine, too. Tommy gave me a lot of credit afterwards for psyching up the team before kick-off. We were trailing 2-0, of course, and I was emphasising the urgent need for an early goal. Actually, I didn't have to exactly work overtime getting the players geared up for this one. With guys such as Tommy Burns around and the determination he possessed, words were often redundant. He and the rest of the players were ready to fight their corner and I remember that being a fabulous evening of entertainment and excellent goals – one a rare header from Tommy for our first. At the end of an unforgettable and thoroughly enjoyable experience I complimented Tommy on his display. He shrugged and said, 'I just did my bit.' You could say he was quite an unassuming kind of guy. He loved the European stage and his skills were tailor-made for this level.

It is so unfair that Celtic were not more successful than they were during his reign as boss. His classy play deserved success, but he came up against a Rangers team that was on a roll. Look at season 1995/96, for instance. Celtic lost only three domestic games – all to Rangers – and it was enough to scupper them in three competitions. That's unbelievably cruel. Celtic went down in the first Old Firm league encounter at Parkhead on 30 September after dominating the match for forty-four minutes in the opening half. Then Rangers full back Alec Cleland, a guy who scored as often as we witness Haley's Comet, went upfield, caught the defence unawares and headed past Gordon Marshall. The second-half saw a typically determined Burns outfit throw everything at their rivals. What happened? Paul Gascoigne broke away and netted the second. It finished 2-0. The other three Glasgow derbies ended in draws, but I'm sure even Tommy might not have minded dropping a couple of points after the exhausting and exhilarating 3-3 draw at Ibrox on 19 November.

That was a Tommy Burns type of game. It encapsulated everything he liked in football; entertaining, attacking, daring play from both sides. And there was a goal from Andreas Thom that will live forever in the memory banks of anyone lucky enough to see it. The German dynamo, another entrancing talent brought to the club by Tommy, cut it from the left and drilled an emphatic effort from outside the box past the helpless Andy Goram. At the end of the campaign, though, the league title was back in Govan and Celtic, after losing one game in thirty-six, were adrift by four points. The champions actually lost two games more, but eleven draws counted against Celtic.

The League Cup draw saw Walter Smith's men travel across Glasgow for the quarter-final. Andy Goram was in an unbeatable mood and a high-flying save from a Paul McStay drive near the end will remain one of the most breathtaking saves I have ever seen. Celtic played well that Tuesday evening on 19 September in the east end of Glasgow, but a wee chap called Ally McCoist was to have the final say. The defence took their eye off him for a moment as a ball came in from the right and the Rangers striker got up at the far post to nod in the only goal of a tense confrontation.

Interest in the Scottish Cup ended at the semi-final stage, beaten 2-1 by Rangers at Hampden. That man McCoist got the opener when Gordon Marshall couldn't hold a hot shot and Brian Laudrup, undoubtedly the sort of player Tommy would have welcomed in any of his line-ups, lobbed in the second. Pierre van Hooijdonk pulled one back and a great chance fell to Simon Donnelly minutes from time. Alas, from only yards out, he contrived to put the ball over the bar. Who would have blamed Tommy for giving up football forever there and then!

Walter Smith, after picking up a league and cup double, won the Scottish Football Writers' Manager of the Year award. I will always remember how he opened his acceptance speech. He said, 'Thank you for this award and for all of those who voted for me.' There was a brief pause before the Rangers manager continued, 'But there is another man who should be here collecting this honour – Tommy Burns.' It was a fabulous gesture from Walter Smith, a man who realised better than most what Tommy was trying to achieve and how he was going about it at Celtic, Rangers' fiercest rivals. Walter would also know the pressure that is relentless on an Old Firm boss. The demands are endless.

Walter Smith, along with Ally McCoist, would help carry Tommy Burns' coffin into St Mary's Church, in the Calton district of Glasgow, twelve short years later. Tommy's ex-Celtic colleagues Pat Bonner, George McCluskey, Peter Grant and Danny McGrain were the other pall-bearers, but the presence of the two Ibrox men merely demonstrated that Tommy Burns transcended the Great Divide in Glasgow. Thousands lined the streets as the cortege made its way from the east end of Glasgow to Linn Cemetery on the south side of the city. There were Celtic, Rangers and all sorts of football fans present to say their last farewells to a great man. There were people there who probably didn't know the shape of a football, but they had turned out to pay their tributes. You need to be special to achieve that.

Tommy Burns was special.

31

TOUCHLINE THEATRICS

I might just have got out of football management at the right time. You see, my lack of twinkle toes means I am never likely to be invited to appear on *Strictly Come Dancing*. I would be a complete waste of time taking part in the touchline cabaret that is now regarded as the norm by team bosses up and down the country on match day. Coaches appear to think they, too, have to be part of the entertainment factor with their dodgy dugout rituals that look as though they have been carefully choreographed beforehand.

There's the pouting, pontificating, gesticulating, leaping, foot-stomping, arms flayling, emotional spasms that we have now come to expect while the focal point during an actual game seems to be swinging to events occurring in the so-called technical areas. Some of the antics seem to be excessively rehearsed by individuals craving the limelight. What's it all about, lads? I don't recall Jock Stein getting involved in a full-blown conga with Sean Fallon and Neilly Mochan during my days at Celtic. Did Sir Matt Busby, the legendary Manchester United gaffer, ever actually sit in the dugout?

Just because some managers are not so actively demonstrative does not mean they are less passionate. I am from the old school that believes you don't have to whisk around like a demented dervish to get your point across. And, as my dear old dad continually repeated, 'Empty vessels make the most noise.' Actually, the best place to watch the team is from the stand. You get a better view, although, once you have been on a touchline for so long, you do have a fair idea of how the game is panning out. When I started out in management at Motherwell I would often watch the match from an elevated vantage point.

One thing you can't do there, however, is make eye contact with someone else. I made that mistake in my first game in charge of Well against Kilmarnock. A Killie supporter caught my attention and he shouted, 'Hay, you weren't a bad player, but you're a dud as a manager if that's how you want your team to play.' I wasn't even into a full first-half in my fledgling managerial career and I was being written off as useless! Actually, I hate to admit it, but that loudmouth had a point. I had set out my team to play offside and, unfortunately, those were the identical tactics employed by our opponents. Sadly, neither team had a player with the pace or the knowledge to spring the trap. That meant there were an awful lot of players congregated in the middle of the park and there was precious little action in either penalty area. It wasn't quite Game of the Century material.

After forty-five minutes of being berated by the Killie fan, I took my place in the dugout for the second-half to get a closer look at the action. There was no ranting, raving or foaming at the mouth. I was there mainly to get my instructions across and there was no bouncing around with rafts of foolscap paper in my hand. Sometimes you can get caught up in the moment, though. I remember the story my old Fir Park boss Ally MacLeod told me about the time he was Ayr United gaffer and he ended up wrestling with his opposite number on the ground. He went for the ball to get it back into play quickly as his team were losing. The manager in the other dugout had different ideas. He stood on the ball and Ally, who was a nervous wreck before, during and after games, went ballistic. He dived at the ball and the next thing both bosses were on the deck rolling around. It's just a pity the TV cameras weren't around that day. Ally was totally animated, a man possessed, on the day of a game while I remained reasonably calm.

I would be no use to TV sports directors or photographers waiting for me to turn purple and explode with rage. I've had my moments, of course, but, please believe me, they have been completely spontaneous. They were never a well-staged act to catch anyone's attention or to show how deeply I was committed to my team. There are other ways of making a radical point to your players or officials and I never believed it was better done while going through the motions of someone who appeared to have just trod on a live electric wire.

I've got a lot of time for Rangers manager Walter Smith. He spends most of the games in the stands these days while allowing Ally McCoist to take care of business on the touchline. If Walter does become demonstrative then you better believe there will be a good reason for it. It's not done for the benefit of the TV people. I don't think you could ever question his commitment to Rangers. It must have hurt him somewhat when he moved out to make way for Dick Advocaat. However, when the Paul le Guen revolution went slightly awry, he was the first man to answer the SOS from his old club. I believe it is a measure of a good manager that he acts with dignity in defeat. Walter has the intellect to carry that out and also, of course, act with the same dignity when his team succeeds. A lot of the present managers appear to be totally absorbed in themselves and some seem to lack the good grace or the manners to spare a thought for their beaten opposite number.

It also looks like they've had to chop down a couple of Norwegian woods for all the scraps of paper managers take into the dugout with them these days. They've got notepads, clipboards, the lot. I have to laugh when I am watching English games on the television. It seems every manager down there, with the exception of a certain Sir Alex Ferguson, has a raft of paper upon which to doodle. What are they writing down? Their list of groceries to pick up from the supermarket on the way home? It's as amusing as it can sometimes be annoying.

I was never one to rub anyone's nose in it when I was a manager. I would like to think I was always courteous. Celtic supporters might now think that I have jumped the fence to the other side, so let me assure them I haven't. However, I have to say I always got on reasonably well with Graeme Souness when he was the Rangers boss. I used to joke he was the man who got me the sack, but, of course, that was nonsense. Scottish football, in fact, had a lot to thank Graeme for when he arrived in the nineties. He was the Scotland international captain at the time and had been hugely successful at Liverpool. He had done well in Italy, too, with Sampdoria and it was a bold move by Rangers to bring him to Ibrox. It was bad news for me, though, when they presented him with an open chequebook.

He was the sort of big name other players respect. Suddenly international stars such as Terry Butcher and Chris Woods were leaving England to play their football in Scotland and that had been unheard of. It was a complete reversal of what we had been used to over the decades. Would I have ever played for Rangers if they had flashed the cash? Quick answer: No. That was never going to happen. I may have watched them as a schoolboy, as I have already admitted, but, once I had played for Celtic, there was no way I would have gone to Ibrox. The sun would have been blotted out by flying pigs before that would have happened!

I've often been asked why I have never been involved in the international set-up. Good question. Gordon Smith is now the Scottish Football Association chief executive and he was my assistant during my managerial stint at St Mirren, so he will have a good idea of how I operate. However, I don't push myself forward and that is not because of a lack of ambition or belief. Far from it. I am not an establishment figure and, to be honest, my grand-sons Vincent and Louis have the same coaching qualifications as me – zilch!

I would always prefer to let my experience speak for itself and there can't be too many out there who have played for their country in World Cup Finals, their club in countless European ties, including a final, performed in England and coached in Norway and across the border while also sampling football – or soccer, as it is known – in the States. And, of course, there is the little matter of managing Celtic, Motherwell, St Mirren, Livingston and Dunfermline. And you can throw in being a chief scout and assistant general manager at Celtic and director of football at Livingston. Oh, and I was an agent, too. I don't think I've missed out too much in a career which, by now, hopefully you will agree has been a fair distance from being dull.

Maybe if I worked on my touchline theatrics I might get noticed. Actually, it doesn't bother me at all. Now where did I put that John Travolta video? I could do with some hints!

32

A CELTIC MAN

When you put on a Celtic jersey you are not just playing for a football team, you are playing for a people and a cause. The words are not mine, they belong to Tommy Burns. I hope he doesn't mind me sharing that exact sentiment.

There is something special about Celtic Football Club. There is an aura about the club and I originally experienced it as a schoolboy all those years ago when I went to the park for the first time to pick up cans to make collections for the nuns. Even after such a long time, it is virtually impossible to define the feeling you get when you walk through those front doors at Celtic Park. I am not being disloyal to any clubs I have been associated with in the past or may be connected to in the future. It is just that there is something very, very appealing about Celtic. It could be their origins, their tradition, their heritage, their worldwide appeal or it could just be the way they are applauded everywhere as a team that will always try to put a smile on football. It's not an obsession, but more of an ingrained admiration.

I've seen poor Celtic teams try to play in an attacking, enter-taining way. It's inbred. It's alien to perform in another manner. Celtic took football by the scruff of the neck in 1967 and knocked it back into shape with the European Cup win in Lisbon. Until then, defensive strategies ruled supreme. The game was being suffocated under a cloak of caution. Inter Milan's much-fêted Helenio Herrera was the coach everyone admired and, unfortunately, copied. His club had won the World Club Championship twice and the European Cup twice in the three years preceding Lisbon. He had perfected a brand of football known as catennacio. Basically, it was a defensive formation that stifled football. Someone needed to come along with the force of a whirlwind and get rid of this attitude. Jock Stein and Celtic achieved that in 1967.

The game throughout the universe owed Celtic a massive debt after that victory. OK, I'm biased, but that performance was up there with Real Madrid in their pomp in the Sixties and that fabulously entertaining Brazil team that won the World Cup in 1970. My big regret was not being there in the Portuguese capital to see it live. I watched it on TV with Catherine in Bothwell, but what I would have given to have been on those terracings alongside all the other Celtic fans. I would have been first over that moat and onto that pitch as soon as the final whistle went. It wouldn't have mattered if there had been alligators in the moat. There would have been no stopping me.

I was nineteen and on the Celtic staff at the time and I had heard a whisper that Big Jock was going to take a handful of youngsters to Lisbon to soak in the atmosphere while gaining some valuable experience. I hoped I might get the nod. I was excited at the possibility, but, alas, I was not in the travelling squad when Big Jock finalised his arrangements. I had left it too late to book flights or even get a ticket, so it was the telly for me.

The score was 2-1 going on 6-1. The historic triumph was achieved very much in the Celtic tradition. I grew up with the Lisbon Lions and it was a genuine pleasure just to mix with these guys in training. I learned so much from them in just what it meant to be representing this special club. So many good things rubbed off and have remained with me throughout my life. You learned how to conduct yourself with a modicum of decorum and remember at all times what Celtic mean to so many. You learn which behaviour is appropriate when representing the club.

As a player and a manager, I always had time for Celtic fans. I've travelled the world attending supporters' functions. I've been away from the club for over a decade now, but I still get invitations from supporters asking me to go along to such and such an activity. I did quite a lot of these while I was a player, but I still smile at the memory of one such function I missed. The fans would always present you with a little memento, cufflinks or suchlike, of your visit to their particular club. On this occasion, though, I simply got my dates mixed up. Someone was far from impressed and telephoned Celtic Park to inform the club I hadn't attended. Then he added, 'And you can tell him he's no' getting his gift!'

I might have upset that particular individual, but I think I had an affinity with more than a few of the fans. I hope so, anyway. There was another night when I was invited to the Paisley Branch of the Celtic Supporters' Association for another function. George Connelly, Evan Williams, Dixie Deans and Lou Macari came along with me. Everything was going well until a punter raced in to tell us some yobs were smashing cars outside the club. There was the unforgettable sight of me and my teammates running out onto the street to prevent our cars from getting tanned. We stood guard at our vehicles for half an hour or so before going back into the presentation. Anyone driving through Paisley that night must have wondered why on earth five Celtic players were milling around street corners!

Celtic, under Jock Stein, broke new ground in football and no one should ever forget that. The very name 'Celtic' is magical. It has a certain ring to it and I will always be more than delighted to be associated with it. I lived the dream when I came into that first team and shared an arena with the likes of Jimmy Johnstone, Billy McNeill, Tommy Gemmell, Bobby Murdoch, Bertie Auld, Kenny Dalglish, George Connelly, Lou Macari, Danny McGrain and so many, many more. I look back on that and it's simply breathtaking.

To manage the likes of Tommy Burns, Paul McStay, Mo Johnston, Roy Aitken, Murdo MacLeod, Davie Provan, Peter Grant, Brian McClair, Pat Bonner and all the others was memorable, too. I won a League championship and a Scottish Cup in a four-year spell in charge before I had turned forty. I am proud of that record and, with a little bit of luck, there would have been other trophies. There is little point in crying over that now.

I can assure everyone that I always did my best for the club closest to my heart. That's just the way it is and it will never change no matter what. I would like to think Tommy Burns identified me as A Celtic Man. That's what I am. It's what I always will be.

33

AWAY FROM IT ALL

I am still surprised I never settled in America. I love the place. When Catherine and I want to get away we inevitably head for the States. Catherine has relatives in Long Island and that means occasional trips to New York, the city that never sleeps, according to a certain Francis Albert Sinatra, who, by the way, just happens to be my favourite singer.

Catherine and I have been to such glorious places like Boston, Cape Cod, Florida and Santa Monica. We were in the Coronado Hotel in San Diego for a break one year and it looked vaguely familiar. I couldn't quite put my finger on it until another guest asked me if I had seen the movie *Some Like It Hot*. It was a typical Billy Wilder comedy which starred Marilyn Monroe, Jack Lemon and Tony Curtis. It was shot at that very hotel. I like to do a bit of driving when we are on holiday and it's always interesting to see a bit more of a country that way. Mind you, I don't mind relaxing by the poolside, either.

My favourite movie star has got to be Jack Nicholson. That guy is immense and has such a range of talents that enables him to play so many different roles. One minute he's trying to break down a door with an axe and giving it, 'Here's Johnny' in *The Shining* and the next he can have you laughing out loud in *As Good As It Gets*. I thought he was brilliant in *One Flew Over The Cuckoo's Nest*, which happens to be up there as one of

the top films I have ever seen. That particular movie could have
been dedicated to some of the football clubs with which I have
been associated! Possibly, I can also identify with the lead character's perceived injustice of it all. Other favourite actors have
got to be Robert De Niro, Al Pacino, James Stewart and Gregory
Peck. Meryl Streep is undoubtedly my No.1 actress although if
I wanted to annoy my wife I might go for Demi Moore. Only
joking, dear!

Relaxing at home is required when you need to recharge your
batteries. You have to have a life away from football or you will
go bonkers. Naturally enough, I watch a lot of sport. However,
I also enjoy American cop shows such as *CSI*, *Law and Order* and
Without A Trace. *Cheers*, set in a bar in Boston, provided some
excellent humour. That was must-see material in the Hay household when it first came out in the Eighties. It had some classic
lines and Ted Danson, as the bar owner Sam Malone, reminded
me of a few blokes of my acquaintance. He had been a top pro
in his day with the Red Sox baseball team and he continually
made references to the good old days when he was 'up on the
mound'.

That was a good mix of characters. There was Norm, who
was the resident barfly, and Cliff the postman who had a view-
point on everything. I recall one little cameo when Cliff asked
Norm for a progress report as he and his wife Vera were trying
for a family. 'I've started putting rhino horn in my coffee,' said
Norm. 'Is it doing any good?' asked Cliff. 'Not really, but I now
have an irresistible urge to charge at buses,' replied Norm.
Marvellous. Of course, *Cheers* then had the spin-off with the
brilliant Kelsey Grammer playing the pompous radio psychi-
atrist in *Frasier*, set in Seattle. I also enjoyed *Friends*, who used
the Big Apple as its backdrop. All were superbly written and
not quite custard-pie-in-the-face *Carry On* material. As a matter
of fact I am more likely to watch repeats of *Cheers*, *Frasier* and

Friends than some of today's so-called comedy shows. There's a lot of stuff I switch off immediately. I know the likes of *Have I Got News For You* has a massive following, but don't include yours truly among that number.

I enjoy a good book and John Grisham's expertly-written courtroom and legal dramas are particular favourites. A book and a cold drink on a balcony on holiday as the sun goes down before going out for an evening's entertainment is sheer bliss. You can feel the aches, pains and stresses ebbing away as you settle into a break away from it all.

Of course, I have enjoyed many a fine lunch with the media in my time and I would like to think I made a few friends in that profession over the years. When we were away from the glare of the spotlight, you could get to know these guys fairly well. Personal favourites were Alex Cameron, of the *Daily Record*, Gerry McNee, who worked with the *Daily Express* and then the *News of the World*, and Alan Davidson, of the *Evening Times*. Sadly, Alex and Alan are no longer with us, but I appreciated their wit and wisdom, especially on foreign trips. I knew Alex as 'The Commander' because he was always immaculately turned out and deserved respect for what he had given sports journalism. He was also known as 'Chiefy' – he was the chief sportswriter with his paper – and some nicknamed him 'Scoop' for all the exclusives he would dig up. Alan was 'Pod'. No matter the weather, blistering hot or freezing cold, he would wrap this gigantic black leather coat around him. He became the 'Prince of Darkness' and that was shortened to Pod. Gerry was the 'Voice of Football', but that was too long so I called him Gerry!

I recall an occasion when I was over at a little trattoria called Enzo's on Glasgow's south side with some of the *Evening Times* sportswriters. John Traynor and John Quinn were among the party. I was the Celtic manager at the time and, let's just say a few aperitifs had been taken by this time, when Traynor challenged me to a keepy-uppy contest outside the restaurant. I couldn't possibly resist, but where was he going to get a ball? Within minutes his sidekick Quinn had produced one. We went out into the street and goodness only knows what the passers-by were thinking as we prepared to go through our repertoire and party pieces. John managed to keep it up for one. It was my turn to show off. I flicked the ball up, waited for it to drop and then belted it as far as I could. The ball was never returned. Game over!

I agreed to do some commentary for Radio Clyde after I had been sacked by Celtic in 1987. I had time on my hands, so I would take the opportunity to take in a game and get paid. Someone at the station obviously had a wicked sense of humour – they sent me to Ibrox for the unfurling of the league flag! Three months beforehand I had still been manager at Parkhead and now I was in Govan with a microphone in my hand and expected to say nice things about Rangers. I queried, 'Should I really be here?' I felt a lot more comfortable doing Celtic TV! I've also done spots on the now defunct Setanta which I enjoyed. I also wrote a column in a national Sunday newspaper for about three years which was insightful, too.

One of the craziest things I ever did with the media was ban a particular group of newspapers from Parkhead on 2 May 1987 for Celtic's last league game of the season. I thought we hadn't been given enough credit or fair and balanced coverage throughout a testing season and, most unlike me, it started to rile a bit. I mentioned it to a newspaperman I respected at the time and he told me I should turf out the sportswriters and not allow them access to the press box. I hadn't thought of taking such drastic action. I can't name the individual, but he normally gave out sound advice. I've always been my own man and stood or fallen by my decisions. I really took my eye off the ball with this one and, unfortunately, I agreed with him. Guys I knew and liked turned up that afternoon to be told they were banned. Falkirk were our visitors and we had been unbeaten at home in the league all season. We had taken four off them at our place earlier in the season. What could go wrong? Everything! We lost 2-1 and, to make matters worse, their winning goal in the fading minutes came from a wee bloke called Jimmy Gilmour, who just happened to be a nephew of Jimmy Johnstone! As I came off the pitch an irate fan in the stand tried to throw his scarf onto the ground. I caught it and walked up the tunnel holding it in my right hand. It was one of my last acts as Celtic manager at Parkhead. I regretted the foolish ban instantly and fell back in with the press pack afterwards.

Another daft thing I tried to do was play golf. Stevie Chalmers won't thank me for this, but I am not a great fan of the sport. I think Stevie must have taken up the sport in his nursery school and he is very good at the game. He plays alongside his buddy Bobby Lennox now that they live beside each other on the Ayrshire coast. Their deadly rivals on the links are their Lisbon Lions teammates Billy McNeill and Bertie Auld. I have tried to get into the sport. Jock Stein was a big golf fan, too, and he expected everyone to join in. We might be down at Seamill and everyone would have their clubs with them. If you didn't participate, you were expected to walk round with the guys who were playing. What did Liverpool's legendary boss Bill Shankly once say? 'Golf is the waste of a good walk.' I'll second that. I believe Graeme Souness also banned his Rangers players from indulging in the sport because they were sustaining all sorts of muscle injuries outwith the usual knocks you get in a football game.

I admit I did decide once to give golf my best shot. After all, I had probably played some form of golf on some of the world's best courses, so I thought I might get involved and find out why this game was so compelling. I got all the gear, new clubs and so on, but I stopped short of the plus fours. We were at Turnberry for a break and physiotherapist Brian Scott and I decided to have a go. Previously, I had practised with Lou Macari and George Connelly at West Kilbride. Lou and George only had a putter each and they simply walked around hitting the ball in the general direction of the hole. I think we were averaging about eight strokes a hole. Anyway, Brian and I were doing our best to put on a reasonable display at Turnberry. There were a couple of Americans playing behind us. I don't think they were impressed. Then in a Yankee drawl, I heard, 'Say, fellas, you're not golfers, are you?' Sharp observation there. 'No, we're footballers,' I replied. There was a pause and then, 'Stick to football, fellas.' By the way, Desmond White, the club secretary, took one look at Celtic's bill for our stay at Turnberry and observed, 'I think we'll go back to Seamill next time.'

I think the reason I didn't take to golf was a simple one; I expected to do well. I had been good at sports at school, running, jumping and the like. However, I just couldn't master that annoying little white ball. It was a wayward, dangerous thing when I was around. Anyway, one day my car was broken into and my gleaming clubs were stolen. I never replaced them and that was me off the circuit. Tiger Woods got lucky!

I've already said Frank Sinatra is my favourite singer of all time and I admit I do listen to quite a bit of music. In fact, I think I've seen Ol' Blue Eyes about four times in concert, twice at the Albert Hall. I was in New York a few years ago and Catherine and I just happened to get off the train at Penn Station, close to Madison Square Garden. Barry Manilow was in town and, acting on impulse, we bought tickets to see him. He was fantastic. He may not be everyone's cup of tea, but the entertainment value that night was something else altogether.

There are a few artists I admire and I'm a fan of the soothing tones of the likes of Johnny Mathis, Andy Williams, Perry Como, Nat King Cole and Harry Neilson. The Beatles and Elvis are on my turntable, too. And I couldn't possibly leave out good old Rod Stewart, could I? You know he is a genuine Celtic supporter when the television cameras pan into the crowd on a cold afternoon at Rugby Park or Fir Park and there is Rod in the midst of the supporters. That's a real fan.

I often wonder if Rod dedicated his massive hit 'Sailing' to Jimmy Johnstone!

34

THE LAST WORD

I have always pushed myself to the fullest extent of my ability to succeed in my chosen profession, whether I've been on the field or in the dugout. I have always had a burning desire to do well, even back to my schooldays in Paisley when I used to scribble in my notebook, 'I want to be the best footballer in school.' I would repeat that line time and time again.

If I ever needed inspiration I could look at my favourite-ever sportsman, the remarkable Muhammad Ali. He was the supreme sports personality to me. When I was training as an accountant, I would go along to one of the Glasgow cinemas that was piping in live pictures of Ali in action. These were the days before pay-per-view satellite channels and if you wanted to see the best heavyweight boxer that ever lived then you had to book your tickets and take your seats for bouts that would start at one or two o'clock in the morning. It was worth staying up late to watch Ali.

I used to go to these early morning treats with a Nigerian pal of mine called Rashid Erogbogbo who was also into accountancy. My friend from Lagos was a big fight fan, too, so I always had company at the old Odeon cinema in the city centre when Ali was enthralling everyone with his amazing array of skills. I saw him fight a guy called Cleveland 'Big Cat' Williams in Houston in 1966. There had been all the usual Ali hype before the bout and there seemed a genuine hatred of each other. I don't think they were trying to sell tickets and it was a fight that packed out the cinema in the early hours of the morning. Ali mania got everywhere! The fight was over in the third round when Ali clubbed his opponent into submission.

Before Ali came on the fight scene it was just about two big guys in the middle of the ring who knocked hell out of each other until one toppled over. There was very little ring craft from the likes of Sonny Liston. Most heavyweights looked as though they headbutted houses for fun. They all appeared to have smashed noses, cauliflower ears and didn't look too dissimilar from your average cave dweller back in the dark and distant past. Ali, as handsome as any Hollywood actor, took boxing to another stratosphere. He proclaimed he was The Greatest and I, for one, was not about to argue with him. However, you could draw inspiration from this colourful and charismatic character. He broke down barriers in sport and gave everyone hope. He was only human, after all.

I mention Muhammad Ali because he was a genuine superstar. There are a lot of footballers out there today who are rated as world class. It's an overused term these days. There are some players performing at present who would do themselves a lot of damage if they ever tripped over their ego. They seem very distant from the man in the street without whom there is no game.

I think I played football in a more genuine era. I wonder what Jock Stein would have made of a little snippet I came across recently. I've already said in an earlier chapter about how our manager detested people turning up late for training. You had to have a right good reason or you knew you were for the high jump. Anyway, I had to smile when I saw this story about a player who arrived extremely late for his team's workout. His excuse was that his electronic gates were malfunctioning and he was forced to wait until his gardener turned up with a key. And who did this guy play for? Would you believe Notts County, who were in England's bottom division at the time! Jock's face would have been a picture if he had been presented with that explanation.

It's merely another illustration that there is an awful lot of money in the game at the moment. Maybe too much, but good luck to the players who are picking up astronomical wages. It's a short career. However, I would like to see the supporters getting more involved with their favourites. Some appear to be shunned and are not on the same level of the players they support through thick and thin. Or, in some cases, thin and thinner! It would be good to see the fans being embraced by the clubs and accorded their proper place. 'Football is nothing without fans,' said Big Jock more than once. He was always aware that they were the lifeblood of the sport. So, let's give football back to the supporters. They should never be forgotten.

Talking from my own experience, I am always happy to chat with football fans. It's mainly Celtic supporters who recognise me, of course. I've a new life now after passing the sixty-years-of-age mark. Not that I'm ready to be put out to pasture just yet, but I can relax a bit more these days than, say, when I was with Celtic, either as a player or a manager. I can often be found in a little hostelry called The Iron Horse in Glasgow's city centre – one afternoon a week nowadays. It's not an all-day session and it's not excessive, but, if I'm not driving, I'll have a pint and, as they say in the States, shoot the breeze with some of the locals. If I'm driving, the Irn Bru comes into play. I still love that stuff!

Sometimes Tommy Gemmell or Bertie Auld will pop in and we can go for a walk down memory lane. Alex Gordon, who helped get my thoughts down in print for this book, and his wife Gerda are companions, as well. Fraser Elder, who once worked with BBC sports and is now a freelance writer, is a welcome addition to our company. There are a couple of guys from other walks of life and it's just good to relax and be normal. You name it, we discuss it.

Every now and again, a bloke, normally of the Celtic persuasion, will come forward, offer me his hand and we'll shake. He'll look me in the eye and say, 'Thanks.' That means everything to me.